ss shall make no law respect-
establishment of religion,
thereof; or abridging the
s; or the right of the people
tition the Government

"In this book, Thane Rosenbaum explores whether the United States is best served by unlimited speech—extended even to terrorists of the left and right, as well as other enemies of the open society—or whether certain restrictions on the First Amendment are necessary for a free society to not be subverted from within.

"With a strong grasp of constitutional and case law, and a keen interest in genuine freedom of speech, Rosenbaum has written an important book that will likely prove controversial to many. His questions and proposed remedies are ones that all those interested in freedom of expression should take seriously. As a free speech absolutist, this has given me great food for thought."

—Ayaan Hirsi Ali, activist, feminist, author, scholar,
former politician, and a Research Fellow with
the Hoover Institution at Stanford University

## PRAISE FOR OTHER NONFICTION BOOKS BY THANE ROSENBAUM

*The Myth of Moral Justice:*
*Why Our Legal System Fails to Do What's Right:*

"Rosenbaum has accomplished what multitudes of professors long for and so rarely achieve: He has set the terms for public debate."

—*The New York Times*

"[A]s a diagnostician, Rosenbaum is on target . . . he exposes a system that encourages lying, permits truth to be stifled and allows evil men to roam free. . . . Rosenbaum should be read by every law student in America."

—*The New York Times Book Review*

"Rosenbaum's book ought to be required reading in law schools and continuing legal educations classes, if only because at least a few of his readers will be humanized by the experience."

—*The Washington Post Book World*

"One of our most original and compelling thinkers about the law and its limitations, Thane Rosenbaum takes on the theme whose name dare not be spoken in polite circles: revenge. With his singular panache and mastery of sources from Supreme Court cases to popular culture to—gasp—life itself, Rosenbaum takes us on a substantive and stylistic tour de force that leads to the 'shocking' conclusion that if the law won't set things right, which it so often fails to do, then it is okay, indeed moral, for us to do so ourselves."

—Daniel Jonah Goldhagen, author of
*Hitler's Willing Executioners:*
*Ordinary Germans and the Holocaust*

"In this brilliant book, Thane Rosenbaum finds language for what all of us, at one time or another, have felt in our bones that there is a law higher than those made by legislatures or courts; and that, when evil appears among us, an appropriate response is the oldest: revenge. Independent thinking at its best, Rosenbaum's fiercely argued text dares to speak truth to cowardice and calls us to understand and accommodate the demand that a punishment that fit the crime and that the score be settled in the Chicago Way."

—Rich Cohen,
author of *The Avengers*

"Rosenbaum inhabits both the fact-based legal world and the emotion-based arts realm, able to address everything from the talion to *The Princess Bride*. His satisfying work gives us permission, contrary to contemporary politeness, to assert 'honor in payback.' . . . Rosenbaum renders a consequential, often gruesome topic uplifting, even fun."

—*Publisher's Weekly* (starred review)

"Rosenbaum spells out the virtually unspeakable in a liberal humanitarian culture: justice is revenge."

—*The Times of London*

"Well-written . . . Rosenbaum convincingly argues for knocking down the false distinction between justice and revenge, for rescuing revenge from its taboo status."

—*The Washington Post*

# Article I

Congress shall make no law respecting an establishment of religion, or prohibiting the free exercise thereof; or abridging the freedom of speech, or of the press; or the right of the people peaceably to assemble, and to petition the Government for a redress of grievances.

# SAVING FREE SPEECH...
## *from ITSELF*

## THANE ROSENBAUM

FOREWORD BY BRET STEPHENS

BEDFORD, NEW YORK

Copyright © 2020 by Thane Rosenbaum

All rights reserved.

Published in the United States by Fig Tree Books LLC, Bedford, New York

www.FigTreeBooks.net

*Jacket design by Christine Van Bree*

*Cover art illustration by Sam Fink*

*Interior design by Pauline Neuwirth, Neuwirth & Associates, Inc.*

Library of Congress Cataloging-in-Publication Data Available Upon Request

ISBN 978-1-941493-26-7

Printed in the United States

Distributed by Publishers Group West

First edition

10 9 8 7 6 5 4 3 2 1

FOR SOLÈNNE ROSE

# CONTENTS

# CONTENTS

# CONTENTS

# FOREWORD

*I*T'S FAIR TO say that I am a strong believer in free speech—not in an absolutist sense (life always must make room for exceptions), but pretty close to it. I want there to be no governmental intrusions on speech. How could I be otherwise? I have been an opinion columnist for most of my professional life. I am paid to speak my mind freely. An anticipated outcome of my line of work is that I might render opinions that offend even my most devoted readers. So be it. Living in a liberal democracy with a free-standing press, I, thankfully, possess the freedom to do just that. Hopefully all readers understand that.

For the past eleven years, in fact, I have directed some of my most withering criticism to the occupants of the White House. One a Democrat, Barack Obama, for the entire eight years of his presidency. At the time I was a registered Republican. With the election of Donald Trump, I forfeited my party membership and joined the ranks of the NeverTrumpers. I have played no party favorites when it came to criticizing two very different leaders of the free world—and for different reasons.

Neither of these presidents have accused me of sedition, (blasphemy, maybe), or have tried to silence me by fiat or edict. I have never been arrested for expressing an opinion. Apart from divulging state secrets, in the United States there is no such crime. Presidents Obama and Trump may have privately fumed. In the case of the latter, orange hair might have looked even more inflamed; an angry tweet could easily have been composed late at night, directed at me but mostly for the amusement of *Fox & Friends* in the morning.

All on account of the First Amendment, and the rampart of powerful news organizations, I have been safe to say whatever I pleased. Yet, I take nothing for granted. I know that in many countries around the world—illiberal, undemocratic, oppressive, authoritarian—I would have long ago been tossed in jail merely for making an unflattering aside.

So why am I writing a Foreword for a book that is asking its readers to take a critical look at freedom of speech?

Well, for one thing, nothing in this book would prevent me or others from criticizing the government. In fact, SAVING FREE SPEECH . . . *from ITSELF* reaffirms most of what we believe to be true about the First Amendment.

I have known Thane Rosenbaum for many years. He is, if nothing else, an original thinker. And a provocative one. And a principled and compassionate writer and friend. If he has a problem with the First Amendment, perhaps we should give it another look.

In reading this book, I am reminded that I, too, have undergone some revised feelings about free speech. And I may probably rethink my position again. Isn't that, after all, exactly what the First Amendment protects?

Years ago, I wrote a column criticizing Columbia University for inviting then Iranian president Mahmoud Ahmadinejad to speak on campus. I compared the incident to whether the university would have extended the same invitation to Adolf Hitler in the 1930s. My objections to granting either of these tyrants an Ivy League platform mirrored some of the points Rosenbaum makes in this book: that if the ideas you espouse are limited to the genocide of a people or wiping nations from a map, then you are disqualified from entering the marketplace of ideas, that what you are offering are not ideas at all, but acts of violence, thuggery, indignity, incitement, and intimidation.

Years later I wrote a column criticizing *The New Yorker* for disinviting Steve Bannon from appearing at its annual festival. Apparently, his inclusion on the roster of speakers was so infuriating to the Twitter universe, and even some staff members of the magazine, that the invitation was rescinded. I wondered what that said about *The New Yorker*'s commitment not just to freedom of speech, but to journalism itself. Regardless of how one felt about Bannon, was he not a person of public interest given the outsized role he played in the election of Donald Trump? And how did Twitter come to influence the editorial policies of a storied magazine?

I was aware of the contradiction between those two columns. A number of years separated their writing, and when I was asked how I could deny free speech to Ahmadinejad while at the same time insist that it be granted to Bannon, I said, among other things, that my thinking had evolved on the subject, and that I had changed my mind.

More recently, I gave up my Twitter account. I have finally decided that the digital discourse that exists on that platform is clearly not the kind of free speech I want to engage in. I would hesitate denying anyone the right to tweet their hearts out, but as Rosenbaum reminds us, the Founding Fathers held out great hope that the First Amendment would lead to a more informed citizenry, and a better decision-making government, influenced by the best the marketplace of ideas had to offer.

I can't say whether Twitter is the modern-day answer to the public square, but I do know that speech, in so many forms and forums, has been less collegial, coarser, angrier, and more mob-like. The heckler's veto is now a full-fledged tsunami of rage. Many are now afraid to speak because the practice of shouting down and drowning out disfavored speakers has replaced common courtesy and true deliberation.

After reading SAVING FREE SPEECH . . . *from ITSELF*, I am listening carefully and thinking a little more deeply when Rosenbaum argues that human dignity should be given the same weight as free speech, that mutual respect is the cornerstone for how ideas can be embraced, and that the marketplace of ideas should be reserved for ideas worthy of entry. This book sharpens your view of the First Amendment. That alone makes it an outstanding contribution to our thinking about free speech.

—Bret Stephens

# INTRODUCTION

The moral legitimacy of free speech no longer makes sense to many people. Its virtues have been thoroughly abused by one set of citizens who have trampled upon the rights of others—fellow citizens who retain rights of their own, rights that should not be subordinated to the First Amendment.

*A*MERICANS HAVE NEVER wavered from their love affair with free speech, the people's choice for the best-known and most revered amendment to its Constitution. It is an entitlement that receives unfailing popular support. And its most-favored nations status crosses party lines. Liberals and conservatives, Democrats and Republicans, find very little common ground in today's political culture. Yet, in the curious alchemy of the First Amendment, they are all unwaveringly united in the principle that Americans possess an absolute right to speak freely without government interference. So profoundly has this right been internalized in the nation's psyche that waving the American flag is tantamount to celebrating the right to free speech.

And, yet, doubt and confusion abound.

This book hopes to begin an honest conversation about what we really mean by free speech—when we invoke the right and trumpet the liberty, when we demand freedom of speech only for the issues personal to us, and when we seek to deny it for others. Do we really want free speech to be limitless? Why does the United States stand out among other Western nations in defending the rights of bullies and bigots to prey upon marginalized groups with weaponized words? Why do we abhor governmental regulation of speech and yet think nothing of speech that is restricted by society at large? How do we account for so much intellectual hypocrisy when it comes to free speech?

This book seeks to answer these important, albeit controversial, questions.

The right to free speech is so often reflexively stated, but not so well understood. Despite all the liberating comfort it evokes, speech is not without cost. Sometimes, the cost is prohibitively high, and when this occurs, society as a whole suffers the consequences. Sometimes gravely. The truth is, speech should not be entirely free.

I can imagine the horrified reaction to this last statement. *How can he say this? Does he not understand what the First Amendment says and what it protects?* I do. But freedom does not have but one meaning— one that derives solely for the benefit of speakers. It also includes the targets of speech who have their own rights. This book is a respectful reminder of those rights, which should not be so casually canceled out by the gluttony and indecency of certain speakers.

I am proposing a new level of moral clarity around the principle of free speech.

It is not an easy undertaking, mostly because it requires that we modify our expectations of what the First Amendment actually guarantees. Doing so will lower the societal costs and improve the climate in which speech is freely offered and received.

I believe it to be a valuable and urgent national project.

We have always been heavily invested, patriotically and emotionally, in the right to free expression. But at this moment in our history, we are actually experiencing a crisis of faith in the First Amendment that is just beginning to emerge in some conversations, and there is confusion over the once-thought absolutism of its meaning.

Addressing this crisis of the inconsistent adherence to the First Amendment is long overdue. And the consequences are great, even if largely unacknowledged. The privileging of free speech has come with much pain, the kind we are expected to endure without complaint. It is a mindset that begins young, embodied in a nursery rhyme that serves as propaganda for the First Amendment:

"Sticks and stones can break my bones, but words will never hurt me."

It is a lovely rhyme and a wonderful thought, but everyone knows that this homespun wisdom is patently false. Words hurt, they can wound, and they can be every bit as lethal as a physical blow. Threats are made through words, fights are instigated, riots incited—words manipulated in the service of violence. The special harm that words cause can linger and are often much more long-lasting than the effects of physical damage.

We have repeatedly confused and conflated hostile acts with free speech. We have allowed the First Amendment to provide cover for those who do violence and disguise it as political expression. The moral legitimacy of free speech no longer makes sense to many people. Its virtues have been thoroughly abused by one set of citizens who have trampled upon the rights of others—fellow citizens who retain rights of their own, rights that should not be subordinated to the First Amendment.

Freedom of expression should not apply to speech that is intended to cause harm—either by threatening and intimidating certain targeted audiences, or by inciting imminent violence against them, or by provoking them into a fight, or when speech is being deployed in order to deprive vulnerable groups of their dignity, self-respect, and social status. Perpetrators of such uncivil and anti-democratic acts against other citizens may feel that laws preventing them from doing so violate their freedom of speech. But what they understand to be free speech would be wholly foreign to the Founding Fathers of this nation who had something entirely else in mind when they enshrined this new freedom in our consciousness and laws. The free speech that they sanctified had to do with the rights of citizens to criticize their government without punishment or recourse. Since that time, however, we have expanded the universe of what constitutes speech to the point where almost anything qualifies for First Amendment protection—whether it be a sincere oration or an accidental burp. Courts should reject allowing the First Amendment to be used not as a defender of liberty but as a weapon against vulnerable groups. The latest studies in neuroscience demonstrate the lasting effect that harmful speech is having on all segments of the population—some more than others. And it is time to give the constitutionality of hate speech codes another look.

But let me make perfectly clear what this book is not about, what I am not proposing, because when it comes to free speech, words can be deceiving.

This book is not about speech one does not like, or disagrees with, or finds offensive, or feels insulted by. This book is not in favor of restricting the free speech of those who wish to openly criticize the policies of the federal government. This book is not meant to serve as marching orders or an operating manual for any political group on any side of the liberal-conservative-libertarian spectrum.

This is a book about the social costs of speech, freely spoken, that causes actual harm—emotional and physical. Speech should not be regulated merely because it insults or offends. As legal scholar Erwin Chemerinsky has stated, "Speech can't be prevented simply because it's offensive, even if it's deeply offensive."[1] But there is a great deal of difference between offense and harm. As long as speech is being offered in a respectful, thoughtful, civilized manner, and its intention is to introduce new ideas or challenge old ones—even if unpopular, even if upsetting—then it belongs in the mythical marketplace of ideas, and I wish such speech good luck in attracting consumers interested in its message.

Colleges and universities have a mandate to serve as catalysts for mind expansion and the search for truth. They should not become incubators of closed campuses specializing in coddled students who do not wish to be challenged or discomforted by disturbing thoughts or insensitive remarks. The whole point of a liberal arts education is the allure of the rigorous argument, the acceptance of contradiction, and the openness to judgments based on the quality and persuasiveness of ideas. The closing of the American mind under the dictatorial edicts of political correctness is fundamentally un-American. But a sensible rethinking of the First Amendment can be accomplished without contributing to this crusade of censorship that has infected American campuses. Here is just one example: An Egyptian Coptic Christian who wrote a book about Islam's centuries-old war with the West was disinvited from speaking at the US Army War College in 2019 because an outside Muslim group protested that he was a "racist" and "white nationalist."[2]

This book is also not making a blanket judgment about any one group. On the contrary, this book is dedicated to the idea that *all marginalized groups of minorities should be protected from true threats to their safety and citizenship*.

This book is categorically neutral between left- and right-wing politics. All political ideas should be welcome in the marketplace of ideas. This book is not choosing sides. At the same time, all groups have the capacity to abuse their freedom of speech—either in the manner in which they speak or in the ferocity with which they censor. Yet groups are not monolithic—there are differences of opinion taking place within them all the time.

In these troubling times of fake news and truth decay, where political debate in the service of representative democracy is most crucial, all speech cannot be (and was not intended to be by the drafters of the Constitution) worthy of First Amendment protection. Ideas are welcome so long as they are actually ideas delivered in good faith to enlighten and persuade, and not to deceive, inflame, incite, and bring about harm.

And because social media and the dark web are both the beneficiaries of free speech and also the chief disseminators of false and harmful speech—not to mention the gatekeepers of terroristic propaganda and home recipes for how to make a bomb—this book supports the sensible regulation of the Internet, as is commonly done in Europe, in the same way that it argues in favor of government involvement in the regulation of harmful speech.

This book is a gut check for America and its love affair with the First Amendment. It is primarily about defining the boundaries and establishing the ground rules for free speech, taking into account the civility, decency, and dignity that gives speech the moral authority to be free.

I know that, for many people, what I am proposing is tantamount to constitutional blasphemy, heretical and dangerous—a throwback to the pre-Enlightenment. Any criticism of the First Amendment is instantly regarded as seditious in our political culture. Sensible reform is reflexively feared. There is a curious and disturbing national groupthink when it comes to the orthodoxy around free speech. More Kool-Aid has been consumed on free speech than on any other public issue. As law professor Frederick Schauer observed, those "on the side of free speech often seem to believe, and often correctly, that it has secured the upper hand in public debate. The First Amendment not only attracts attention, but also strikes fear in the hearts of many who do not want to be seen as opposing the freedoms it enshrines."[3]

I realize that when it comes to books about free speech, very few of them reevaluate the very premises of the First Amendment itself. Nearly all of them have nothing critical to say about the Free Speech Clause and how it is commonly applied. Most books about the First Amendment are really celebrations of free speech. This one, however, is more like an autopsy of an amendment. I am well aware that a discussion of the high costs of free speech will be a hard sell for many in a marketplace of ideas where all participants have bought into a happy monopoly with an efficient market immune from government regulation. If you are among such satisfied consumers of free speech, I respectfully ask you to withhold judgment. Let me try to sell you something else.

Would that not be the perfect demonstration of why we have freedom of speech to begin with?

# FREE SPEECH RECONSIDERED

[T]here are also speakers like the ones who gathered in Charlottesville who cynically weaponize the First Amendment in order to provoke a fight, incite lawlessness, and threaten vulnerable minorities.

*I*T MUST BE a terribly confusing time for free speech enthusiasts—especially in America, where the Bill of Rights remains the enlightened testament to a secular religion unlike any other in the world. Among the precious freedoms Americans cherish, one stands out above the rest. One liberty, embodied in the First Amendment, is first for a reason. It is lodged in the hearts of citizens and engraved as an endowed birthright in their memory. Indeed, for most people, it is the supreme virtue of American society, defining what it means to be a citizen of the United States.

Before they attended to the matter of bearing arms, unreasonable searches and seizures, trial by jury, compensation for property taken by eminent domain, and cruel and unusual punishments, the Framers of the Constitution, our Founding Fathers, were under pressure from some states to create a general right of expression, declaring that "Congress shall make no law . . . abridging the freedom of speech."

It is a pretty dramatic opening statement, followed by a catalog of rights and freedoms that would make the Constitution of the United States arguably the most celebrated and contested governmental contract with its people the world has ever known.

And it all starts with free speech.

But the free speech we enjoy today is very much unlike, if not altogether unrecognizable from, what the Founders envisioned. Never before has the Free Speech Clause of the First Amendment elicited so much ambivalence and bewilderment. Nearly everyone seems to have a strong opinion about the sanctity of free speech. But the consensus that was once absolute now has skeptics. More and more are recovering addicts from the drunken free-speech hedonism of the past. The new normal of self-doubt and second thoughts has left many people unsure of how they really feel about the First Amendment. Constitutional certainty has given way to more complicated and nuanced assessments of right from wrong.

During the summer of 2017, an assembly of several hundred assorted white supremacists, KKK, neo-Nazi, and Alt-Right agitators staged a rally in downtown Charlottesville, Virginia, under the slogan, "Unite the Right." The ostensible purpose for the march was to protest the decision by the city to remove a statue from a University of Virginia park honoring the Confederate general Robert E. Lee. As the rally commenced, the protestors almost immediately started chanting, "Jews will not replace us!" Obviously, nostalgia for the Confederacy and the preservation of General Lee's statue was not the only item on their list of grievances. The connection between a statue of a man who probably had not met many Jews in his lifetime and the world's oldest prejudice was not immediately apparent. What occurred, however, and what could have easily been predicted, was the usual chaos that emerges from a gathering mob with a hateful agenda. The white supremacists came prepared for the night and for a fight. There were counter-protests by self-proclaimed anti-fascists, violent skirmishes, and one death.

The city had tried to avoid a calamity by moving the rally to a different location—a larger park a mile away where the statue of General Lee was not located and where, arguably, the rally would be less pitched for violence. Those efforts were blocked by a federal judge who ruled that the city must grant the white supremacists a permit to exercise their right to freedom of speech—at the very location where their assembly would have the greatest effect and meaning.[4]

Standing beside their clients in court and prevailing on their behalf, not unlike forty years earlier when they represented neo-Nazis in Skokie, Illinois, were lawyers from the American Civil Liberties Union (ACLU). And once again, as in Skokie, the ACLU faced harsh criticism for representing the instigators in Charlottesville. After all, the ACLU bills itself as a progressive legal entity that is supposed to champion the rights of the oppressed, the marginalized, and the mistreated. Why, after all these years, do they still find themselves vindicating the rights of Nazis when their overall mission is to promote diversity, equal protection, and mutual tolerance? It has been reported that some of its supporters called to express their outrage and cut off further donations. That, too, happened in Skokie decades earlier. One current board member of the Virginia chapter resigned, but not before writing on Twitter: "I won't be a fig leaf for Nazis. Don't defend Nazis to allow them to kill people."[5] Former board member Wendy Kaminer wrote that, going forward, the ACLU might just hesitate in taking on free-speech cases that "advance the goals of white supremacists or others whose views are contrary to our values."[6]

What was different this time, however, was that it was not only ACLU donors and former board members who were questioning the judgment of an organization that refuses to prioritize the speakers they routinely defend. After all, some speakers express an actual idea that contributes to public debate and enriches an informed society. But there are also speakers like the ones who gathered in Charlottesville who cynically weaponize the First

Amendment in order to provoke a fight, incite lawlessness, and threaten vulnerable minorities. For them, the First Amendment is a convenient and effective cover to spread mayhem. Would it not be a better use of legal resources, and a more righteous calling, if the ACLU focused on assisting the first group of speakers and left the second group to fend for themselves without top-notch legal representation?

This time, in Charlottesville, it was not just their benefactors but the ACLU itself that was having second thoughts about how to define its core mission. Earlier in the year, the organization had filed a lawsuit on behalf of British, far-right political commentator Milo Yiannopoulos' right to speak at the University of California in Berkeley. Now they found themselves successfully representing white supremacists in Charlottesville. Staff lawyers began to grouse. Had the ACLU become just a *pro-bono* sap for right-wing agitators, those for whom the Constitution was not a sacred document but rather an operating manual for undermining democracy and imposing the will of an angry mob? Here they were, mounting a legal defense for racist and anti-Semitic groups whose civil liberties were directed toward saving a statue of a man who had led an army that defended the slavery of an entire people—America's original sin.

Some of the ACLU's internal conflict may have begun in 2008 when, following the election of Barack Obama, it defended four students who spray-painted "Hang Obama by a Noose" and "Let's shoot that nigger in the head" on a wall at North Carolina State University. The organization also lent its services in 2015 to defend the Washington Redskins football team in its effort to retain its nickname despite mounting pressure from Native Indian-Americans who believe that such misappropriation represents a desecration of their cultural history.[7]

Perhaps for the first time in its history, the ACLU wondered whether it had forfeited the greater good of its progressive agenda merely to remain true to its First Amendment bona fides. Is it not also an organization dedicated to equality and racial justice? As evidence of this newfound moral revulsion at work, more than 200 staffers (out of a total of 1,300) signed a letter to the ACLU's executive director, questioning whether the rigid stance it had historically taken in defense of free speech was now eroding its moral authority to advance the arguably more laudable goals of social justice and equal protection. The letter recommended that the ACLU become more discriminating in the kinds of First Amendment cases it takes on in the future. After all, as one ACLU staff attorney said, "The ACLU can have a proactive First Amendment stance without giving free legal services to Nazis."[8]

On May 1, 2018, without fanfare and perhaps so as not to highlight that it had lost some of its First Amendment mojo, a committee of the ACLU that had been established to address the concerns expressed in the joint letter released new guidelines on how the organization would decide upon which free-speech cases to litigate. The most important change in policy: It would no longer represent clients who choose to test the limits of the First Amendment by marching with guns in order to express their views.

The fact that the letter was written and signed by so many, and that some action, albeit quietly, was taken, suggests that even die-hard free speech absolutists may now be willing to concede that not all speech, by all speakers, is worth defending. A soul-searching experience such as this, taken by even a single ACLU lawyer forty years ago during the Skokie litigation, would have been unimaginable.

And the ACLU is not alone. Confusion about free speech abounds everywhere. And not only from those who make their living defending it. Many question what free speech really means in a world of social media trolling, cyberbullying, cloak and dagger hacking of America's presidential election, militant protest rallies by groups that spread hate, incitement to violence, the spreading of fear, and college campuses that are repressing the openness of mind that was once the whole point of a liberal arts education.

These feelings are deeply felt but not often publicly stated. But it is there, a clear signal that the First Amendment is flawed. We have been applying it too rigidly and permissively, and in ways that our Founding Fathers would have found not in keeping with its original purpose. So much energy has been expended on limiting any restriction on free speech and defending the First Amendment from any deviation that we have desecrated and complicated its essential meaning beyond recognition. Civil liberties reflected in free speech is one thing; uncivil insanity typified by harmful speech is quite another.

Our Founding Fathers believed that free speech would make the government more responsive to the people by empowering ordinary citizens to make their displeasure with the government freely known. And free speech would enable the people to become better citizens, fully engaged in a government by the people, fully participating in democracy from the soapbox to the ballot box.

How do marching Nazis, Klansmen, and White Supremacists who hate Jews, blacks, and Muslims have anything to do with those noble intentions?

Free speech absolutists are its loudest defenders, but free speech does not mean that we must be forcibly exposed to so much violence as noise—the kind that benefit only First Amendment blowhards. Being loud and berating is not the same as being right. Free speech absolutism is not a virtue; it is a cult. Most people, fortunately, do not live in a world of absolutes. Absolutism is the tyranny of the fanged few—the ideological bullies feasting on the masses of less impassioned public opinion. There have always been legal limits to free speech, even as some pretended that the First Amendment allowed for no exceptions—a short text with an elongated sense of personal liberty that now, perhaps, finally needs to be reexamined.

I will discuss this in greater detail later, but shouting "Fire!" in a crowded theater is not protected speech, nor is libel and defamation, obscenity, "fighting words," incitement to imminent lawlessness, and true threats of violence. There is already precedent that makes speech less free than we have for so long been taught to believe.

Ironically, given that speech was ushered to the head of the line alongside the freedoms of religion, press, and assembly—all designated as first among equals—it was the people, and not even the Founders themselves, who insisted on singling out this particular right from the rest. The original draft of the Constitution did not include free speech at all. Charles Pinckney, a South Carolina legislator, proposed adding a free speech clause to the Constitution. A slight majority of the eventual signers, among whom were Alexander Hamilton and James Madison, rejected it. It was the pesky and persistent representatives of four states—Virginia, New York, Rhode Island, and Maryland—that made the insertion of free speech into the Constitution a condition of their adoption.[9]

The deliberations surrounding free speech preceded the creation of this country. Granting this liberty top billing on the grand marque of the Age of Rights was itself, appropriately, the subject of fierce democratic deliberation. Free speech has always informed the debates of the United States and, in fact, made them possible. Indeed, what eventually became the centerpiece of our democracy—the guarantee of free speech—was the subject of passionate debate. And that is what the Founding Fathers believed to be the political essence and moral imperative of free speech: citizens engaged in healthy debate, trading arguments like currency—a harmless exchange of words that form ideas, all for human betterment and good governance.

America's free speech guarantee is the very cornerstone of its liberal tradition, the primary calling card of its democracy, and the embodiment of its noble experiment in self-rule. In 1937, Supreme Court Justice Benjamin Cardozo described free speech as "the matrix, the indispensable condition of nearly every other form of freedom."[10] Nothing else threatens the sensitivities of American exceptionalism as much as impinging on free speech. And it accounts for why this nation is willing to celebrate free speech with patriotic fervor even when courts so often end up protecting speech that is anti-American both in word and deed.

Perhaps the best example of this apparent paradox reveals itself in the burning of the American flag. In *Texas v. Johnson*, decided in 1989,[11] the Supreme Court ruled that burning the American flag, rather than saluting it, waving it, or watching it unfurl in the wind, is protected expression under the First Amendment. Expressive for sure, but also arguably an act of aggression, infuriating and harmful to anyone who has had a loved one die in battle defending that very flag. And yet, extreme tolerance for political dissent, even as it provides a platform for anti-American animus, is what distinguishes the United States from most nations around the world. We prefer patriotism, but it is not un-American to criticize the government— even in vociferously vulgar terms. Totalitarian societies demand total conformity and national obedience. A truly democratic society, however, if sincere in its beliefs, gives dissidents the freedom to speak their minds—disloyal though they may be, and hostile in the manner by which they choose to express their opposition.

The American colonies had lived in terror of a British monarch who saw subversion lurking in every shadow and who was quick to charge sedition with every benign protest. The first order of business in forming a new nation was to make sure that paranoid tyrants could no longer stand in the way of a citizen's right to speak freely. We have come a long way since the restive days of King George III. Today, denouncing the president is a quasi-spectator sport. Protestors, under certain limits, are all welcome. *Saturday Night Live* is a weekly television takedown of Oval Office pretensions. Showtime's *Our Cartoon President* is a devastating parody of the president, his family, and government insiders. Donald Trump may possess the thinnest of skins, and his wishes for censorship linger beneath the surface of a fragile ego. Nonetheless, we are living in a golden age of irreverent presidential mockery—megalomania be damned.

Democracy, after all, is a messy state of affairs, and that mess, for most Americans, also accounts for its allure. The patriotic love for this country carries with it the obligation to protect the rights of even those who despise this country and who feel compelled to make their antipathies widely known. Over the years, the Supreme Court has invalidated laws that would ban neo-Nazis from marching in Skokie, Illinois, which was once a hamlet of Holocaust survivors,[12] or punish those who would deliver a hateful message in the form of a burning cross on an African-American's lawn.[13] The father of a dead marine who sought to bury his son was denied recovery of damages for the emotional distress he suffered when a church group picketed the funeral in order to voice their objections to gays serving in the military. They were holding signs that read: "God Hates Fags" and "Thank God for dead soldiers."[14] The soldier was not a homosexual, but his funeral, along with other final resting places for soldiers around the United States, have become protest venues of choice for this particular church. Other signs read: "Thank God for 9/11" and "God hates America."

And for the majority of constitutional scholars, the ACLU, and eight of the nine members of the Supreme Court who set aside the monetary award received by the father of that dead marine and upheld the right of the church group to ruin the one opportunity he had to say goodbye to his son who had served his country with honor and distinction, these rulings make perfect sense and are consistent with the meaning and purpose of the First Amendment. After all, shouldn't neo-Nazis, the Ku Klux Klan, and homophobic houses of worship be permitted to voice their opinions—in nearly any fashion they choose—even if that means communicating their message to land a specific blow for maximum effect? These are not acts of expression meant for the general public. They are intended for a particular listener, often delivered right to their faces and, in the case of the neo-Nazis in Skokie, right on their village green. The speaker always selects the right targets—people who are vulnerable to harm due to historical, racial, and biological factors beyond their control. And the harm is real, both in its psychological and physical dimensions, enough so that it manifests itself in emotional scarring and bodily sickness, leaving citizens debilitated by the harmful expression of another. The medical research supporting these findings is beyond dispute and will be discussed more fully in later chapters.

And yet, in the case involving the church group and the aggrieved father, the Chief Justice of the Supreme Court, who wrote the opinion, delivered a tutorial on the First Amendment, reminding everyone—as if anyone needs any further reminders—why this decision was legally correct and consistent with the free speech priorities of the United States.

Many call this glorification of unfettered speech, this slavish devotion to the First Amendment, free speech absolutism. It is a default position that favors, reflexively, the rights of the speaker over the listener, regardless of what the speaker has to say, how he or she may choose to say it, and the effect the speech ultimately has on the recipient of his or her message. For many Americans, the First Amendment's Free Speech Clause is inviolable. Yes, begrudgingly, some free speech diehards recognize a handful of proscribed categories of speech that are without constitutional protection and are therefore considered non-speech.

Saying openly that one believes in hate speech codes or the censorship of nearly any form of speech is not the way to get invited to fashionable parties. It was not always this way. During the 1960s, with protest movements and social upheavals marking a new political consciousness in America, courts began to apply the First Amendment more strictly, and consistently, against government attempts to restrict the free speech of its citizens. Burning a draft card, wearing a jean jacket emblazoned with the message "Fuck the Draft," even torching an American flag were ruled to be constitutionally protected communications of a political nature that, while offensive to some, ultimately addressed serious issues of public concern.

Before then, and especially during both World War I and II, the First Amendment did not come to the rescue of those accused of rousing public sentiment with grand gestures of political dissent that might serve to expose the nation to foreign threats. Going back even further, the Alien and Sedition Act of 1798 during President Adams' administration and the suspension of *habeas corpus* in 1861 during the Civil War under President Lincoln, were not declared unconstitutional even though these measures criminalized political activism and completely laid waste to the Free Speech and Assembly clauses of the First Amendment. Most Americans at the time wholly supported the Sedition Act even though today such a governmental maneuver would be denounced as fascist censorship of the first order and a blatant disregard of constitutional guarantees.

In fact, the First Amendment did not produce much case law at all during the first 160 years of its existence. Free speech was always regarded as a virtue of American democracy, but actually placing restrictions upon governmental prior restraints was far less developed and hardly ever occurred. Free speech was surely a feature of the Bill of Rights, but the government felt equally free to curtail speech during times of national emergency. It was not so obvious to ordinary citizens that, should they ever find themselves arrested for protesting the government, the First Amendment would always be available for their defense. Similarly, a citizen's free speech liberties were never regarded as being so versatile and potent that they could be deployed to help bring down the democracy.

If it were possible for the Founding Fathers to drop in on modern times and observe how their Constitution was now being interpreted, they would be appalled to learn that neo-Nazis, cross burners, and homophobic churchgoers were exploiting their First Amendment freedoms to prey upon vulnerable citizens. Surely that is not what they had in mind when they codified free speech as a central tenet of American democracy. What was initially conceived as a bill of right against a tyrannical king who punished his subjects for speaking their minds, and which was created to enhance self-government and democratic deliberation in all forms, is now being used by illiberal, intolerant, and undemocratic citizens to cause harm to those they do not like, depriving them of the dignity and tranquility they otherwise deserve.

Surely this is a misapplication of the First Amendment, a distortion that privileges speech over other civic values—namely, mutual respect, civility, common decency, and equal protection. These, too, were intended to be virtues of our democratic culture. The aspiration, after all, was always to create an environment that enabled and motivated citizens to participate in self-governance. How can one meaningfully avail themselves of democratic participation if they are being singled out for disrespect, if they are made to feel threatened, fearful, anxious, and without access to the public square? When it comes to a standoff between those who wish to assert their right to free speech in a hostile manner and those who merely wish to enjoy the privileges of citizenship, our legal system, generally, sides with the speaker.

The rebellion against King George III and the Revolutionary War that ensued coincided with the Age of Rights, inspiring a new nation with a living Constitution founded on humanistic, enlightened principles of liberty. But these new people of the Americas, now called the United States, walked away from the experience of living under the British crown determined to enjoy liberties previously unknown to them. The revolution was hard-won, and the rights they fought for would never be taken lightly. But some rights were weighted over others, with conflicting claims in a liberal society. Speech inexplicably has become a zero-sum game, a trump card that a cynical speaker always knows can be played to his or her advantage. *"My free speech will cancel out your rights to experience your own brand of American freedom."* Frightened and emotionally traumatized citizens, assaulted by another's speech, are not free.

Free speech, paradoxically, leads to a one-sided conversation. The constitutional right to speak is being exploited by bullies granted a bully pulpit, courtesy of the First Amendment. Law professor John A. Powell wonders, "What would it look like if we cared just as deeply about equality? What if we weighed the two as conflicting values, instead of the false formalism where the right to speech is recognized but the harm caused by that speech is not?"[15] In allowing for such disparate treatment, by extending rights that favor speakers regardless of their effect on listeners, we have enabled a good deal of humiliation, indignity, and actual harm—to both the body and tranquility of mind—to flourish with the blessing of the First Amendment.

But this is a modern constitutional innovation at the federal level. The language adopted in the 1821 New York State Constitution, for instance, which eighteen other states followed and which is still in existence today, reads: "Every citizen may freely speak, write, and publish his sentiments on all subjects, being *responsible for the abuse of that right.*"[16] Pennsylvania was the first state, actually, to incorporate the expressed "abuse" exception, back in 1790. The "abuse" of the right to free speech was always contemplated as a check upon a liberty that could very well interfere with the citizenship of another. The abuse was never excused; it always balanced out the right—until more recent times.[17] Indeed, this parallel duty not to abuse the right of free speech seems to have been forgotten. It is, however, very much present in the laws of Europe.

# AMERICAN OUTLIERS:
# SPEECH AS ROBUST RIGHT

*The First Amendment has become a ridiculously overhyped and manipulated freedom.*

NOT WIDELY KNOWN is that other nations around the world, including democracies fashioned from the cradle of the Enlightenment, adopted the teachings of the same worldly philosophers as did the United States—Locke, Rousseau, and Kant—and somehow managed to avoid the free speech madness that is as tightly woven into America's democracy as are the Stars and Stripes. The United States has an unsurpassably more exuberant appreciation of free speech than other democratic countries. Nations such as Germany, England, Belgium, Brazil, France, Canada, India, Ireland, Israel, Cyprus, Australia, Italy, the Netherlands, New Zealand, Austria, Sweden, Denmark, and Switzerland all have hate speech laws that restrict free speech. Marching neo-Nazis in Austria and Germany—two nations for whom brown shirts and the chanting of "Heil Hitler" is not some quaint trip down memory lane—get marched right to jail for up to three years. The Germans also recognize free speech, but they made an ideological if not humanistic decision that the protection of human rights was a more important defining feature of German citizenship. They did not see a reason why a commitment to free speech necessarily meant an obligation to tolerate hate speech. Brazilians regard the issue similarly and, unlike the circumstances behind the neo-Nazi march in Skokie, Illinois, Brazil is no refuge for Holocaust survivors. Brazilians simply know that Nazis—whether they be old or new—marching in any direction is not good for society. The interest that Germany, Austria, or Brazil has in making such expressive speech or conduct unlawful has less to do with protecting a vulnerable minority (because relatively few Jews actually live in these countries) than it does with safeguarding the overall political climate from a group that is only up to no good.

Just imagine the public sphere as a rain forest: Brazilians see both environments as worthy of protection from different but equally hazardous forms of pollution.

In France, Dieudonné M'bala M'bala, a comedian who popularized an inverted Nazi-style salute and whose comic material often includes the wish fulfillment of sending Jews back to the gas chambers, is routinely banned from performing in his native country and, occasionally, from entering the United Kingdom. He has been convicted of engaging in racial hatred in France repeatedly. He was even sentenced to serve two months in a Belgian prison and pay a $10,000 fine for inciting hatred stemming from racist, homophobic, and anti-Semitic comments made during his act.[18] More recently, he faced seven years in prison for a Facebook posting that mocked the Jews killed in Paris during the *Charlie Hebdo* terrorism attack and for identifying with and showing sympathy for their murderer.[19] The French, with their own rich liberal traditions and a revolution fought for liberty dating back nearly as far as our own, sleep well at night knowing that such laws are in place preventing Dieudonné from inciting hatred and causing harm to France's Jews. The deprived free-speech right of the comedian is apparently not central to their consideration of overall liberty. France remains a free society even though an anti-Semitic agitator may feel otherwise. The manner in which he chooses to communicate his hateful message has consequences—even in a society that values free speech.

In explaining why Dieudonné is treated differently from the cartoonists who drew for *Charlie Hebdo*, Emmanuel Pierrat, a French lawyer who specializes in free speech issues, said, "Freedom of expression stops where it starts to encroach upon the freedom of others."[20]

In Germany, in 1994, the Constitutional Court ruled that freedom of speech is not available as a defense to those who propagate the "Auschwitz lie"—the absurd falsehood that the Holocaust never happened. In 1995, a state court in Berlin convicted a neo-Nazi leader who greeted visitors outside of Auschwitz by telling them that the Holocaust was pure fiction.[21] Germans who wish to promote a false "idea" in contravention of the historical record—that the gas chambers of Auschwitz either never existed or that Germany had nothing to do with them—are not permitted to do so without risking criminal punishment. No one questions Germany as a mainstay of liberal democracy. And its sensitivity to Holocaust memory is now a first principle of its nationhood. And, yet, as a free society, it is comfortable denying the right to free speech for those who wish to introduce such pernicious and harmful falsehoods into the public sphere.

Both of these German cases took place nearly fifteen years after the Skokie decision. German lawmakers and judges were no doubt aware of this inconceivable American free speech case that had no counterpart on the European continent. To a European, *Collin v. Smith*, the federal court Skokie decision, was not so much a federal case as a freak show. Why in the world would Americans allow neo-Nazis to march in front of Holocaust survivors? What next: Feed Christians to lions? Where is the civic virtue in such bread and circuses? America's reputation for First Amendment excess precedes itself. And it does not seem to mind its outlier status as a nation where free speech is much more than a mere figure of speech. America takes great pride that anyone and everyone has an absolute right to speak their mind—even if they are out of their mind. And for decent people everywhere, it boggles the mind.

One can imagine that the surreal events in Skokie presented affinities too close for Germany's comfort. A suburb of Chicago is quite a distance from any city in Germany, but even in 1977, before the digital highway of the Internet, news traveled fast, and this type of news was of the especially rapid sort. Nazis will forever be Germany's most raw nerve—an Achilles' heel that covers the entire body. Germans know what comes out of the mouths of Nazis when given the chance to speak freely. Perhaps for this reason, Germany did not respond as if it had anything to learn from America's often perverse affection for its strict interpretation of the First Amendment. For Germans, the Skokie decision was a legal anathema—a quirk of national naiveté, the innocence of a country dimmed by the good fortune never to have experienced how speech can overthrow a republic.

This is one of the things that European nations understand about free speech that the United States does not. America stands alone among advanced democracies in rejecting hate speech laws on constitutional grounds. Law professor Jeremy Waldron called this "American exceptionalism with a vengeance."[22] What is it about the First Amendment that is not appreciated from afar? The concept of natural rights began in Europe and evolved in the United States with a Jeffersonian, Madisonian, Hamiltonian twist. One obvious novelty was an exaggerated holiness involving free speech. But even that did not manifest itself until after nearly two hundred years of its existence. Free speech absolutists in the United States constantly quote the British writer Evelyn Beatrice Hall, who wrote in her *The Friends of Voltaire*, "I disapprove of what you say, but I will defend to the death your right to say it." This statement is often misattributed to Voltaire himself. Ironically, however, this clever quote has had no influence on the British and French. Yet, Americans who have never even heard of Voltaire recite a phrase he never said as if it were their very own personal mantra.

All kinds of catchy slogans about free speech are celebrated in the United States and yet hold no sway in other democracies. They are invoked to justify and protect what is sometimes intolerable speech. And they are each composed with the smug moral authority of a people certain that theirs is the correct reading of liberalism. They believe that democratic self-government is simply not possible unless the most odious members of society are given their chance to spew their hatred of others.

Time and again, we hear:

"Good speech will cancel out bad speech."

"How does one draw the line between good and bad speech?"

"Allowing racists to speak freely brings them out into the open where they can be challenged and defeated."

"Having to tolerate the free speech of bigots is the price we all pay to live in a free society."

"Sunlight is the best disinfectant"—a quote from Supreme Court Justice Louis Brandeis in 1914 on how best to fumigate the harm that speech sometimes brings.

How that actually works in practice is not so obvious to a targeted individual situated in the middle of a riot.

British novelist Salman Rushdie stated in 2012 that "bad ideas, like vampires . . . die in the sunlight." This is an odd thing to say coming from someone who, because the Prophet Muhammad made an appearance in his novel *The Satanic Verses*, had a *fatwa* placed on his head by the Iranian cleric Ayatollah Khomeini. Rushdie was driven into social exile for years. No amount of sunlight shielded him from the darkness of Khomeini's idea that apostates should die a violent death. All kinds of sadistic behavior take place in the plain light of day. ISIS has beheaded hundreds with the sun beaming overhead, the blood flowing, the world watching, and the message clearly and freely communicated.

European lawmakers and jurists are of the view that bad ideas are bad for a reason: They are not really ideas at all. Just because they are spoken, or written out, does not automatically qualify them to be emulated, adopted, debated, or seriously considered. They do not meet the high standards required of ideas found worthy of sharing space in the public sphere. As law professor Eric Posner wrote in response to Rushdie, "Bad ideas never die: They are zombies, not vampires. Bad ideas like fascism, communism, and white supremacy have roamed the countryside of many an open society."[23]

The rest of the free world largely agrees. Even our bordering neighbors have a lower tolerance for speech intended to cause harm. "Canadians do not have a cast-iron stomach for offensive speech," said Jason Gratl, a lawyer for the British Columbia Civil Liberties Association. "We don't subscribe to the marketplace of ideas. Americans as a whole are more tough-minded and more prepared for verbal combat."[24] There is a strong global consensus that democracy is not enhanced whenever neo-Nazis, skinheads, and extremist right-wing or terrorist groups are nearby and taking their turn at the microphone. The more recent electoral successes of extreme right-wing parties in Europe is raising a continental cause for alarm.[25] These anti-democratic groups are not known to make any contribution to the "marketplace of ideas." How do you know this to be true? Does anyone think for a moment that a vigorous debate involving the deranged "ideas" of the KKK, neo-Nazis, and practitioners of Islamic terror would result in everyone conceding that they were right all along?

For several decades now, the Western world has been awash in moral relativism—the concept that all cultures, and the morality that guides them, exist relative to one another. None are better or worse. President Obama's skepticism about American exceptionalism was of a piece with this idea. Cultures are equipped with their own logic. What makes sense to one might offend all norms of another. What one culture does with its women, children, elderly—and their unique rites of passage and rituals—might seem barbaric to another culture, but that does not make it wrong. It is a judgment-free ethos, where the passing of judgment is itself a sign of post-colonial arrogance. Is it female genital circumcision or mutilation? Is the wearing of a burqa a cultural and religious norm, or is it the dehumanizing subjugation of women?

The moral relativist insists that no one is ever in a position to really know.

But being able to judge the conduct of another, fairly and correctly, is the cornerstone of liberal thinking. Evaluating options, weighing values, drawing conclusions, and making assessments is what liberal thinkers are expected to do. A philosophy based on the relativity of cultures undermines our moral duty to make fundamental distinctions between right and wrong.

A type of moral relativism fuels the folly that all ideas start out the same until they run the gamut through the marketplace of ideas. They have no currency at all at their inception, so they cannot be judged. Only through this mythical marketplace can valuations be assigned, where the bad ideas are identified and discarded like rotten fruit. But is that really necessary? Must a notably bad idea be given access to this public market? Can it not be called out for what it is from the very start—a flagrant violation of social and intellectual norms? Should we not be able to unequivocally agree that a white supremacist's ideas should not be allowed to become mainstream?

The only reason for the existence of extremist hate groups is to foment social unrest, incite violence, and promote disharmony among citizens. The responsibilities of citizenship, the rights and duties it imposes on all members of society, are truly foreign to them. Hateful advocacy is a blanket condemnation of civilizing norms. It is the very opposite of democratic participation. The propagation of hate has no interest in the pursuit of objective truth or the general improvement of society. The aim is to falsify and destroy; it is a disagreement with life itself.

Europeans take full measure of the social cost of harmful speech. And they also account for benefits that accrue to a society from speech. After a balancing of values, these other liberal democracies conclude that there should be no distinction between ordinary physical harms that governments are obligated to punish and prevent, and harms that arise from speech. Injurious speech is deserving of no special exemption. Reckless driving receives none either. Main Street and the public square should be made safe from either of these dangers.

In America, however, when it comes to the First Amendment, we treat every voice as precious; all opinions are equally valuable regardless of what is said or how it is said. It does not have to be this way. We can make choices and determine what is an acceptable public utterance. We do not have to be imprisoned by them. Voicing an opinion need not be a free-for-all. Some make no pretense that their actions and utterances are motivated by the life of the mind. They are not aiming for a civic award; elevating society is not their concern. Their world is visceral and impulsive. The gutter is their preferred domain; the endgame is to bring everyone down to their level. There is simply no moral or legal reason why they should be heard in a public setting. They do not have to be rewarded with a soapbox, unless the soap is being used to wash out their mouths.

It is for this reason that Europeans refuse to sweat the line-drawing and slippery-slope anxieties about restrictions on speech. They recognize that free speech ought to come with limits and that the reasonable regulation of speech is no less a governmental obligation than making sure that food and drugs, the securities markets, and the bridges and roadways are safe for public consumption and use. In parts of the United States where marijuana is still illegal, its recreational use results in a criminal conviction. Meanwhile, burning a cross in front of African-Americans to drive home the point that they are unwelcome in the neighborhood is constitutionally protected. Taking an action, like drug use, that might harm only oneself is against the law. Yet, tormenting a family and destroying their sense of tranquility and social status as citizens triggers no legal sanction. Try explaining this to a European. No wonder other nations are mystified by our misplaced priorities when it comes to free speech.

Within the constellation of natural rights, the freedom to speak freely is, arguably, the most natural right of all. But that does not make it dominant. Other rights and liberties are manifested in personal autonomy, dignity, and tranquility. The dignitary and equal protection rights of citizenship are no less natural to human existence. Privileging the First Amendment rights of the speaker while relegating the target of his unwelcome speech a second-tier citizenship is unjustified. The First Amendment has become a ridiculously overhyped and manipulated freedom. The United States could stand to reconsider whether its outlier devotion to the First Amendment still makes sense and whether it is finally time to take proper measure of the true costs of free speech.

# SILENCED SPEECH ON THE AMERICAN COLLEGE CAMPUS

No matter how the First Amendment is viewed by the general public, freedom of speech is symbolically dead in the one place where it was once most alive.

UNSTATED THOUGH IT may be, never before have Americans been this confused, or profoundly conflicted, over the abuses of free speech. A cultural shift has already occurred. There are many examples in recent years of Americans expressing ambivalence about the excesses of speech. And there is hypocrisy in professing to be in favor of free speech while at the same time silencing or condemning the politically incorrect speech of another. Free speech is being tested. The right, left, and center of the political spectrum are having trouble distinguishing their right from their left on the free speech divide.

In September 2017, the Brookings Institution released a survey entitled, "Views among college students regarding the First Amendment." Historically, free speech has been at its most vibrant on university campuses. Institutions of higher learning are presumed to offer platforms where ideas are vigorously debated and discussed. The whole point of a liberal arts education is to teach students to be open to conflicting points of view and challenged by different ways of thinking. And public universities, as state institutions, are strictly bound by the Constitution and its free speech guarantees. Private universities are no less obligated to maintain intellectually open places of learning.

Yet, the survey revealed that a plurality of college students today—fully 44 percent—do not believe the First Amendment protects "hate speech"—even though courts have unequivocally ruled that it does. And these findings were consistent among Democrats, Republicans, and Independents. Female students, however, were particularly insistent that the First Amendment did not protect those who resorted to hate speech, by a margin of 49 percent to 38 percent. Even more surprisingly, a majority of students—51 percent—were of the mindset that a student group should be allowed to shout down a speaker simply because they disagreed with his or her views. Apparently, according to a younger group of our citizens, the First Amendment protects those who disrupt debates. The debaters are left to fend for themselves, rendered speechless.

It gets worse. An astonishing 19 percent agree that, rather than just drowning out the speaker by making noise, opposing student groups also have the right to resort to violence to prevent the speaker from possibly ever speaking again.[26] Surveys conducted independently by the Knight Foundation and Gallup revealed that 69 percent of college students believe that their colleges should impose restrictions on "slurs and other language on campus that is intentionally offensive to certain groups." More than half said that the climate on their campus "prevents some people from saying things they believe because others might find them offensive."[27] And the Foundation for Individual Rights in Education ("FIRE") conducted a survey of colleges and universities in 2015 and discovered that 55 percent of these institutions maintain speech codes that control what can be said in a university setting.[28]

So much for free speech on college campuses and respect for the First Amendment.

Anyone paying much attention to life in the ivory tower and on the campus square must have noticed that students have been demonstrating their misapprehensions about the First Amendment for several years now. The answers to these survey questions are symptomatic of real-world attitudes straight out of collegiate playbooks. Invited speakers have been heckled into silence, forced to take their seats, ushered into hasty exists, escorted by armed guards—all because students refused to hear what the speakers were expected to say and attended the lecture precisely to sabotage it.

"Shut it down!" has replaced the polite applause or silent treatment and become the new rage on campus.

All across the United States, a majority of students no longer believe in the free speech rights of invited, outside speakers. Worse still, the right of their fellow, more open-minded students to hear the speaker is of little interest to them, too. Such was the experience of Israel's former ambassador to the United States Michael Oren at the University of California, Irvine, in 2010. There was nothing diplomatic about the hostile reception the ambassador received. The hecklers prevailed, and he never got a word in edgewise. The irony is that the ambassador was prepared to take questions from members of the audience who opposed his government's views; that simply was not good enough for the "no free speech for you" crowd, exercising their combative hecklers' veto.

Matters were even worse at the University of California in Berkeley in 2017, when rioting broke out before a scheduled protest against right-wing ideologue Milo Yiannopoulos. Both his speech, and another from conservative provocateur Ann Coulter, were cancelled.[29] Ironically, Berkeley is the birthplace of the Free Speech Movement, which galvanized the counterculture of the 1960s and defined the progressive politics of the era. Today's version of progressive politics, however, resembles a movement far more interested in selective speech than in free speech.[30]

Even more recently, in January 2018, at the University of Chicago—where only a year earlier the dean of students, John

Ellison, penned a letter to incoming freshmen informing them that creating "intellectual safe spaces" and providing "trigger warnings" were anathema to university life, and that Chicago would not cancel the appearance of invited speakers—students and faculty rallied together to rescind an invitation made to former White House advisor Stephen Bannon to speak at a town hall debate on campus. Over one hundred faculty members signed a petition objecting to Bannon's appearance, stating, "The defense of freedom of expression cannot be taken to mean that white supremacy, anti-Semitism, misogyny, homophobia, anti-Catholicism, and Islamophobia must be afforded the rights and opportunity to be aired on a university campus."[31] This from one of the few universities that truly values academic freedom and where the premises of "intersectionality" and the suffocations of political correctness have not been allowed to dominate campus culture. If the University of Chicago is rescinding invitations made to controversial speakers, then the First Amendment is truly undergoing a profound rethinking of constitutional priorities.

We are seeing more and more examples of speech being silenced and genuine confusion as to how free speech actually works in a society that is showing little tolerance for opposing points of view. Discussions are brought to an end before they even begin. The First Amendment, with all its free speech fanfare, sometimes appears to be nothing but a paper tiger.

Berkeley may still be the epicenter of New Left nostalgia—but not in ways that would be familiar to the leaders of the students who, in the 1960s and 1970s rallied against the Vietnam War through the exercise of free speech. In 2017, hundreds of thousands of dollars were spent on security measures to make it safe for conservative politico Ben Shapiro to deliver a speech on campus. Bomb-sniffing dogs had to be deployed.

Some college speakers never even make it to the podium to experience the indignity of being denounced. Some are fortunate enough just to make it out of campus alive. This is what happened in 2017 in separate incidents involving two very different types of speakers: conservative commentator Heather MacDonald at Claremont McKenna College; and libertarian political scientist Charles Murray at Middlebury College. Neither got a chance to speak. Both were secreted off campus to ensure their safety. Allison Stanger, a professor who was scheduled to moderate the conversation with Murray, and who did not share many of his views, was attacked by an angry mob of students and ended up in the hospital—all because it was she who helped whisk Murray out of the auditorium.[32]

There is a disturbing 2015 video of a Yale professor, Nicholas Christakis, shouted down and condemned by students for calmly attempting to defend his wife, Erika, who was the subject of angry criticism for believing that students who were offended by certain Halloween costumes were taking the matter too seriously. Neither husband nor wife are at Yale any longer.[33]

And it is not always students caught up in a censorial mood. University presidents may also need a refresher course on old-school free speech guidelines. Two members of the Sigma Alpha Epsilon fraternity were expelled by the president of the University of Oklahoma in 2015 for leading a racist chant that referred to the lynching of African-Americans. The incident was odious and reprehensible, for sure, but what happened to the First Amendment rights of those two students? It is one thing to have them morally shunned on campus—called out for their un-collegial, racist behavior. But expulsion for exercising a constitutional right would seem to some as positively un-American. And they were expelled from a publicly financed, state university, where the speech guarantees of the First Amendment clearly applied. The fraternity itself could have been banned for racial discrimination because they were, apparently, disallowing African-Americans from joining.[34] But merely boasting about such exclusion is not unlawful. And neither is a racist chant in support of lynching—not in

America, at least. After all, what makes their racist chant any less worthy of First Amendment protection than burning a cross on an African-American's lawn? Both are utterly despicable. To an African-American, cross-burning and a song celebrating lynching are internalized in equally devastating ways. Neither should receive First Amendment protection, and at least one president of a public university agrees. But in the process, he might have violated the First Amendment guarantees of those two former students. But why then did no free speech absolutists rise to their defense?

Sometimes universities have engaged in self-censorship, restricting their own ability to speak, instead of standing firm on First Amendment principles. Yale University Press, for instance, published a book in 2009, *The Cartoons that Shook the World*, which surveyed the global mayhem that arose from the twelve cartoons appearing in a Danish newspaper in 2005, depicting, and in some cases mocking, the Prophet Muhammad. Many Muslims in the Middle East, Persian Gulf, and Africa found these cartoons to be blasphemous. And they made their displeasure known. The outcry over the cartoons resulted in rioting in the streets and the vandalizing of foreign embassies. In the end, about two hundred people were killed, and the Western world was placed on notice that its belief in freedom of expression—artistic or otherwise—was not shared by much of the world's Muslim population. The publication of such insulting caricatures was greeted not with counter-cartoons in a robust debate of inky aesthetics, but with the terrorism of Islamic extremism.[35]

Worldwide anger over the incident did not die down. In fact, it formed a link within the chain of events that led to the mass killings at the French satirical newspaper *Charlie Hebdo* in early 2015, where a different group of cartoonists lost their lives for the Sharia crime of blasphemy against Mohammad. Yale, obviously, got the message. It went ahead with its plans to publish a book about the affair in the face of this known risk. But it capitulated to the threat of terrorism by relinquishing its academic mission to pursue truth.

Nowhere in the published book could the offending cartoons actually be found. The book came with a provocative title promising cartoons, but one would have to look elsewhere to view the pictures that ignited all of this Islamic rage. Perhaps Yale's publishing arm decided to show sensitivity to the feelings of Muslims, which is why a book about a controversy over cartoons contained lots of words but no cartoons. More likely, however, they had a reasonable fear that terrorism would visit the university, and neither academic freedom nor truth-telling was worth losing life and limb.[36]

Yale should either have published the book with the cartoons or not published it without them. Cowardice in the defense of liberty weakens democracy and enables the opponents of free speech to shut down debate through violence—a tactic that worked for King George III until he lost the American Colonies. This nation was built on the very lesson Yale failed to learn.

Elsewhere on the campus scene, several commencement speakers slated to receive honorary degrees were unceremoniously told that the university had changed its mind on account of words spoken or actions taken that some students would find to be unacceptably offensive. Exercising their freedom of speech had bizarrely disqualified them as graduation-day speakers. Distinguished, but nonetheless disinvited because students and faculty objected to the content of a message delivered in the past. Silencing and wholesale condemnation has become the new ethic at the academy. Holding two conflicting arguments at the same time has become a disfavored intellectual exercise. Feminist and human rights activist Ayaan Hirsi Ali, a known critic of the misogynistic treatment of women in Islamic societies, was told by Brandeis University that her commencement address and the receipt of her honorary degree were both cancelled. Similar snubs occurred with former secretary of state Condoleezza Rice at Rutgers, International Monetary Fund managing director Christine Lagarde at Smith College, and former University of California, Berkeley chancellor Robert Birgeneau at Haverford. The list of withdrawn invitations to speakers includes: former secretary of state Henry Kissinger, former Harvard University president Lawrence Summers, actor Alec Baldwin, DNA co-discoverer James Watson, Indian prime minister Narendra Modi, filmmaker Michael Moore, conservative Pulitzer Prize–winning columnist George Will, liberal Pulitzer Prize–winning columnist Anna Quindlen, and comedian and talk show host Bill Maher.[37]

This is a group of people who would not agree on very much if you shoved them all into one room. And, yet, none of them was acceptable to college students who show such seething contempt for anything outside of their comfort zone. Whether a speaker is on the right, left, or in the center, many students and faculty do not want to hear it, will not allow anyone else to hear it, and just might decide to shout it down. It is as if discourse has been replaced by discord.

And to prove that this is no joke, comedians Jerry Seinfeld, Chris Rock, and Larry the Cable Guy have forsworn performing at colleges altogether. These professional joke tellers, whose job description demands that they occasionally wade into politically incorrect territory to get a laugh, believe that their kind is no longer welcome on such severe ivy-covered places where speech is less free and more scrutinized than ever.[38]

So much for free speech and artistic liberty for visitors to universities and colleges. What is happening inside the classrooms is far worse. What is being taught is often dictated not by what students should know but by what will not offend them. Professors anxiously modify their lectures, making sure to issue "trigger warnings," not committing "microaggressions," and ensuring that "safe spaces" are available to their students—places where upsetting ideas cannot hurt them. In many cases, academic freedom no longer applies to a course syllabus, and professors are afraid of their students. At the University of Illinois, a professor was fired for teaching the Roman Catholic perspective on homosexuality, and a University of Kansas professor was suspended for an unflattering tweet about the National Rifle Association (NRA).[39]

Has the American mind become officially closed? When it comes to the classroom, self-censorship has become an unspoken campus crusade. No matter how the First Amendment is viewed by the general public, freedom of speech is symbolically dead in the one place where it was once most alive. And even avowed liberals are having difficulty accepting the lack of independent critical thought. *New York Times* columnist Nicholas Kristof wrote of how, even in his own household dedicated to progressive politics, he and his daughter were at odds about the absence of ideological diversity on campus.[40]

# 4.

## THE GENERAL PUBLIC, AND KEEPING YOUR MOUTH SHUT

*Speech may still be free, but opening one's mouth now carries much greater risk.*

EVEN OUTSIDE OF university life, the spirit of the First Amendment could use a refresher course. All sorts of people have lost livelihoods and commercial endorsements because of loose lips that get tongue-tied all on account of political incorrectness. There is a general intolerance for speech that may inadvertently offend. Retractions are everywhere.

NFL quarterback Cam Newton from the Carolina Panthers made a sexist remark during a post-game press conference in 2017 and paid a stiff price in the withdrawal of one of his commercial endorsements. In response to a question from a female reporter wondering about the route-running of his wide receiver, Newton chuckled and clumsily said that it was funny to hear a woman ask such a complicated football question. The quarterback made no inappropriate pass. He just fumbled the question, as if it never occurred to him that female reporters who cover the NFL actually understand the nuances of the game. In a league that has had its share of troubles with outright sexual violence against women, this was a relatively harmless moment. Newton apologized the next day, but the damage was already done in a nation no longer in a forgiving mood about errant speech. Speech may still be free, but opening one's mouth now carries much greater risk.

What happened with comedienne Roseanne Barr in May 2018 was somewhat different. An unfortunate exercise of free speech led to an abrupt end to the revival of her hit TV show, *Roseanne*. She sent out an undeniably and deplorably racist tweet about former Obama White House advisor Valerie Jarrett. No one fed her this line. She claimed that her tweet was only a joke. Shouldn't her network, ABC, have simply considered the source: a crude comedienne mouthing off, not unlike the character she was paid so handsomely to re-create weekly? Why were free speech advocates not coming to her rescue? Had she simply crossed a line that even the First Amendment could not support?[41]

James Damore had been gainfully employed as a software engineer at Google for four years until he was abruptly dismissed from his job in 2017 for having written an internal memo that eventually went viral. He naively believed that he was safe to exchange ideas with his colleagues. Apparently, however, holding challenging views at a tech giant is best left inside the trash folder on one's desktop. In response to the increasingly delicate issue of gender diversity in the workplace, Damore argued that women were underrepresented in the technology industry not necessarily due to discriminatory hiring practices, but because of biological differences. He intended to provoke an "honest conversation" within the offices of Google about the reasons for the gender gap and why workforce disparity is inevitable. Google's chief executive did not agree, writing that Damore's memo advanced "harmful gender stereotypes" of women too anxious to perform well in high-pressurized work environments. Google's many engineers, mathematicians, and computer scientists—all fearless when it comes to defending marketing practices—were now revealed to be dangerously fragile when faced with offensive opinions. Damore filed a complaint against Google with the National Labor Relations Board just before being fired. The Board did not protect his putative free speech rights either.[42]

Google is not alone in policing the speech of its employees. In fact, at Mozilla, where its Firefox browser competes with Google in the search engine arms race, the CEO of the company, Brendan Eich, lost his job when it was discovered that in 2008 he had donated $1,000 in support of California's Proposition 8, which sought to ban same-sex marriage in the state. A private donation, made as an exercise of political opinion having nothing to do with his corporate responsibilities, was a fireable offense.[43] Dan Cathy, the president of Chick-fil-A, similarly spoke out against same-sex marriage in 2012 but managed to keep his job, although not without a lot of anguish and backlash for expressing such an unfavored opinion.[44]

It does seem that 2017 was the year where saying even the most innocuous thing could land the speaker in the apology penalty box, where fairly innocent statements required the kind of *mea culpas* that are never extracted from hard-core felons. Just consider these swift disavowals from speakers who were spooked by the disapproving reactions to their remarks: At the 2017 Oscars ceremony, actor Michael Keaton accidentally conflated two films with African-American themes, *Hidden Figures* and *Fences*, and said "*Hidden Fences*." An effusive apology was issued the very next day. The same thing happened to actors Hilary Duff and Chris Hemsworth, both of whom attended separate Halloween parties in 2017 dressed as Native Indian-Americans.[45] Artistic expression, even on Halloween, cannot include cultural appropriation—even if innocently and harmlessly undertaken. Singer and actor Justin Timberlake made the mistake of sending out a tweet in which he expressed admiration for a particular African-American. What offense that caused is difficult to fathom, but the very next day he was fast at work composing an apology by professing his love for all peoples.[46]

Defenders of President Trump, arguably misguided, have come to learn that speaking favorably about the president's misconduct or other undisciplined behavior will not be tolerated as merely a matter of opinion. In June 2018, Kanye West was besieged by Twitter trolls for having tweeted his support for President Trump. The country singer Shania Twain, who happens to be Canadian, felt compelled to apologize for saying that, had she been allowed to vote in the 2016 presidential election, she would have supported Donald Trump.[47]

I am not a spin doctor for celebrities, nor am I leaping on a soapbox to advocate support for any of the preceding statements—whether from Cam Newton or Shania Twain. But if one were to separate the statements from the bold-face names who said them and just examined the comments themselves, it would be hard to imagine the kind of public outrage that these statements actually elicited. They are pretty inoffensive, actually. In a nation purportedly enamored with the First Amendment, how did we become part of this cult of denunciation, all the while professing an allegiance to free speech?

And that is the point.

These very recent anecdotes of speech in retreat hint that a shift of some kind is taking place, where speech absolutism is looking a lot more like rejectionism. Some might say that these are mere aberrational detours from America's otherwise long-standing First Amendment commitments. They do not reflect a fundamental change in the nation's romance with free speech. What we are experiencing is a momentary fascination with political correctness and its call for multicultural sensitivity. After decades where speech took liberties with prejudices both pernicious and benign, America is finally being given a crash course in the unspoken rules of pluralism. We are undergoing a cultural moment, trying to correct for years of self-perpetuating stereotypes and ethnic, racial, sexual, and gender injustices. This is not a trivial reordering of national priorities. The imperatives of free speech are getting in the way of this new national project. For well over fifty years, the First Amendment stood as a colossus over all other rights and values. It never took a back seat to any other of America's catalog of freedoms; the singularity of speech was never challenged.

Until now. Perhaps political correctness has led to a new social consciousness, one that involves a backlash against free speech, fearlessly taking on the pieties of the First Amendment. But if that is true, the consequences this presents to the values behind free speech have not yet been acknowledged or fully examined. One can speculate that Donald Trump's presidential victory, with its open disdain for political correctness, serves as its own free speech countermovement, poking the sleeping bear of the First Amendment in hopes of arousing its dominance and quashing this new sensitivity toward censorship. In the meantime, to suggest that America remains a beacon of free speech fixation, without reservation, is false.

# 5

# FREE SPEECH MAY BE LESS AMERICAN THAN FOOTBALL

*Words better left unsaid remain just that.*

L EGALLY SPEAKING, NONE of these examples of America's sudden free-speech phobia actually involve the First Amendment at all. In the case of Cam Newton, a corporate sponsor can decide that a celebrity no longer possesses the right image to represent its product. The lesson for all professional athletes: Press conferences have consequences—be careful what you say. There is no First Amendment play for this quarterback to call from the Bill of Rights playbook. Similarly, a professional sports league comprised of individual owners can decide that the personal conduct of a fellow franchise owner (such as Donald Sterling, who made some private bigoted remarks) has become detrimental to the NBA's brand, and they can take action and force a sale. Sterling may have had any number of antitrust and contractual claims against the league for having his team wrested away from him all because of a racist rant recorded by a vindictive mistress. But his First Amendment rights were surely not one of them. And Google, subject to anti-discrimination employment laws, can decide who among its employees are worth promoting and which deserve to be let go. They can also decide what constitutes inappropriate material for inter-office memos. In such a private, corporate setting, Damore possessed no free speech claim that would protect him from losing his job. The First Amendment was not implicated in either of these cases. The First Amendment applies only to governmental restraints on speech, but most people invoke the right and believe in the principle no matter who is seeking to silence them.

The NBA and Google are free to tell their franchise owners or software engineers, respectively, to keep quiet, without violating the First Amendment.

Many people are confused as to how the First Amendment actually works in practice—not as a philosophical principle but as a legally enforceable right. Two people having an argument on a street corner where one says, "Shut up! Stop talking! I don't want to hear from you anymore," and the other replies, "Wait a minute, this is a free country: I have a First Amendment right to free speech, so I can say whatever I want!" clearly would benefit from a refresher course in American civics. The First Amendment has little to do with friendship.

That is because the First Amendment, like all amendments to the Constitution, is a negative right, rather than a positive or affirmative one. No one has a right to free speech in absolute terms. We all speak at our own risk. *The right only applies when the government prevents citizens from exercising their right to speak.* Understood in this way, the First Amendment is less of an affirmative right than a defense against government's attempt to silence us. Americans have no constitutional right to verbally pummel away at each other without regard to other values, such as civility, truth, and mutual respect. We can, of course, behave boorishly with insults and weaponized words, but not because of any constitutional claim of right. We do not legally assert our rights to free speech against each other. We just do it anyway without legal justification. The right to speak is one we take for granted, not unlike the right to breathe air.

The existence of the First Amendment provides Americans with the self-assurance that this is a nation of free speakers. Protesting the government is not a treasonous act but an act of civic participation. Speaking one's mind, for the most part, is not a crime. But recently we have been treating certain people as if it is.

The First Amendment has little to do with nongovernmental actions that interfere with speech. A speaker who resorts to dangerous, threatening, and harmful speech is not acting under the protection of the First Amendment. Freedom of speech was envisioned to protect words and conduct that contribute to the pursuit of knowledge, human betterment, and the general welfare. Words better left unsaid remain just that.

At the start of the National Football League's 2017 season, all eyes were not on the field, but rather the sidelines, as individual players decided whether to support the Black Lives Matter movement, and show solidarity with former NFL quarterback Colin Kaepernick, by refusing to stand during the singing of the national anthem. The season before, it was just Kaepernick and a smattering of a few other players who took a stand by kneeling and choosing the pre-game ceremonies to symbolically protest police brutality against African-Americans. During the 2017 campaign, however, perhaps in reaction to President Trump's reprimand that players who disrespect the flag should be kicked off their teams, more players around the league joined in on this new ritual in defiance of the president and as an act of collective protest. It has been said that some Americans, for whom patriotism is a higher aspiration than a Super Bowl–winning season, exercised their rights as consumers and cancelled their season tickets and/or turned off their TVs, lodging their own protest against the protestors. Football might be America's game but, in the estimation of some of its fans, not when the players engage in perceived anti-American activities. Finally, Jerry Jones, the owner of the Dallas Cowboys—sometimes referred to as America's Team—decided to put an end to this sideline sideshow. He placed his own players on notice that if anyone refused to stand for the national anthem, they would not play in the game.[48]

Many NFL players around the league groused that such a punitive action by a franchise owner violated their constitutional rights. After all, this was a political protest, dealing with a political matter against the police, a governmental entity. Is this not the appropriate occasion in which the First Amendment can be called upon?

Jerry Jones is a private citizen, and it is his team. The players work for him and must answer to him. Actions that he takes or rules that he enforces against his players might violate the Collective Bargaining Agreement that the NFL has negotiated with its players. He may or may not have breached a contract, but he surely did not violate the Constitution. An employment contract with a private employer does not necessarily guarantee the freedoms that citizens possess under the laws of the United States. Damore, the Google software engineer, discovered that very thing.

Players have a right to express their opinions about racial injustice as citizens of the Unites States. But that right does not extend to game time as team members of the Dallas Cowboys. At that point, they are on the clock—for all four quarters. Jerry Jones has a right to mandate the color of the uniforms his players wear during the game or even the business suits they may be required to wear to and from the game. He can also decide how he wants his team to be presented to the fans right before kickoff. And, apparently, he wants them lined up and standing respectfully during the playing of the national anthem. The First Amendment has about as much involvement in this matter as do the rules of rugby—neither apply. Unless the State of Texas passes a law requiring all those who attend football games within the state to rise during the anthem, black lives will surely matter, but the First Amendment does not apply to this entirely private and corporate dispute.

Let me be clear: I am absolutely not denigrating or trivializing the Black Lives Matter movement. That is not what the above paragraph says. The issue is, quite simply, that standing or kneeling for the national anthem does not fall under the umbrella of the First Amendment while at work in the private sector. The Founders intended for the First Amendment to permit citizens to criticize the government in the public square and not be punished for it. It never occurred to them that citizens, while on the job, could force their employer to grant them the time to make a political statement and then assert the First Amendment in order to prevent their firing.

There are those, however, who insist that kneeling in protest during the national anthem is precisely what the flag exemplifies and the First Amendment guarantees. Maybe so, but it still does not give the players a constitutional right to express their political opinions in this fashion—in such a time, place, and manner. And NFL fans, by turning away from the game, were saying that free speech is not absolute, and listeners have rights, too.

An employer, and the general public—even social media trolls—have their own ways of censoring speech without violating the First Amendment. Speech can be abridged by other citizens. There are costs to speaking, imposed by everyone except the government. A Google engineer loses his job; an NBA franchise owner loses his team; and celebrities of every stripe are compelled to apologize for making statements that runs afoul of the moral censors of the moment. Perhaps we are not a nation of free speakers, after all; perhaps our indulgences with free speech come qualified with restrictions—whether governmental or societal.

As a constitutional amendment, it is best to think of the Free Speech Clause of the First Amendment as something we keep tucked away safely in our back pocket. We know as Americans that it is always available to be used in our defense should the government seek to thwart our freedom of expression. The First Amendment is, practically, not so much a license to speak as a legal defense that can be asserted against the government should it try to impose a cost—by way of fines, jail time, or permits denied—on speech. But many incorrectly believe that the right under the

Constitution to speak freely is limitless and that it can be used at any time and without moderation or even good manners. They can unleash themselves onto the public square—without quality controls, guardrails, or common courtesies. This misperception, and the abuse that follows from it, has eroded our social cohesion and political engagement. It has forced many citizens to withdraw from civic life because the risk of becoming the target of another's First Amendment fury is too great and, in many cases, inevitable. And citizens who are forced to live in fear of indignity are not citizens at all.

All speech is not fair game, and government interference is not off-limits. This unrelenting exposure to the harm that speech can cause is not the price we all pay to live in a democracy. We should not be compelled to move somewhere else, to a more sensitive society that protects emotional well-being along with bodily harms.

In a nation notorious for reckless speaking, speakers do not always have the right of way. We have never been that free with *any* liberty—especially not speech.

# 6

# WHERE IT IS PERMISSIBLE TO SAY: SPEAK NO MORE

There are, after all, common sense, best practices, and rules-based restrictions on speech that everyone understands and consents to freely.

NEARLY EVERYONE KNOWS that falsely shouting "Fire!" in a crowded theater is not legally protected expressive activity. (Of course, *truthfully* shouting fire in a crowded theater is both legal and deserving of a medal, whereas shouting fire in an empty theater is legal although mentally suspect.) This limiting rule about free speech, at least when it came to theaters set on fire, was pronounced by Justice Oliver Wendall Holmes Jr. in his seminal 1919 decision in *Schenk v. United States*, the first of several Supreme Court cases that established sensible limits on our right to free speech.[49] Justice Holmes would probably also agree with the statement that one does not possess a right to scream in an area where there is a risk of causing an avalanche.

Not every word out of a person's mouth, however, needed to be subject to Supreme Court review. There are, after all, both commonsense best practices and ruled-based restrictions on speech that everyone understands and consents to freely. For instance, a party to an action in a criminal trial or civil lawsuit, or even a witness, a juror, or a spectator watching from the gallery, cannot just stand up in open court and make his or her opinion known about the proceedings. Nor can one even calmly profess his or her innocence or deny liability without being called out of order and fined for contempt. Law professor Stanley Fish has observed that the regulation of "hate speech" is "no more or less difficult than the question of whether spectators at a trial can applaud or boo the statements of opposing counsels."[50] If those who sit in courtrooms are required to comport themselves with decorum, why should we not demand anything less from those who cannot seem to get through a day without resorting to injurious speech in order to make their feelings known?

Speaking of courtrooms, if free speech applied to them during trials—if everyone simply was given a chance to have his or her say, at any time and without restriction—there would be no reason to have evidence rules, which determine what gets said during trial and the manner in which it gets said. Jurists do not take kindly to people disrupting the proceedings in their misguided belief that they have the right, as Americans, to speak their mind whenever they wish. No one has such rights. Those charged with the responsibility to interpret the Constitution do not allow for the liberal exercise of free speech in their own courtrooms.

Judges are not alone. Students who interrupt teachers and disrupt classrooms that are in session are disciplined. Students who believe they have First Amendment rights, especially in public schools where the Constitution surely applies, cannot object that their rights have been violated by an imperious, rule-enforcing teacher. Free speech does not extend that far. Anyone who has ever been to a public or private library knows that there are monitors hired to *shush* anyone who tries to speak above a whisper. The First Amendment will not rescue a noisy talker. Employees can be terminated at will for openly criticizing their employers. Job seekers and applicants for funding can be snubbed in the hiring process, or deprived of a grant, if positions they have taken publicly (or ill-advisedly on Twitter or Facebook) end up not be-ing viewed favorably by a prospective employer or grant-making entity. No employer is under any legal or moral obligation to overlook a candidate's idiotic tweet by saying, "Well, he does have a First Amendment right to his opinion, so I can't hold that against him." Publishers, broadcasters, and Internet service providers can be fined or sanctioned for violating certain standards of decency or engaging in defamatory conduct. However, none of them can point to the First Amendment to excuse not measuring up to those standards.

There are limits to the First Amendment, categories of pro-scribed speech—"fighting words," libel and slander, "the incite-ment of imminent lawlessness," intimidation and "true threats"—that are essentially deemed as non-speech and therefore are outside the operation of the First Amendment. There are cate-gories of speech that do not receive constitutional protection, such as blackmail, bribery, perjury, harassment in the workplace, plagia-rism, child pornography, some forms of panhandling and telemar-keting, and lying to government officials, along with restricted speech in the military and penal institutions.[51]

The Supreme Court has held that flag-burning is protected First Amendment activity because it, purportedly, constitutes an ex-pressive political viewpoint. But while burning the Stars and Stripes is regarded as permissible symbolic speech, an American citizen who does not agree with the direction the country has taken cannot express his discontent by assassinating public officials. Yes, that, too, would be a politically expressive act, but it is not a constitutionally protected one.

Professor Alexander Tsesis has remarked that there are no First Amendment guarantees for speech intended to solicit votes within one hundred feet of polling places on election day, or for the oper-ating of some adult theaters, burning draft cards, and disseminat-ing pornography. Given that some forms of speech are already regulated, why then should hate speech, for instance, receive greater rights under the First Amendment than any of these other categories of political speech? "Arguably, like obscenity or threats made against the President," Tsesis writes, "hate speech has little or no social and political value. . . . [H]ate speech is either non-speech, and therefore not protected by the Constitution," or it offers nothing that could possibly "elicit democratic values."[52]

The First Amendment's grant of rights is inapplicable when applied to non-speech. In the prior examples, the right to speak is rejected in favor of other considerations: the right of litigants to receive a fair and orderly trial and not have the proceeding taken hostage by a narcissistic heckler; the right of students to be taught by an undistracted teacher rather than having their day interrupted by a petulant classmate; the right of employers to maintain control over their work environments and to make hiring decisions based on complete knowledge of past conduct; the right that the general public has not to be exposed to smut; the right of an individual to privacy and to have his or her reputation protected from falsehoods; and the right of an official not to be attacked. For those who like to see movies on sold-out opening nights, rest comfortably in knowing that your right to not get stampeded is valued more than a dangerous prank of shouting "Fire!" To allow otherwise would be an abuse of the First Amendment. How absurd would it be if our obsession with free speech gave the speaker leeway in any of these situations? The exploitation of free speech is not a political virtue. It is a capitulation to harmful noise—and that noise can have injurious physical and emotional consequences.

These examples also demonstrate that we are entirely capable of making choices between competing rights—of balancing the interests of speakers against listeners and of labeling some speech as not being speech at all, but rather the narcissism of a nitwit or the rantings of someone with no intellectual aspirations to advance a worthy idea or contribute to meaningful public debate. We should judge them as illegitimate speakers. No one is automatically made better when they open their mouths. We, therefore, should treat them no differently from toxic polluters—in this case, those who cause environmental damage to social tranquility and human dignity. There are "time, place, and manner restrictions" on speech, where courts have ruled that the government is permitted to narrowly restrict even political speech, provided that it is not on account of the content of the message being delivered. But how about simply displaying good manners when exercising one's citizenship and in respecting the citizenship of others?

The sensible regulation of speech already exists—in case law—without offending liberty. Yet, we could all benefit from a renewed understanding of the First Amendment and how it should apply in the modern era, consistent with our founding democratic values, common sense, and human decency. And we may require more regulation of speech to preserve our democracy.

# 7

# WHAT IS THE
# MARKETPLACE OF IDEAS?

*The more speech to which we are all exposed, the more ideas that are conceived and circulated, the more truth, ultimately, is revealed, and the better decision-makers we all become.*

*I*N A COMPETITIVE, consumer-oriented society like the United States, where zero-sum, winner-take-all contests are rites of passage and where even happiness is pursued rather than bestowed (thank you, Thomas Jefferson), is there any wonder that the exercise of free speech, too, must pass the test of survival of the fittest? The Neoclassical model of economics, with its rational markets, invisible hands, and *laissez-faire* attitudes about government regulation, has its hand in the speech business as well. Ideas emerge from their own natural selection, the evolutionary travails that lead to all truths.

At least that is what free speech absolutists have been accustomed to believe.

Under the First Amendment, as judges and scholars have interpreted its meaning, free speech is regarded as not so much a right as a consumer product, not unlike toothpaste and breakfast cereal. It has its own supply-and-demand curve, shortages and scarcities, externalities and transaction costs. And, most of all, speech—whether through spoken words or symbolic conduct—exists within a competitive market that is robust, fluctuating, and, at times, ruthless.

This should not be all that surprising. In America, healthy competition is a national ethos. Of course, that all depends on whether the contest to be decided is actually healthy. Speech, sometimes, when taken to extremes, when words are intended to wound, is bad for your health. And a marketplace of ideas, governed by nothing other than an invisible hand, is likely to be as indelicate as showing someone the back of the hand.

If you are one of those who believe there is already enough competition in America without having to throw speech into the fray, then the person to blame is perhaps this country's best-known former Supreme Court Justice, Oliver Wendall Holmes Jr. In one dissenting opinion, he established the dominant metaphor for why Americans rely on the First Amendment to distinguish truth from falsehood and why so many argue that governmental efforts to regulate speech must be resisted at all cost. In *Abrams v. United States*, a case brought under the Espionage Act of 1917 against Communist sympathizers, the Court upheld the convictions of the defendants, but in dissent Justice Holmes wrote:

> [W]hen men have realized that time has upset many fighting faiths, they may come to believe even more than they believe the very foundations of their own conduct that the ultimate good desired is better reached by *free trade in ideas*—that *the best test of truth is the power of the thought to get itself accepted in the competition of the market* and that truth is the only ground upon which their wishes safely can be carried out. That at any rate is the theory of our Constitution.[53]

Ironic that a Supreme Court case from a century ago, arising from a long-forgotten war and expressing the opinion of one dissenting justice, somehow became immortalized as the strongest justification for what makes unfettered free speech so vitally important to the body politic. Defining speech as "the free trade in ideas" inside a marketplace from which truth emerges is still very much the prevailing theory behind the First Amendment.

Holmes introduced a concept that, like other goods and services exchanged in a competitive economy, speech operates in a marketplace of its own. What people say, the formulations of their mind, does not come with price tags, but the consumers of speech—those listeners within earshot, assimilating what was said—nonetheless know how to assess their relative values and how they compare with other speech offerings within the market. Indeed, consumers know whether the quality of expression even belongs in the competitive arena of speech. Perhaps it should be heavily discounted, or tossed out altogether, like stale bread or last year's model. Like the buying and selling that occurs in all markets, consumer demand will determine the fate of speech that is offered for sale in this mythical market.

Yet Holmes was careful to describe only a certain category of speech as being worthy of free trade. Not all speech would necessarily qualify. What he imagined was a marketplace of "ideas." Speech that does not convey an idea—no pretense to human betterment, a casual remark that cannot possibly enlighten the mind or fire the imagination, an emission from the mouth that is no more precious than a hiccup—does not gain entry into this particular marketplace. Ideas are the specialty items in an elaborate boutique of mind expansion. They are to be deeply valued and fiercely traded in this robust, competitive arena. Ideas are the coin of the realm in the speech economy. They are the stock and trade of this marketplace. And for this reason, in the interest of consumer welfare, government should never interfere with the free-flowing emanation of ideas. Thinking about free speech in these terms—as the delivery system for the creation of ideas—is a unifying principle that has shaped First Amendment jurisprudence for nearly a century. Indeed, Holmes forever solidified the marketplace of ideas metaphor, and its hold on the First Amendment, as "the theory of our Constitution."

What a factory and fount the First Amendment is. A marketplace of ideas is not just some showcase that operates beyond the reach of common men, like an auction house for race horses or fine art or an exclusive clearinghouse for rarefied commodities that only a certain segment of the public can bid on or partake in. A marketplace of ideas is a truly democratic engine for social change. It is not limited to the philosophically inclined. What gets exchanged in this market is at the center of the moral and political universe. Ideas raise the valuation of all human capital. Everyone benefits when the best and most original ideas are brought to market. It is only through ideas that discoveries are made and political truths verified. In fact, *truth* is the endgame of this market—the grand prize—what all of these verbal transactions are directed toward. The bill of sale is a receipt for enlightenment. Free speech as a kick-starter of ideas becomes the essential ticket to the discovery of truth. The more speech to which we are all exposed, the more ideas that are conceived and circulated, the more truth, ultimately, is revealed, and the better decision-makers we all become. As legal scholar Alexander Meiklejohn has written, establishing truth through the marketplace of ideas "is not merely the 'best test.' There is no other."[54]

The Supreme Court continues to invoke this metaphor so frequently that the marketplace of ideas has become enshrined in both our jurisprudence and national consciousness. And for this reason, America's market economy has come to resemble its political economy, with a *laissez-faire* approach to government regulation common to both. The Court has often stated that it should play no part in policing speech, especially if that means regulating the content of what is being said and, invariably, favoring one idea over another. From a 2008 Supreme Court decision, for instance, "The First Amendment creates an open marketplace where ideas, most especially political ideas, may compete without government interference. It does not call on the federal courts to manage the market by preventing too many buyers from settling upon a single product."[55]

Justice Louis Brandeis, who concurred with Holmes in his dissent in *Abrams*, would, eight years later, add his own rhetorical flavor to the free speech debate that encouraged even more feverish trading within the marketplace of ideas. In a concurring opinion in *Whitney v. California*, a case upholding the conviction of a California heiress who founded the Communist Labor Party of America, Brandeis wrote his most memorable defense of free speech—especially when such speech is unpopular and arguably dangerous: "Discussion affords ordinarily adequate protection against dissemination of noxious doctrine, . . . the path of safety lies in the opportunity to discuss freely supposed grievances and proposed remedies, and that the fitting remedy for evil counsels is good ones. . . . If there be time to expose through discussion the falsehood and fallacies, to avert the evil by the processes of education, *the remedy to be applied is more speech, not enforced silence.*"[56]

Two giants of the Supreme Court with a great deal of faith in the functioning of a marketplace of ideas, the virtues of deliberative democracy, and the citizenry as rational and sensible consumers of speech locked us into a freewheeling vision of free speech that was destined for abuse. Holmes conceived of a market where speech that constitutes an idea leads to truth; Brandeis introduced the concept that more speech is always the antidote for bad speech. Indeed, a society can never get enough speech. For Brandeis, speaking freely about the politics of the age is the truest test of democracy at work because more speech invariably leads to more truth, and the marketplace is an efficient clearinghouse of information. Under this framework, all ideas are welcome because they always contain their own truths. In such a truth-friendly environment, there is no risk of being exposed to too much of a good thing. This optimism about free speech has guided many decisions of the Supreme Court for decades. In 1974, the Supreme Court ruled, "Under the First Amendment, there is *no such thing as a false idea.* However pernicious an opinion may seem, we depend for its correction not on the conscience of judges and juries but on the *competition of other ideas.*"[57]

Taken together, the happy amalgam of speech, truth, and ideas lies at the heart of why free speech is treated so permissively by American courts and why American citizens must endure so much unwelcome speech without recourse. The prohibition against allowing the government to regulate the content of expression, and the legal system's unwillingness to develop a more listener-friendly paradigm of the First Amendment, is what privileges speech with the presumption that more of it is always better—even if crass, boorish, or dangerous. In almost any form, speech has value in the marketplace of ideas because it always receives the benefit of the doubt of rising *to* an idea, so the theory goes.

# 8

# IS EVERYTHING THAT SPILLS FROM THE MOUTH OF A SPEAKER AN IDEA?

Given the all-forgiving ground rules and the "anything goes" alibi of this liberty, free speech becomes a fight that the victims of harmful speech cannot win even if they choose to return fire.

THE MARKETPLACE OF ideas is the reason why we have all become a captive audience to the excesses of the First Amendment. Perhaps it is time to take a critical look at this bizarre bazaar of unmoderated, often reckless modes of expression. So many of the misgivings about free speech can be traced to a marketplace where few rules apply and where lawlessness is seen as a virtue. We are told that speech can only flourish in improvisational surroundings. We are admonished to defer to the speaker. Inform the listener that if he or she does not like what is being said, he or she can have a turn, too, in order to rebut and reply and to introduce a counter-opinion.

There is a casualness and smugness about the extent of the listener's burden. The speaker's prerogative is urgent; the listener's pain is ignored, as if his complaint is somehow churlish and un-American. How is this a workable or fair environment for public discourse? Speakers are disproportionately favored with no incentive or requirement to modulate their speech. Meanwhile, the targets of their speech-making become frontline casualties, forced to endure the burdens of the First Amendment like cannon fodder.

For nearly one hundred years after Justice Holmes first analogized a free trade of ideas to other capitalistic enterprises with their market forces and failures, rational consumers, and unseen transaction costs, free speech was unleashed upon society, tossing speakers and listeners into a steel cage match.

Given the all-forgiving ground rules and the "anything goes" alibi of this liberty, free speech becomes a fight that the victims of harmful speech cannot win even if they choose to return fire. After all, harms cannot be remedied simply by resorting to more speech—tit for tat. When hatred and its accompanying harms are directed at citizens, how are they expected to defend themselves in the marketplace of ideas? Respond with reciprocal hate? Try to reason with murderous adversaries? Offer to debate in a civilized setting? Answer with words of love and the assertion of dignity?

It is difficult to compete in such well-fortified, hostile arenas immune to mediating charms. To a neo-Nazi who wishes to re-blast the furnaces of Auschwitz in the United States, a Klansman who would like nothing better than to string up an African-American on a tree branch, or a nativist waging a local turf war against Muslims, what, exactly, is a fitting retort in the marketplace of ideas? This competitive marketplace of ideas, so American in its muscular appeal with its winner-take-all, scorch-the-earth ground rules, is an ill-suited forum in which those being threatened with violence and intimidation can reasonably protect themselves or sensibly respond.

As social anthropologist Sindre Bangstad observed in 2014, It has become something of a liberal platitude to cite the great US Supreme Court judge Brandeis . . . that the answer to hate speech is more speech. . . . [R]acist and/or discriminatory speech is not *per se* motivated by any attempt to further the cause of democratic deliberation. Racist speech does not function as an invitation to conversation. It does not offer reasons or arguments with which its audience can engage; and the visceral hostility it expresses effectively forecloses, rather than opens, the opportunity for further discussion. . . . If more speech or counter-speech is in fact the great solvent that the free speech absolutist thinks it is, what, then, is the reasonable and appropriate response to being called a rat, vermin or to being threatened with anal rape? . . . To date there has been no great liberal debate in which racists, fascists, neo-Nazis and their targets have engaged one another in democratic deliberation."[58]

The free market analogy was always an imperfect one. What kind of market did Holmes actually envision? A marketplace of ideas operates very differently from most other kinds of shopping and trading experiences. The valuation of and trading in ideas cannot really be structured like other mercantile exchanges. Holmes truly was comparing apples and oranges. After all, stocks and bonds, oil and natural gas futures, gold and other precious metals, cotton and coffee, even Bitcoins, are traded in genuine world markets. Someone is *actually* ringing up purchases and making change. Anyone with a computer or smartphone can receive instantaneous valuations, capitalization, trading volume, and price range. With a licensed broker or a seat on an exchange, a market participant can post trading instructions—when to buy and sell, with prices rising and falling and computer terminals blinking to reflect those transactions. Investors in such markets can experience the exhilaration and heartache of fluctuations in value caused by any number of factors: world events, monetary policy changes, foreign currency manipulation, outright fraud, political coups, and shortages and scarcity caused by bad weather and failing crops.

In what way does the marketplace of ideas share these vagaries of supply and demand? Instead, it features an invisible hand that is spasmodic and twitchy—it is actually more like a sleight of hand. Unlike other markets that trade in actual assets—stocks, bonds, commodities—and that require some regulation to ensure fairness and efficiency, the one Holmes conjured for ideas has neither a physical place nor the machinations of market-making. It is more like a phantom market—a pop-up where bullies pop off.

Without boundaries or oversight, exposure to harmful speech is inevitable. Free speech operates in its own metaphysical universe. Establishing the valuation of an idea is done without metrics—without data to support the substance of the idea. There are no guidelines or benchmarks to assess whether the speech even qualifies as an idea. It is a market operating blithely without quality controls or security cameras. With neo-Nazis and hatemongers galore, why would any sensible person shop for ideas among such a motley crew of predatory merchants?

The Food and Drug Administration (FDA), the Securities and Exchange Commission (SEC), the Commodities Futures Trading Commission (CFTC), the Consumer Financial Protection Bureau (CFPB), and other regulatory agencies seek to eliminate these standardized risks in other markets. Commercial speech is subject to some governmental regulation and oversight, too. For instance, drug advertisements cannot be so expressive or factually reckless as to run afoul of FDA rules. But no such government regulator is permitted to safeguard against dangerous speech. Bullhorns are essentially handed out to any lunatic who has something he wishes to get off his chest.

Even if such a marketplace actually existed with speakers peddling their ideas for sale, it would hardly provide a pleasant shopping experience. It would constitute an uninviting place of total chaos with injuries traded too fast to restock the shelves.

This madness of a marketplace is what a former supreme justice once wished for us? Does it at least carry liability insurance? Extremist groups feel at home in such a climate. Like manic shoppers on Black Friday, they cast about not for bargains but for victims. They traffic in fake ideas, counterfeit knockoffs—a Fort Knox of bounced checks and snake-oil salesmen hawking ideas in name alone. One wonders whether Justice Holmes had ever actually gone shopping in a legitimate establishment—for anything. Ideas cannot be transacted just like any ordinary consumer good. Speech, more often than not, is decidedly not consumer friendly. The best ideas are not ceremoniously crowned after vigorous thoughtful debate. They generally emanate out of more serene, less gladiatorial settings.

We need to become more honest about the horrors of Justice Holmes' mythical marketplace of ideas. It is not an intellectually inspiring arena. Market participants are easily cast out, and some are shouted down. There are actually two speech markets. One is boorish and base, low-rent, and wholly inappropriate, featuring the worst kind of non-speech and non-ideas. The other hosts those with genuine ideas in an atmosphere of mutual respect. First Amendment absolutists see no difference between these two and play no favorites. All speakers are treated as first among equals. But making no distinction between these two market participants bestows an unwarranted legitimacy on the purveyors of hate. They are the duplicitous beneficiaries of a right being dispensed far too liberally—a liberty trivialized rather than treasured.

Did Holmes actually believe that all manner of speech should count as an idea worthy of this market? Did Brandeis not consider the possibility that bad speech introduced into a marketplace already besotted and besieged with more of the same does not purify the intellectual environment? It only compounds the problem, crowding out actual ideas that will never find buyers. Former attorney general Jeff Sessions stated, "There are those who will say that certain speech isn't deserving of protection. They will say that some speech is hurtful—even hateful. . . . But the right of free speech does not exist only to protect the *ideas* upon which most of us agree."[59]

Simply stated, not all speech automatically qualifies as an *idea*. This is the confusion that Justice Holmes set in motion that persists to this day. Apparently, even an attorney general of the United States can get easily tripped up, granting all speech the presumption of an idea. But that is an overly generous and simplistic assessment of the virtues of speech—any speech at all. There is idea-laden speech, and there is speech that has absolutely nothing to do with ideas. Actually, most speech does not come close to offering up an idea; it was never uttered for that purpose.

Like most things, speech has many grades. It can inspire and beguile, educate and enlighten, clarify and inform, placate and subdue. Speech can come in the form of cautionary words as well as sound the alarm of the town crier. But it can also coarsely degrade, denigrate, humiliate, and spread malicious gossip.

And it can most certainly cause harm, as we shall see.

# 9.

## AN IDEA BY ANY OTHER NAME

Is it not time that we finally . . . become more intellectually honest about just who and what we are protecting with our First Amendment?

YES, SPEECH ALWAYS has the potential to express an idea, but it most often falls short. Most of what we hear all day are empty words—chitchat, nonsense, shooting the breeze, talking about the weather, and just making conversation. That is how most people spend their day while engaged in speech. It is true—small talk occupies most of our audible space. The Founding Fathers did not fight a revolution and secede from an empire so as to make idle, superficial, and banal talk a favored liberty in this new nation. The liberty they envisioned applies only to speech infused with a loftier purpose. Most people do not open their mouths with the aim of contributing to the public discourse. Most people are not aspiring for a Patrick Henry moment, seeking to persuade others or protest their government. Lacking oratorical ambition does not make them less valuable citizens. But it does mean that the First Amendment probably will not need to be called upon to defend what they have to say. *Speech directed at the government is precisely what the First Amendment was drafted to defend: a*

*citizen's right to openly criticize the political leadership and direction of*
*the United States, to meaningfully engage in civic, democratic participa-*
*tion.* The First Amendment does not apply to the mundane and
quotidian. Neither "Pass the ketchup" nor "Jews to the Gas!" are
ideas, and surely the impulse to speak such words is not the reason
why we have free speech.

Speech that strives for seriousness still might fall short of an
idea. No matter. Effort counts. One should be credited with having
ventured into the marketplace of ideas in good faith. The marketplace of ideas sometimes offers only a meager shopping experience. Some speech, through artifice and pretty packaging, not to
mention nativist thinking and other distorting prejudices, may appear to be an idea from a reputable vendor. The Supreme Court,
in fact, has contributed to false labeling, allowing loathsome,
head-scratching behavior to pass as an idea under the First Amendment. Stanley Fish has observed this misdirection, with the First
Amendment being played like a "marvelously flexible instrument,"
a game of three-card monte with courts picking and choosing between speech and non-speech, simply by designating the expression as an idea. For instance, here Fish provides a humorous
sampling of "ideas": "the malicious depiction of a man having incest
with his mother is an idea; . . . the repeated portrayal of women as
appropriate objects of degradation is an idea; . . . that the genocidal
message of Nazis who wanted to march through Skokie is an
idea."[60]

He is right: Arguably none of those examples represented an
idea, and yet the Supreme Court treated each speaker—an assortment of white supremacists and Nazi wannabees—like an Edison
or Einstein. Ideas can be both false and bad and come in many va-
rieties. Nazism was surely no repository of refined, enlightened
thought. "The Final Solution to the Jewish Problem" is not an idea
but a euphemism for Jewish genocide. "Ethnic cleansing" is presumably an idea, too; so is "re-indoctrination" and "resettlement."
All of the aforementioned ideas are uniquely bad in both

conception and practice. If the marketplace of ideas operated like a true clearinghouse, these ideas would be vanquished in short order. Consumers would express their preferences and reject them. And that would be the end of it, like the recall of a car or the public rejection of a newfangled flavor, like New Coke. But that is now how it happens. The marketplace of ideas is powerless to police itself, and the unregulated freedom that characterizes this marketplace ensures that bad ideas will flourish and be indistinguishable from good ones.

Nazi Germany, for instance, featured neither a marketplace of ideas nor a democratic system of civic and political participation where free speech was welcome. Would we today grant the murderous ideological agendas of Hamas, the Taliban, al-Qaeda, Boko Haram, and ISIS access to a marketplace of ideas simply because their madness is framed as an idea? Is there an invitation to debate mentioned in any of their death chants? They do not seem to be very much interested in free speech for their own people. Winning over the populace is accomplished with terror, not persuasion. Does anyone believe that the odious ideas of the Iranian regime could capture minds in a free marketplace? When Hamas defeated Fatah in the first democratic elections held in Gaza, the terrorist group celebrated not by welcoming Fatah as the loyal opposition but by tossing its members off rooftops and shooting them in the street. This is a marketplace where only barbarians need reply.

Philosopher John Stuart Mill was also overly optimistic in his belief that bad ideas might contain an element of truth that sharpens our understanding of the world. I think it is more likely that bad ideas given access to the public sphere corrupt truth and muddy moral clarity.

In *United States v. Dennis*, a case brought during the Cold War against eleven members of the American Communist Party, the government alleged that the defendants had conspired to violently overthrow the United States. In affirming their convictions, Judge Learned Hand of the United States Court of Appeals for the

Second Circuit warned in 1950 against a First Amendment smugness—the paradox of allowing the enemies of democracy to benefit from First Amendment freedoms they would most assuredly eliminate should they ever rise to power. Such naive permissiveness is suicidal during times of national emergency when threats against the United States are not abstractions, but are real and lethal.[61]

Judge Hand wrote: "That may be a proper enough antidote in ordinary times and for less redoubtable combinations; but certainly, it does not apply to this one. *Corruptio optimi pessima* (Corruption of what is best is the worst tragedy.) True, we must not forget our own faith; we must be sensitive to the dangers that lurk in any choice; but choose we must, and we shall be *silly dupes* if we forget that again and again in the past thirty years, just such preparations in other countries have aided to supplant existing governments when the time was ripe. Nothing short of a revived doctrine of *laissez-faire*, which would have amazed even the Manchester School at its apogee, can fail to realize that such a conspiracy creates a danger of the utmost gravity and of enough probability to justify its suppression. We hold that it is a danger 'clear and present.'"[62]

Treating the marketplace of ideas as an intellectual sandbox where everyone, including all schoolyard bullies, is invited to play without restriction is a foolproof way to one day being remembered as a "silly dupe."[63] Judge Hand openly mocked this *laissez-faire* commitment to the First Amendment, the all-too-casual belief that more speech is the antidote to bad speech, and that liberty at all cost is better than a more measured approach to freedom—one that exercises caution above reckless absolutism.

Of course, *Dennis* took place during the worst manifestations of Cold War hysteria. Many believe today that it was wrongly decided. The First Amendment, after all, in addition to free speech, also grants citizens freedom of assembly. If the *Dennis* defendants wanted to join an American communist party and read Karl Marx for kicks, is that not the ultimate expression of political engagement and personal liberty? Should we not all applaud their right to read whatever political treatise they wish and join whatever party suits their political orientation? Yes, of course, if the intent of such groups were to engage in an open debate as to their view of a better way of governing.

But where speech crosses the line from debate to terrorist actions, most Americans would not be sympathetic to the activities of cells operating in the United States where its members, American citizens or foreign residents, watched bomb-making instructional videos on YouTube and listened to sermons of how to bring about the most mass death. Should such videos as the ones from Islamic cleric Anwar al-Awlaki, which are easily available on the Internet, and are quoted by his followers, be protected under the First Amendment? Are they not the very definition of incitement? In the days and months after 9/11, there were far fewer absolutists taking up a rallying cry on behalf of freedom of speech and assembly for such activities. But as time passes, abstract liberties get mugged by the reality of murderous foes who have no stake in liberal values and who would not hesitate to invoke the First Amendment as a defense to any governmental action taken against them.

Justice Holmes envisioned his marketplace of ideas as a courtroom with an orderly presentation of argument, organizing rules and a resolution that unveils the truth.

Good luck with that.

Those were different times, and hindsight can be a convenient luxury.

Speakers in the marketplace of ideas, exercising their rights under the First Amendment, can nearly say whatever they wish in whatever manner they choose to express themselves. They are unbounded by evidence or procedural rules. There is no judge who will call them out of order. The balancing of the scales of justice has no counterpart in the marketplace of ideas.

Opinions can be lopsided and offered from many directions so that their origins are likely to be unknown. It could just as well be called a marketplace of chaos. Intellectual rigor or internal consistency is of no concern. The more clashing the speech, the more chaotic this marketplace seems to function. And everyone seems to be fine within the frenzy—all except those who are unwillingly dragged into the fray. In such a disorderly place of colliding speech, with declarations whizzing like projectiles, one can choose to avoid what they do not wish to hear or only take in what confirms what they already believe to be true or, worst of all, have neither the timing nor the dexterity to get out of the way.[64]

If the marketplace of ideas is not an arena of rigorous debate and respectful dialogue held before an audience shopping for essential truths, then what good is it—how does it promote democracy or enhance ideas? Bad ideas are entering the mainstream through a marketplace that is indifferent to what is actually being exchanged. Imagine a stock market that did not trade in shares of actual companies or a futures trading exchange without commodities. No one seems to mind that hollow ideas infiltrate the market of ideas like dummy corporations. Speech that incites violence or threatens already marginalized groups is granted the legitimacy of ideas. Harmful speech receives a First Amendment seal of approval within the charade of a fail-safe marketplace that is anything but safe and very much prone to failure.

Just as there are permissible barriers to entry in other markets, so, too, should speech be subject to some form of sensible regulation. Justice Holmes did Americans no favor with his mythical marketplace. It surely has not made America smarter or richer in ideas. At least one legal philosopher, Alexander Meiklejohn, acknowledged that, for all the luster and bluster of the "marketplace of ideas," it is not a particularly helpful doctrine for assessing differences between right and wrong and true and false.[65]

And what is worse: This marketplace lacks the one concrete feature that gives meaning to an actual marketplace—a final verdict issued by the consumer. In actual markets, consumer goods, stocks, bonds, and commodities, should they elicit little or no interest, will decline in price, become discounted, get rejected, or be recalled. They disappear from the market never to be seen again. They might be sold for scrap. Of course, the idea behind them can be tinkered with and improved upon. Remember the Palm Personal Digital Assistant and the Walkman? They morphed into smartphones such as Apple's iPhone. Some renewed consumer interest might emerge. But the product in its original form is usually gone for good.

That is how true markets function.

The marketplace of ideas is much more forgiving of its wares. Ideas that are roundly rejected somehow get to hang around, like hoodlums lurking in the dark, the ash still flickering from cigarettes clinging to their lips. They live to fight another day. Sometimes they are tidied up, made to look and sound more presentable. An odious edge is softened. A spin doctor gets called in for a house call. (Think of "anti-Zionist" becoming a convenient way to avoid being labeled an "anti-Semite.") But mostly they simply reappear at the speaker's corner or the public square, exactly the same as before, with their jackboots and nooses at the ready, seeking a permit to march or create some other mischief. This is, after all, what Hitler himself had in mind with intimidating tactics that incited a beerhall putsch or a Kristallnacht. Justice Robert Jackson, in his dissenting opinion in *Terminiello v. Chicago*, wrote that extremist groups "resort to these terror tactics to confuse, bully and discredit those freely chosen governments. Violent and noisy shows of strength discourage participation by moderates in discussions so fraught with violence, that real discussion dries up and disappears. And people lose faith in the democratic process when they see public authority flouted and impotent."[66]

Jackson, who was the lead prosecutor in the post–World War II Nuremberg Trials, surely understood that marching goons dressed up to intimidate and spread fear have very little interest in deliberative democracy. Indeed, the ostensible purpose of their assembly is to end democracy itself—a foreshadowing of things to come. Is it not time that we finally reconcile ourselves to this unfortunate fact and become more intellectually honest about just who and what we are protecting with our First Amendment? We need to start making distinctions between the motives of speakers and stop trying to elevate evil intentions and placing them on par with those with whom we are merely having a disagreement. There is an underworld of difference between a rabble-rousing bigot and a Cicero, between the primal violence of brown-shirted Nazis and the Lincoln-Douglas Debates. Martin Luther King Jr. and the Klan relied upon radically different methods of persuasion, and it is a gross insult to King to treat him as if he were deserving of no more rights and protection than the Klan.

Back in the late 1970s, the Jews of Skokie, Illinois, a mere thirty years after the end of World War II and the liberation of Auschwitz, must have wondered why the pernicious "ideas" of the Nazis had returned, this time with a "neo" prefix, yet there was nothing new about their abhorrent anti-Semitism. Had their ideas not already been rejected in the marketplace? How can Nazi propaganda actually still be for sale? After losing the war and having been judged guilty of committing crimes against humanity, the Nazis had already lost the argument, their ideology thoroughly rejected, their ideas deemed without redemption.

What kind of a sleazy marketplace is this?

Justice Holmes believed that even the views we detest must be given an opportunity to succeed, to find followers. But for how long must this go on? Our tolerance for bad ideas is so great, we permit them to be reintroduced over and over again—recycled anew and then rejected as old. Do ideas, especially odious ones, deserve such a long shelf life? In every other marketplace, a vanquished competitor is forced to go away. In the marketplace of ideas, noxious views linger.

There is, however, no legal or moral justification for protecting bad ideas for eternity. The right to free speech is not a license to forever taunt those who simply wish to live their lives peacefully, in full enjoyment of their own rights.

# 10

# A MARKETPLACE OF IDEAS FOR THE DUMBFOUNDED

If everything is worthy of being an idea, and a majority of buyers in such a marketplace are sympathetic to a murderous agenda masquerading as an idea, what, absent government regulation, is to prevent a society from acting upon this idea if it prevails in the market?

ORSE STILL, IT is not at all clear that the marketplace of ideas can actually lead to the emergence of truth and better decision-making. Justice Holmes assumed that human beings behave like rational actors in a market devoted to speech—similar to the way that economists apply the rational actor model in analyzing other markets. Justice Brandeis took this faith in rational actors a step further. For him, the marketplace of ideas was the arena whereby citizens exercised their political duty to engage in public discourse, a task they performed as rational beings on their way to becoming informed citizens. Law professor Lyrissa Barnett Lidsky credited justices Holmes and Brandeis for establishing a First Amendment doctrine "that rel[ies] on a model of the audience as rational, skeptical, and capable of sorting through masses of information to find truth."[67]

These assumptions, however, do not necessarily work in practice, even in mercantile markets. The market analogy, derived from the neoclassical model of economics, is based on a premise that rational consumers are capable of judging the quality of the ideas that are produced in this competitive marketplace. Rational consumers will ensure that only the best ideas emerge from the tussle, provided that an intrusive government does not interfere with the *laissez-faire* virtues of allowing consumers to distinguish for themselves what is true from what is false.

Except for one thing: People are not naturally good at making decisions, and they are even worse at recognizing truth even when it is right in front of them. As Professor Derek Bambauer has written, "The weakness of the marketplace of ideas is the consumers who shop within it. . . . [W]e do not consistently discover truth and discard false information. . . . The marketplace of ideas does not describe how humans behave, and should thus be discarded as a framework for decisions about regulating communications."[68]

We do not know even what we think we know. A marketplace that consists of only good ideas might not successfully cancel out bad information because we are all prisoners of cognitive biases, predispositions, and distortions that too often dictate our thinking. We believe that past events will reoccur, or hope that they will, even if we are in possession of new facts that demonstrate that our prior views were mistaken all along. For instance, many people still believe that the decision to invade Iraq in 2003 was necessary because Saddam Hussein possessed weapons of mass destruction.[69] That was false. Many people still believe that one of the reasons Al Gore lost the 2000 presidential election was because he took credit for inventing the Internet—and that made him look foolish, deluded by his own sense of grandeur. But he actually never said that. What Vice President Gore did say was that when he was a young congressman, he was involved in legislative measures that helped fund the Internet, thereby making it more functional for commercial purposes.[70]

There is no shortage of information in the marketplace of ideas that would, quite easily, debunk these false notions—especially in the age of the Internet. A perfectly efficient and cost-less marketplace of ideas should stand as an information mecca for a better-informed citizenry. Why, then, do rational consumers forsake this marketplace and choose instead to believe in convenient but incorrect falsehoods? Perhaps because the presumption of rational consumers operating within a free market of ideas is itself false. An overabundance of faith in the rational actor model has grave consequences when applied to ordinary markets; it is especially misguided when dealing with free speech. Unfortunately, however, the same overconfidence in rational consumers guides the *laissez-faire* thinking about the First Amendment.

Many people are ignorant of basic facts about the world in which they live. And even worse, they hold irrational beliefs that cause them to make decisions based on incomplete or distorted information. Human beings frame their understanding of events in ways that are not always faithful to the facts. These framing devices make it easier to take mental shortcuts. For instance, most people are more likely to remember events that are either vivid or emotionally charged. Events that are rich in color and steeped in emotion are naturally more memorable. This is one of the reasons why people believe that cars are safer than planes, incorrectly attributing fewer casualties to vehicular deaths than the number of people who die through commercial aviation. Plane crashes conjure a level of horror that exceeds the controlled imagination of a fender bender. These and other cognitive biases distort our capacity to process the truths we need to know and the decisions we would otherwise make. The inevitability of these cognitive mistakes puts the lie to the rational actor model. We are not always guided by rational thinking even when we have all the facts. As Barnett Lidsky has written, "Cognitive biases threaten one of the foundational assumptions of the marketplace of ideas; namely, that humans are rational actors, capable of sifting through information, sorting the wheat from the chaff, and ultimately reaching truth."[71]

Here is a sampling of what people believe in spite of the availability of a marketplace of ideas where knowledge is plentiful and the discovery of the truth is, as Justices Holmes and Brandeis so believed, a moral justification for the First Amendment:

In the 2008 presidential election, 59 percent of respondents knew virtually nothing about the position of the candidates; 12 percent believed that Barack Obama was a Muslim.[72] In 2011, *Newsweek* conducted a poll of one thousand Americans to see how they would fare on a standard citizenship test. Here are some of the results: 29 percent could not name the vice president; 73 percent had no idea why the United States had been in the Cold War; 44 percent were completely mystified by the Bill of Rights, not sure what rights were even included in them.[73] Only one in six Americans and fewer than one in four college graduates can find Ukraine on a map even though it is the largest country in Europe. The majority of respondents were off by 1,800 miles. So much for the First Amendment's (or the Internet's) contribution to the state of general knowledge in America.[74] Only one out of four people can name all three branches of government, with one-third unable to name even a single branch. And when it comes to America's favorite constitutional amendment? A little more than one-third can name only one of the rights contained in the First Amendment. A slight majority believe that the media is not permitted to report on national security matters without first receiving the government's approval—partly because they do not know that the First Amendment includes freedom of the press!

According to Steven Sloman, the editor of the journal *Cognition*, each year human beings know even less about their world because we rely on the expertise of others to do the work for us. For instance, a hunter-gatherer from the Stone Age was actually quite self-reliant. He or she made clothes, started fires, hunted for food, and managed to avoid getting eaten by predators. Today, Sloman writes, most people cannot explain how a zipper actually works. It turns out that inundating people with facts has the opposite effect: They have little interest in consuming and learning from them, and their intellectual laziness makes them feel stupid and resentful. The availability of information is just another reminder of what to avoid.

Even our present commander-in-chief, Donald Trump, seems positively bored by the nitty-gritty details of how the world works. He does not appear to have a ready command of much knowledge at all. Anyone who watched the 2016 presidential debates knows that Trump consistently received the most sustained applause, which translated into a majority of electoral college votes. Instead of raw data, or a wonky recitation of policy, he mostly delivered bombastic, easy-to-remember slogans, like: "Make America Great Again," "Build That Wall," and "Lock Her Up!" The masses repeated them in unison. Despite what Justice Brandeis believed, public debates are not necessarily won by the candidate with the superior grasp of facts. It does not come down to a contest of ideas at all. The marshaling of the right emotional levers will surpass data every time in winning over voters. Perhaps we would all be better served with a marketplace of emotion instead.[75]

What would people know if they did not have the benefit of this fabled marketplace and its ever-replenishing warehouse of ideas— this miracle of self-government that leads to essential truths and greater civic participation? Could it get any worse if the market-place closed for the winter, took off holidays, and shut down during elections? The state of popular ignorance offers no reassurance that simply by introducing more speech into the public discourse, Americans are destined to become a better-informed electorate. Cluelessness seems to be our most natural state of being, even with the vast resources of the marketplace of ideas at our disposal. Columnist Nicholas Kristof observed ruefully that "Americans are as likely to believe in flying saucers as in evolution."[76]

And often the marketplace of ideas is rigged by political forces that control the flow of knowledge, even though there are competing ideas that could be used to rebut the incorrect information that is being presented as absolute truth. Prior to the Civil War, golden-tongued but racist Southern legislators, such as John Calhoun and Henry Wise, duped Northerners and flooded the Southern marketplace of ideas with proslavery nonsense, such as the ruse that plantation owners treated their slaves benevolently as if they were their own children. Abolitionists like Frederick Douglass, William Lloyd Garrison, Theodore Weld, and Angela and Sarah Grimke were apparently exercising their free speech rights at the same time, but the marketplace of ideas was inundated with supremacist thinking, and anti-slavery voices had a difficult time competing for attention.[77] The marketplace of ideas has never been open for business on a level playing field. This point was made by law professor Charles R. Lawrence III, in asking, rhetorically, whether "racial insults are ideas? Do they encourage wide-open debate?" He added the racial observation that, from the very beginning, "the American marketplace of ideas was founded with the idea of racial inferiority of nonwhites as one of its chief commodities, and ever since the market opened, racism has remained its most active item in trade."[78]

As we all know, slavery ended not because of passionate oratory—not even the emancipatory words of Abraham Lincoln carried the day—but only after the bloodiest war in American history. The democratic virtue of the First Amendment is a romantic concept, but political truth and transformational change is often more likely to come by way of force than through the rhetorical finesse of heated debate.

After a century of genocides around the world, and new ones that have already marred the twenty-first century and revealed no great improvement, one can surely conceive of majoritarian preferences that arise out of the marketplace of ideas that, for instance, favor the genocide of a minority population. If everything is worthy of being an idea, and a majority of buyers in such a marketplace are sympathetic to a murderous agenda masquerading as an idea, what, absent government regulation, is to prevent a society from acting upon this idea if it prevails in the market? Majority preferences are not necessarily the "best step to the truth," despite what Justice Holmes may have believed.

And this fantasy about the panacea of more speech, and the bonanza of truthful information it provides, does not lead to better decision-making—even among experts. Evidence seems to show that the more choices we have at our disposal, the more prone we become to decision paralysis. Presented with an endless variety of ice cream flavors creates a sugar rush and a mind freeze—and an impulse to simply choose vanilla. All these flavors become mind-numbing. It is the curse of having too many options. Research indicates that employees are less likely to participate in 401(k) plans the greater the selection of investment funds that are offered to them.[79]

A marketplace of ideas that resembles the Wild West for its "anything goes" ethos—the absolutists' ultimate Hollywood fantasy—has little chance of creating a better-informed electorate or interrogating the truth, which was the wish of our Founding Fathers. Bombarding the public with crisscrossing pseudo-ideas that causes most people to duck is not the way to run a pluralistic democracy.

The Internet is not helping matters. The digital age has democratized knowledge and made it much more accessible. It has also led to information overload. All this data is, for most people, incoherent. Human beings cannot even begin to process and digest all that is made available—much less make sense of it. Given the widespread hostility to government or editorial oversight and digital censorship, there are no filters in place to parcel out what is of value from what is mere noise. A Google search makes no qualitative judgment when spitting out primary sources and inane blog posts. Algorithms are not programmed for quality control. Consumer protection is not binary. The result is a cornucopia of crap. And it is a modern problem without precedent.

During the natural life of the First Amendment, newspaper editorials were the primary sources of printed opinion, which depended on owning a printing press—a prohibitive start-up cost that clearly divided actual publishers from those who were reduced to simply submitting Letters to the Editor. Sure, there were some private pamphleteers, sandwich board-sign walkers, and speech makers standing on soapboxes shouting loudly at the public square until they became hoarse. Demonstrators and symbolic speech makers—cross-burners, flag-burners, those inciting violence, and others wearing jean jackets with patches that read "Fuck the Draft"—tested the contours of the First Amendment in various ways. But generally, those were the days of a far more innocent First Amendment. Free speech, today, has lost its innocence, with cyberbullying on social media platforms, terrorist bomb-making instructional videos, and presidential elections being hacked by online pirates. Self-expression requires little more than a smart-phone. Incitement to violence can be instigated without leaving one's bedroom and without getting ink or blood on one's hands.

On October 29, 2017, CNN's Senior Technology Correspondent, Laurie Seegal, filed a report on websites devoted to the enabling of hate online. Specifically, she focused on two sites: PewTube, which is devoted to posting racist videos whose content is so vulgar they do not meet the standards of YouTube and invariably get taken down; and Hatreon, a crowdsourcing website where extremist political and controversial content receives online funding. For instance, white supremacist Richard Spencer, and Andrew Anglin, the founder of the neo-Nazi website The Daily Stormer, are partly funded by donations made through Hatreon. The Daily Stormer receives $7,800 each month thanks to its crowdsourcing campaign.

Google, which owns YouTube, and Facebook are faced with the dilemma of how to treat such provocateurs on the Internet. More recently, they have tried to marginally balance free speech with the responsible monitoring of their platforms even if it results in cen-sorship. PewTube and Hatreon openly say that they are responding to the restrictive content policies of these major digital information providers—essentially, filling a need. Possibly true, but they have also become cyber-havens for racists, anti-Semites, homophobes, Islamaphobes, violent content producers, terrorist propagandists, white supremacists, and online cyberbullies of every denomination.

While watching two of the offerings on PewTube, videos with provocative titles such "Ovens of Auschwitz" and "Black Lives Don't Matter," Seegal correctly observed, while scrapping all journalistic objectivity: "This is just so offensive. A pretty horrific title for a video. Oh, wow . . . so racist, anti-Semitic images. As a Jew, this is pretty offensive. Actually, I don't want to watch this. This is pretty awful. . . . Oh, my god, I want to stop this. It's not just people with different political ideas . . . this is a platform that enables and allows some of the most racist, anti-Semitic, racist images. . . . I don't believe these people deserve a platform. And neither do some of the tech companies, either."[80]

First Amendment absolutists hold fast to the marketplace of ideas even though free market enthusiasts, generally, have come to realize that blind fidelity to all that is *laissez-faire* reveals market imperfections that do not advance the interests of consumer welfare. It goes beyond economic lexicon; some things are simply beyond the pale. Tim Squirrel, a former president of the Cambridge Union, a group that does not shy away from political debate, said, "Every time you invite . . . a racist or a homophobe, you're not endorsing his views, but you're legitimating their views as something that's up for discussion."[81]

# 11

# WHAT IS SO BAD ABOUT THE REGULATION OF SPEECH?

It may be necessary, at times, for the government to tinker with the ground rules for how free speech can be exercised. Doing so does not automatically convert the United States into a nation of despotic tyranny, but rather one where sensible citizens are profoundly aware of both the freedoms and responsibilities that come with the privilege of free speech.

NEARLY ALL ECONOMISTS agree that some government involvement in the free market is essential to correct for transaction costs caused by the fidgety operations of the invisible hand. The neoclassical theory of economics is elegant in design but flawed when exposed to the full sweep of irrational human behavior. Absolutism is viewed as a quaint artifact of Adam Smith—a nice theory but a disaster in practice. For this reason, some government intervention is welcomed in the purely economic—goods and services—spheres of life.

But when it comes to the marketplace of ideas, free speech can tolerate absolutely *no* regulation. Why is that? What makes free speech so antiseptically hands-off? As law professor Jerome Barron presciently understood many decades ago, "the idea of a free marketplace where ideas can compete on their merits has become just as unrealistic in the twentieth century as the economic theory of perfect competition."[82]

The externalities and transaction costs that are rampant in the marketplace of ideas are real and just as distorting as those found in marketplaces of pure commerce. In addition to cognitive biases and irrational consumer behavior, the marketplace of ideas is also always vulnerable to those who deliberately pollute the market with false information, exercising the heckler's veto and conspiring to shut down speech. These are serious and undeniable market failures. They have the same effect as flooding the music and fashion industries with bootleg recordings and counterfeit merchandise— with far more pernicious consequences. A knockoff Fendi purse can at least carry a small iPhone. Floating an "idea" that all Muslims are terrorists, however, is a falsehood with profoundly more dire implications. We recognize the imperfection of markets that cater to consumer goods, yet we idealize the marketplace of ideas as if it functions with total perfection. There is no justification for this disparity and for treating free speech as if it must be exempt from outside interference and beyond the reach of any regulator.

The economist Ronald Coase dedicated his professional life to finding ways to address the problems of transaction costs and externalities in markets. He criticized "intellectuals [who] have shown a tendency to exalt the market for ideas and to depreciate the market for goods."[83] Most people would not elevate the importance of ideas above food, drugs, or their financial investments. Why then should ideas be immune from government regulation when the FDA and the SEC, for instance, set best practices and stand guard over illegal and anti-competitive behavior committed by those who would introduce untested drugs and deceptive investments into the commercial marketplace? Coase wrote in 1977, "There is simply no reason to suppose that for the great mass of people the market for ideas is more important than the market for goods. But even if the market for ideas were more important, it does not follow that the two markets should be treated differently."[84]

And the government already intervenes in matters related to speech that makes it far less free than absolutists would like.

Beginning in 1949 and until 1987, the Federal Communication Commission (FCC), for instance, interceded in order to make sure that consumers had access to complete information on controversial issues—especially when it came to political affairs. The FCC established the "Fairness Doctrine," which obligated broadcasters to present issues of public interest and to ensure that contrasting viewpoints were properly represented. Yet, during the time that the doctrine remained in force, it inevitably abridged the constitutional guarantees of free speech. The government essentially dictated what content broadcasters were expected to produce and disseminate across the airwaves. The owner of a small-town radio station did not have the right to exercise his or her free speech in whatever manner he or she chose. For instance, if he or she opposed the Vietnam War, a controversial topic to be sure, he or she was still obligated to present contrasting viewpoints. The government's position was that if one receives a license to broadcast over the public airwaves, the broadcaster had a duty to the public to thoroughly cover the issue rather than presenting a purely partisan treatment. Depriving the broadcast license holder of its First Amendment freedom actually served the public good. And it was consistent with the broader historical objectives of free speech—to inspire public debate by exposing radio listeners to a range of consolidated thinking on the subject.

The Fairness Doctrine treated the airwaves like a supermarket required to stock its shelves with produce and frozen food, canned goods and choice meats—and, yes, some organic food, too, in the interest of consumer choice. A supermarket filled only with sugary breakfast cereal is not in the public interest. The Fairness Doctrine inevitably limited the guarantees of the First Amendment. But so what? There is no point to having free speech if the marketplace in which it is presented is of such disarray and uncoordinated chaos that truth is not to be found there. It may be necessary, at times, for the government to tinker with the ground rules for how free speech can be exercised. Doing so does not automatically convert the United States into a nation of despotic tyranny, but rather one where sensible citizens are made profoundly aware of both the freedoms and responsibilities that come with the privilege of free speech.

The Fairness Doctrine was eventually revoked, which explains why American broadcasters such as Fox News and MSNBC can seemingly curate the day's news so that it aligns with the views of their partisan listeners. The same is true with talk radio shows where divergent opinions are not part of the programming ethos. The repeal of the Fairness Doctrine also made it possible for the Sinclair Broadcast Group, the largest owner of local television stations in the United States, to mandate in April 2018 that two hundred of its anchors read essentially the same script. All this uniformity was intended to send a message to competing broadcasters and assorted media outlets that they were disseminating "fake news," and could not be trusted to inform the public. Yet, by hearing identical scripts across the country, the public ended up shortchanged, even though Sinclair's gambit pleased Donald Trump to no end.[85]

Are we really better off today without the Fairness Doctrine even though, during its time, it placed some restrictions on free speech?

The Fairness Doctrine was not the only instance in which the government retained some control of how freedom of expression is, in practice, exercised. The Supreme Court has held that public schools can function as free speech regulators when a student's desire to speak at will interferes with the broader obligation of the school to educate its students. In *Bethel School District No. 403 v. Fraser*, decided in 1986, a student was suspended after delivering a sexually suggestive speech. The First Amendment applies to public schools, but the right cannot be unlimited, otherwise schools would become the Speakers' Corner for unruly students and lose the authority to compel them to quietly stand in the corner.[86] In *Hazelwood School District v. Kuhlmeier,* decided in 1988, a principal removed two articles from a school newspaper. The students' First Amendment claim was rejected in favor of the principal's right and obligation to maintain school decorum.[87] Yes, it was a public school, but not everything in a high school newspaper involves investigative reporting deserving of a Pulitzer. On the scales of censorship and prior restraint, this was hardly a constitutional catastrophe.

And yet, an incident that took place in a small town in Wisconsin in the spring of 2018 was troubling to most and confusing to many. A photo captured outside of a courthouse before the junior prom of a public high school showed more than sixty students engaged in performing a Nazi salute.[88] After the photo made its rounds through social media and became an Internet sensation, outrage and handwringing echoed even in places where free speech is considered sacrosanct. Many felt that the students—some of whom had already graduated; others were still at the school—should be disciplined. The school district, however, ultimately decided that the students may not have known the implications of their act, and even if they did, they had a First Amendment right to exercise their political beliefs. But there was no evidence that the students were engaged in an act of political expression. As Professor Kathryn Schumaker wrote, "If the salute was not political expression, it does not merit special protections of the First Amendment. There is no constitutional right to be a jerk at school."[89]

Similarly, public universities are granted leeway to decide what materials the curriculum should include. Students do not possess a First Amendment right to dictate to their colleges what they are required to read. And not having a say in the curriculum is not a violation of free speech. On a campus, the marketplace of ideas is restricted to what the university believes should be taught there. The marketplace is not wide open: It has hours of operation, and not all ideas will receive a hearing. Universities set the terms of how speech is freely exercised, not the students; the university is permitted a role as regulator of speech for outside speakers— which include time, place, and manner restrictions on public lectures held on campus. A university also has the right to prevent a student group from staging a protest in ways that interfere with campus life—and the First Amendment is no worse for wear.

There are permissible restrictions placed on speech and conduct that occurs off-campus as well. The Supreme Court has over many decades upheld the right of cities to impose time, place, and manner restrictions on speech, not because of the content of what is being said or the viewpoint expressed, which would be unconstitutional, but on account of general public welfare considerations. For any number of reasons, including crowd control, safety, and other law enforcement priorities, the government has the right to determine the appropriate time, place, and manner in which a speech or a march should take place. The form and packaging of speech matters. The manner and presentation of the ideas matter, too. If the speaker is inciting his audience in a hostile way, if good manners are beyond his or her control, or if he or she is begging for a fight, then some forfeiture of First Amendment protection should be expected, and the government is not overstepping its regulatory bounds by insisting that the speech take place elsewhere, or not at all.

# 12

# SPEECH THAT IS NON-SPEECH

Society has an interest in civility for many reasons but most especially because ideas are unlikely to find acceptance in uncivil environments. . . . The First Amendment does not entitle a speaker to violate the prevailing social norms of civilized life.

HERE ARE CATEGORIES of proscribed speech that do not receive First Amendment protection at all. The failure of *laissez-faire* forces the government to step in and declassify some speech as non-speech. The invisible hand does not deliver on its claimed efficiencies. Externalities and transaction costs arise. The government regulates by denying entry into the marketplace of ideas.

Speech-related market failures are often found in the context of emergency situations. In such instances, courts regard speech to be of such low value that regulating even the content of what is being said does not present a constitutional problem. An entire doctrine of "low-value speech" has evolved that essentially created a two-tiered category: speech that has social value and speech that does not. As law professor Genevieve Lakier has written, "The doctrine of low-value speech allows the government to do what it is not supposed to be able to do: that is, to remove ideas it dislikes from *public circulation in the marketplace*."[90]

Courts are not averse to acting as referees when it comes to pumping the breaks on free speech. And they do not necessarily object to wading into the constitutional arena even when it means restricting the content of the speech. Occasionally, judges play favorites—privileging some ideas over others, acting with full confidence that they can evaluate the "seriousness" of the ideas presented, their "societal costs," or whether they even amount to ideas at all.[91]

The Supreme Court already makes distinctions between full-fledged ideas and speech unworthy of First Amendment protection. Unworthiness is labeled as having low value—meaning that First Amendment safeguards do not apply to speech that presents more social costs than it is worth. Take obscenity, for example. The Court has ruled that "[a]ll ideas having even the slightest redeeming social importance—unorthodox ideas, controversial ideas, even ideas hateful to the prevailing climate of opinion—have the full protection of the guarantees . . . [b]ut implicit in the history of the First Amendment is the rejection of obscenity as *utterly without redeeming social importance*."[92]

Obviously, there is a standard for ideas—and the standard begins with the imperative that they have "redeeming social importance." Does cross-burning? For that matter, does flag-burning? In later obscenity cases, the Court established the *Miller* test for distinguishing what has value and what is nothing but smut. The test was designed to determine whether the offending material lacks "serious literary, artistic, political, or scientific value."[93] The justices on the Supreme Court are not necessarily snobs, but they do have some taste, and the *Miller* test demonstrated that the Court at least knew what to look for. And one thing is for certain: The Supreme Court has little regard for speech that originates from and appeals to low-value, guttural sensibilities. It believes that the First Amendment was designed for a more valuable purpose: to uphold speech that has serious literary, artistic, political, or scientific value. What does not make the grade is speech with an avowed purpose to cause harm to another. Such speech is without redeeming social importance, and no worthy ideas can possibly spring from it.

Without at least some government intervention, all markets fail—and that is especially true in the marketplace of ideas. To account for monopolies dominated by thugs and speech that produces no truth, the Supreme Court created categories of speech that simply cannot avail themselves of the First Amendment protection reserved for actual ideas.

In *Chaplinsky v. New Hampshire*, decided in 1942, the Court held that "[t]here are certain well-defined and narrowly limited classes of speech, the prosecution and punishment of which have never been thought to raise any constitutional problems. These include the *lewd and obscene*, the *profane*, the *libelous* and the *insulting* or *'fighting words'*—those *by which their very utterance inflict injury* or tend to *incite an immediate breach of the peace*."[94] The Court went further in explaining what makes these proscribed categories so anathema to free speech—why they default to the status of non-speech once they enter the public sphere: "[S]ome utterances are *no essential part of the exposition of ideas, and are of such slight social value as a step to the truth* that any benefit that may be derived from them is clearly *outweighed by the social interest in order and morality*."[95] The Court then quoted *Cantwell v. Connecticut*, decided two years earlier, which ruled that, "[r]esort to *epithets or personal abuse is not in any proper sense communication* of information or opinion *safeguarded by the Constitution*."[96]

The language of *Chaplinsky* says a great deal about why free speech should not be limitless. Courts are not powerless to regulate low-value speech that has no business in the marketplace of ideas. Judges have an obligation to categorically state, as a matter of law, that when "utterances are no essential part of the exposition of ideas, and are of such slight social value as a step to the truth," the First Amendment guarantees that apply to sincere speakers are absolutely *not* available to those who speak in a manner that clearly deteriorates the "social interest in order and morality." Society has an interest in civility for many reasons, but most especially because ideas are unlikely to find acceptance in uncivil environments.

Other Supreme Court opinions have also noted civility as a constitutional commitment. A few months after *Chaplinsky* was decided, the Court once again explained that freedom of expression can never be completely absolute because the government must "ensure orderly living, without which constitutional guarantees of civil liberties would be a mockery."[97] Even in the Supreme Court decision that upheld the right to burn the American flag as an act of political expression, the Court recognized that the "First Amendment does not guarantee that other concepts virtually sacred to the Nation as a whole . . . will go unquestioned in the market-place of ideas."[98]

The Founding Fathers did not intend to omit human decency and mutual respect as affirmative duties of citizenship. The First Amendment does not entitle a speaker to violate the prevailing social norms of civilized life. The Founding Fathers imagined the First Amendment as elevating the quality of public debate. If a speaker refused to rise to the occasion and rejected all possibilities for civil discourse, then that speaker was on his or her own. The risk that speech might cause harm was his or her burden to bear. Citizenship is not a one-way street paved with rights without reciprocal obligation. Lakier observed in 2015 that "*Chaplinsky* made it possible for the government to prohibit speech not only when it threatened violence and disorder, but also when it violated dominant social norms of civility, piety, and decency—for example, by depicting sex in an obscene manner, or by speaking of others in an uncivil manner, or by addressing another in words calculated to cause offense."[99]

The language of *Chaplinsky* establishes reasonable limits for curtailing the abuses of the First Amendment. Low-value speech that does not contribute to the marketplace of ideas is not "part of the exposition of ideas," and its exclusion "has never been thought to raise any constitutional problem." And the truth-seeking agenda of the First Amendment is thwarted when what is being introduced into the marketplace of ideas has only "slight social value as a step to the truth."[100] *Chaplinsky* does not mince words. It confronts directly the transaction costs of speech that has no legitimate claim to the marketplace of ideas. Those transaction costs include not just emergency situations that present a "clear and present danger," but also speech that causes injury, incites violence and immediate breaches of the peace, along with speech that undermines civil society's interest in public order and morality. Law professor Brian Leiter wrote what can best be described as a manifesto against the overprotection of free speech and concluded that, "Most non-mundane speech people engage in is largely worthless, and the world would be better off were it not expressed."[101]

Requiring common decency and mutual respect before entering the marketplace of ideas does not erase liberty from the free speech equation. There is nothing wrong with demanding civility in a marketplace that ultimately depends on trust among participants. True ideas, after all, are born with the aim to persuade and inspire, not to spread fear and alienate. With respect to the heckler's veto, Chief Justice Vinson wrote in *Feiner v. New York* in 1951 that "[i]t is one thing to say that the police cannot be used as an instrument for the suppression of unpopular views, and another to say that, when as here the *speaker passes the bounds of argument or persuasion* and undertakes incitement to riot, they are powerless to prevent a breach of the peace."[102] And in the infamous "seven dirty words" case (which is popularly remembered as the words that George Carlin used in his comedic act and which then, because of the Supreme Court, transformed him into a free speech icon), the Court, in 1978, reasoned that "a requirement that indecent language be avoided will have its primary effect on the form, rather than the content, of serious communication. There are few, if any, thoughts that cannot be expressed by the use of less offensive language."[103]

Is that really too much to ask? If you have something to say, deliver your communication in a form and manner calculated to change minds, choosing your words wisely so that they will be acceptable to the sensibilities of most people and will not be inconsistent with the norms of polite society. Disagreeing with an idea should be done in the spirit of a civilized, mutually respectful exchange. Ideas are, in essence, invitations. They should be presented with the hope of convincing open-minded listeners.

Ideas thrive only in environments that are conducive to intellectual engagement. As law professor Frederick Schauer once wrote, "Free speech is about a certain kind of environment in which we learn from each other, deliberate with each other, and engage in various forms of collective communicative activity. . . . [T]he actively hostile audience challenges not only the speaker but also the particular free-speech inspired legal and social rules according to which the speaker is protected in the first place."[104]

The pristine sanctity of the marketplace of ideas is deemed so inviolate, we have lost the commonsense wisdom that arose out of these earlier First Amendment cases. More often than not, the *Chaplinsky* standard is ignored and "utterances [that] are no essential part of the exposition of ideas" are typically treated as if they *actually* belong in the marketplace of ideas. We are told that ideas come in different forms and urged not to be too judgmental in dismissing them. Gangsta rap, for instance, is idea rich but indecently presented. It still qualifies under the First Amendment. Extremist groups, after all, have ideas—extreme and murderous though they may be. You just have to peel away all the layered hate. An entire theory of moral relativism exists to impose a judgment-free zone around the acceptability of ideas. Under this framework, all ideas are worthy of the First Amendment. The government must never be allowed infinite powers of censorship and the state policing of thought.

This makes no sense.

One wonders whether these fears are more imaginary than material. Is it really so difficult to label some forms of expression unfit for a public hearing? Writing on this subject, journalist Kalefa Sanneh observed that, "free-speech advocates need not pretend that every provocative utterance is a valuable contribution to a robust debate, or that it is impossible to make any distinctions between various kinds of speech."[105]

Perhaps we have finally reached the tipping point where the sanctity of the public sphere is deemed as important as a solitary citizen's right to free speech. The public square, like all public accommodations, should be open and safe for common usage. Stronger measures must be taken to correct the imperfections of an unregulated marketplace of ideas. Writing about the way in which social media and Russian and Chinese hackers succeeded in hijacking the 2016 American presidential election by exploiting the freedoms of the First Amendment, law professor Tim Wu wrote, "It is time to recognize that the American political process and the marketplace for ideas are under attack, and that reinvigorating the First Amendment is vital. . . . Some might argue, based on the sophomoric premise that 'more speech is better,' that the current state of chaos is what the First Amendment intended. But no defensible free-speech tradition accepts harassment and threats as speech, treats foreign propaganda campaigns as legitimate debate or thinks that social-media bots ought to enjoy constitutional protection. A robust and unfiltered debate is one thing; corruption of debate itself is another. We have entered a far more dangerous place for the republic; its defense requires stronger protections for what we once called the public sphere."[106]

The marketplace of ideas is not some sacred, inviolable place that functions perfectly and produces costless outcomes. On the contrary, it is imbued with error, biases, prejudices, monopolies, harmful merchandise, transaction costs, and externalities aplenty. It is a mythological entity screaming for some sensible supervisory oversight to make sure that buyers and sellers are bidding on the very thing that this market is purporting to sell.

In November 2017, the president of Rutgers University in New Jersey, Robert Barchi, spoke at a town hall, sponsored by the student government, ostensibly about the right to free speech on a college campus. Rutgers had been the focus of unwanted media attention all related to three professors who had been accused of spreading anti-Semitic, homophobic, misogynistic social media postings, and anti-Israel misinformation, either on their social media platforms or through their academic writings and lectures.

Barchi used this opportunity to defend the three professors based on their First Amendment rights and the academic freedom granted to them as members of a university community. One of the professors, Michael Chikindas, who taught microbiology, wrote on social media that Judaism was "the most racist religion in the world." He also blamed the Armenian genocide on Turkish Jews. Barchi noted that Chikindas made "crude jokes about Israel, Judaism, women, homosexuality, and a whole lot of things which most of us would find repugnant." One of the other professors, Jabir Puar, in a 2016 lecture, stated that Israel used the bodies of "young Palestinian men . . . [to] mine for organs for scientific research." The third professor, Mazen Adi, defended Palestinian terrorism in class and once stated that Israel had trafficked in children's organs.

All of these claims are preposterously false and unbecoming of anyone purporting to be an academic and holding a position at a university.

After setting forth the complaint against these professors, each of whom had engaged in different forms of what most would describe as both hate speech and unprofessional scholarship, the president of Rutgers decided to lecture the audience on his understanding of the Bill of Rights. "On the other hand," he said, referring specifically to Chikindas, "they are also things that are covered by his First Amendment right to free speech. You may not like what the guy says, but you have to like the fact that he can say it."[107]

If the purpose and effect of certain speech is to cause harm, spread lies, incite violence, and threaten and intimidate, then it is naked of ideas and unworthy of the First Amendment—most especially on a university campus. No, we do not "have to like" it, and the president of this university should not be enabling it, lecturing those who wonder why he is excusing and defending shoddy scholars who teach blatant falsehoods and treating their incompetence as a First Amendment issue rather than as grounds for termination. What is the meaning of such derangement in a public university?

In 1963, the Yale Political Union invited the segregationist governor from Alabama, George Wallace, to speak. A few weeks before his scheduled visit, the KKK bombed the 16th Street Baptist Church in Birmingham, Alabama, killing four African-American schoolgirls. Appearing outside the Alabama State Capitol building, Governor Wallace had once infamously declared, "Segregation now, segregation tomorrow, segregation forever!" Many blamed him (indirectly) for the church bombing.

The acting president of Yale at the time, Kingman Brewster Jr., and New Haven's mayor, Richard C. Lee, rescinded the invitation, saying that Wallace was "officially unwelcome" at Yale.

Pauli Murray, a female African-American lawyer and civil rights activist pursuing a graduate degree at Yale Law School, wrote a letter to Brewster, urging him to allow Wallace to speak on campus and present his views. This might seem odd given that fifteen years earlier she spent a night in jail for refusing to sit on broken seats on a segregated bus in Virginia, and as a law student at Howard University she participated in sit-ins to integrate whites-only restaurants in Washington, D.C. Yet in her letter to Yale's president, she wrote: "I would be among the first to picket such a meeting [referring to the planned Wallace visit]," and urged Brewster not to "compromise the tradition of freedom of speech and academic inquiry" by preventing Wallace from appearing on campus.

Brewster did not change his mind. It is unknown what consequence would have occurred had Wallace been granted a Yale audience. Might he have incited a riot? At that time, Wallace was a segregationist of the highest order, and despite the blame he received for the church bombing in Birmingham, he was not known as an instigator of imminent violence. For her part, Murray was a true free speech absolutist. She wrote to Brewster: "The possibility of violence is not sufficient reason in law to prevent an individual from exercising his constitutional right." She was incorrect under the law, but she was perhaps right in thinking that Wallace's opposition to racial integration was an opinion protected under the First Amendment. But what if the Wallace speech had actually taken place, and what if, in making his argument, he decided to toss a noose over a tree branch or burned a cross on Yale's lawn? Those are surely not ideas—either in content or delivery—that the First Amendment was ever intended to protect.[108] Allowing such violence into the marketplace of ideas does not foreshadow First Amendment progress. It more accurately suggests that free speech has regressed as an ideal, something is amiss, and the First Amendment could benefit from a second look.

# 13

# DIGNITY BY RIGHT

Everyone has the right to expect to be treated with dignity. What is the point of having freedom if it means that more aggressive citizens will use theirs to strip others of their self-worth? Free speech absolutism, as practiced in American society, is inconsistent with a no less important and equally non-negotiable right: one that protects the intrinsic value of the self.

OR ALL THOSE bullies and brutes who cannot resist the impulse to harm another human being with unremitting insults and humiliation, it is a good thing they do not live under the moral and legal maxims of the Talmud—the primary source of Jewish law and theology. Unlike the First Amendment, Jewish law does not have a similar get-out-of-jail-free card for everlasting free speech or an automatic exemption for lethal and malicious slips of the tongue. Most other countries, free societies, too, have a greater appreciation for the damage that can be done by words and signage alone. The weaponizing of "sticks and stones" is unlawful under many legal systems, including in the United States. Taking a bat to someone's head is aggravated battery. Some legal systems, however, are more progressively inclined to criminalize words used as weapons, too. And boorish behavior unbecoming of an advanced society should not deserve a pass, either.

There is a wonderful Talmudic commentary about the legal implications of causing humiliation in a fellow human being. It is no small transgression. Indeed, it is referred to with the same dramatic impact as if the injured party has been drained of his or her own blood. There is even a physiological demonstration to prove this point. An embarrassed victim immediately turns red-faced after being humiliated—the natural outcome of being shamed, especially in public. Soon thereafter, however, one notices that all color is gone, and an ashen pale complexion sets in. The disappearance of color—the turning to white—mirrors the shedding of blood. It is the look of abject dishonor. The injury has lost its outward manifestation and has now become fully internal. It is no longer capable of leaving a bruise, but there is a good chance that it might cause an ulcer.

A Midrashic commentary (on Jewish scripture) from the Babylonian period, attributed to Rabbi Menachem L'Beit Meir, which has universal appeal since everyone has, at some point, been embarrassed, said that "[o]ne who is humiliated, his face first turns red, and then turns white, because due to the magnitude of the shame, his 'soul flies away,' as if it wanted to leave the body... once the blood returns to its source, the face turns white, like someone who has died." Others attribute a similar commentary to Rav Nachman bar Yitzchak.[109]

Talmudic scholars have devoted centuries to examining the legal and moral implications of this tortious act—the humiliation of another person. If blood is shed—internally released and symbolically expelled—then why should humiliation be punished any less harshly than a homicide? Must blood only be splattered on the street before the law takes notice? Yes, of course, a body pronounced as dead is no longer among the living. But that is also true for many people who are, technically, among the living. There are people walking around who have suffered profound emotional damage from humiliation and indignity, betrayal and loss, and although their bodies are in motion, they are not experiencing the full sensations of a living being. Writer and Holocaust survivor Primo Levi once described such damaged souls as the "hollow man."[110] Many movies and TV programs are in vogue about the walking dead. One does not have to be an actual zombie to be incapable of life. There are the lifeless among us who are perfectly healthy in their vital signs. It is just their inner worlds that are numb and without vitality. They are hollowed out, so empty and bereft inside they might as well be dead. Scholars of legal history, however, know well that the murder of the soul is not a common law crime. Law professor Patricia Williams noted this absence when she referred to racist verbal violence as "spirit murder."[111] The Talmudic mandate that regards the humiliation of another human being as a blood-shedding act is a medieval object lesson in progressive wisdom: Injuries caused to human dignity ought to be taken as seriously as damage done to the body. Ancient rabbis were clearly onto something.

After all, dignity matters. The psychological and physical impact of indignity and the overall damage to the human body and brain that arises from it is considerable, largely misunderstood, and wholly underappreciated.

One of my earlier books, *The Myth of Moral Justice: Why Our Legal System Fails to Do What's Right*, focused on the legal implications of violence, inwardly experienced, that leaves no bruise to the body but still has devastating effects on human life.[112] A more recent book, by psychologist Lisa Feldman Barrett, made a similar claim about the trivialization of emotional harm under the law. "The law protects the integrity of your anatomical body but not the integrity of your mind even though your body is just a container for the organ that makes you who you are—your brain. Emotional harm is not considered real unless accompanied by physical harm."[113]

There is a fundamental paradox at the heart of the American legal system: A good deal of conduct that causes harm to another human being has no remedy under the law because the wrongdoer's action was verbal, and not physical, in nature. Our legal system has adopted all manner of criminal statutes, tortious liability rules, and case law, and applies each of these rules severely against those who bother to leave physical, material, and external evidence of the damage they cause. Yet, when it comes to wrongdoers and tort-feasors who do violence in more invisible, but no less annihilative ways, there is an indifference—a social allowance and legal exemption—as if such injuries are beyond the capacity of the law to both judge and punish. Harm done by speech does not even rise to the level of a misdemeanor, while even minor damage done to the body can raise all manner of felonious outrage.

How is that justifiable?

This dichotomy between the physical and spiritual spheres of life, the tangible and intangible, the external and internal, and the objective and subjective, has many facets that plays out to dramatic effect under the law. We all know that the legal system conventionally addresses tangible harms and material damages—broken bones, breached contracts, theft of property, homicides, the negligent performance of affirmative duties. These are all crimes and torts that leave demonstrable evidence of themselves.

Morally, however, we are all even more familiar with conduct that results in damaged dignity through overt humiliation and the disgrace that comes with being dishonored. Such actions admittedly leave less of a detectable mark—without the bandages and breakages that constitute the bread and butter of a forensic examiner—but nonetheless still produce even longer-lasting effects on the victims of such behavior. After all, scars fade with time and bruises simply disappear, but emotional harm is never erased from the memory bank and often carries a physical dimension that results in actual sickness. Wounded dignity is relived easily with a casual recall. Dishonoring someone, especially in front of family members and others, causes immeasurable injury far beyond any material harm. Broken bones do not have the same levels of staying power nor do they leave any lasting impression on psychic health—unless they coincide with psychological harm, where verbal violence combines with a physical assault. But in situations where there is just physical injury, the brain does not reexperience or

recall the moment of breakage. There are no splints for such injuries. A broken arm by itself, years later, will never become the
source of an ongoing traumatic memory. Pain of this sort is rarely
remembered. Only the cast serves as keepsake.

And yet the law, at least its American variety, seems to have no
interest in making an offense against dignity actionable.

All of this is especially relevant in the realm of the First Amendment. After all, free speech, by definition, allows for the taking of
liberties when it comes to expression, and those liberties may
cause all manner of emotional distress, indignity, and dishonor.
Understood in this way, the First Amendment, freshly minted
within the Bill of Rights, was an injury waiting to happen right
from the very beginning of the constitutional era. It was a liberty
born to create offense and to be used offensively. "Congress shall
make no law abridging . . ." is, by itself, affirmative and declarative.
Speech is the given; the hold is placed on the government to refrain
from the abridgment of speech.

Dignitary rights, by contrast, go unmentioned. They are internal
in nature, purely possessory and passive. Dignity is upheld and
maintained even for those who wish its diminishment. To sustain
one's dignity, one must be willing to defend it. Speech is asserted,
often full-throated, sometimes with voices raised and high-pitched
and thrust upon unwilling listeners.

When speech is on the offense, dignity digs in to play defense.

The problem is that America is not one of those societies where
dignity is spoken of as a claim of right. The legal implications of
trespassing on private property is well understood; trampling
upon someone's dignity sounds more like the making of a
nineteenth-century duel—pistols at dawn, count off ten places,
turn and fire. Dignitary and emotional harm do not expressly fall
under the protection of the Constitution. Unless speech threatens
or incites imminent violence, intimidates, or provokes a fight, a
speaker is relatively free to insult the dignity of another without
violating the Constitution. The word does not appear in any of

America's founding documents—neither in the Declaration of Independence nor in the Bill of Rights.

It is a startling omission. Any society that prides itself on the promotion and preservation of liberty is fully aware that exercising rights is only one phase of the democratic process. Rights fall within a matrix of competing values, and the rights possessed by others must cohere into a workable social arrangement. The social contract has many signatories. All that decorative penmanship sometimes results in sharp elbows. Each has surrendered private rights for the public good and general welfare of society. A truly liberal, pluralistic, and democratic system of law should also expect its citizens to perform reciprocal duties as part of the privilege of possessing those rights. Living within a democracy is more than merely claiming the rewards of citizenship. There are also burdens—surely, the payment of taxes and the defense of the homeland—but also a fellowship among citizens, affording to each other the mutual respect that is an essential consequence of the consent to be governed.

Everyone has the right to expect to be treated with dignity. What is the point of having freedom if it means that more aggressive citizens will use theirs to strip others of their self-worth? Free speech absolutism, as practiced in American society, is inconsistent with a no less important and equally nonnegotiable right: one that protects the intrinsic value of the self. The German philosopher of the Enlightenment, Immanuel Kant, was the godfather of human dignity, elevating it to a categorical imperative. He famously wrote in 1785 that a human being "is not to be valued merely as a means to the ends of another or even to his own ends, but as an end in himself, that is, he possesses dignity (an absolute inner worth)."[114] This principle only has meaning if all citizens understand that the dignity of others is not to be trifled with. Damage done to dignity is rarely self-inflicted—it comes from the outside and destroys a person's inner worth.

Kant wrote that "[e]very man has a legitimate claim to respect from his fellow men and in turn is bound to respect every other."[115]

The essence of citizenship hinges on the possession and protection of personal dignity. Kant further wrote that "no man in a state can be without any dignity, since he has at least the dignity of a citizen."[116] For Kant, upholding one's honor often requires measuring one's worth in relation to others in the community. That is difficult to do in a society where self-respect can easily be undone by indignity and humiliation. Injury caused by speech—"verbal injuries"—has the potential to strip victims of their sense of honor and do damage to their inherent dignity.[117]

And yet, the word "dignity" appears nowhere in America's vaunted catalog of rights.

In 1942, the anti-Nazi dissident group known as the White Rose, comprised of a mere five students at the University of Munich, typed up leaflets with inspiring words warning Germans not to relinquish their liberal, humanistic culture to the death cult of the Third Reich. Jews and the disabled were already being murdered in what was still the early days of the Final Solution. The White Rose's second leaflet addressed the situation faced by the Jews, but the focus was on something even more elemental than mass murder. "Here we see the most frightful crime against dignity, a crime that is unparalleled in the whole of history. For Jews, too, are human beings."[118] When humanity sinks to its lowest depths, what is noticed first, and lamented most, is the disappearance and annihilation of human dignity.

Law professor Steven Heyman was probably not thinking of the Talmudic injunction not to symbolically drain the blood of another human being through humiliation, but he might as well have been when he wrote, "When the speech degrades the individual in front of others, it also constitutes an attack on social personality that is analogous to defamation." Yes, defamation, not because of an untruthful accusation, but because what was published or said was dehumanizing—the annihilation of the human personality itself. We all possess an inviolability of personality, our lifeblood and life force, the essence of who we are as individuals. "The law would be deficient if it failed to protect against such affronts, which cause injury far beyond any tangible harm."[119]

Dignity and equality are not separate facets of citizenship. In fact, they are codependencies, symbiotic—the diminishment of one calls into question the existence of the other. No one treated with indignity can feel like anyone's social equal. And true equality requires mutual respect and the dignity afforded by citizenship. Treating people with contempt constitutes a denial of their worth as human beings. And speech that targets a person's right to equality is anathema to democracy. There is no greater offense to our pluralistic tradition than the desecration of citizenship itself. The psychologist Kenneth Clark astutely observed, "Human beings . . . whose daily experiences tells them almost nowhere in society are they respected and granted the ordinary dignity and courtesy accorded to others will, as a matter of course, begin to doubt their own worth."[120]

The civilizing of society is like a vast public works project. Roads and dams, bridges and buildings—but dedicated to the dignification of people. One facet of civilization is the expectation that citizens can leave their homes without fear that their property will be invaded or plundered. Another is that, once outside their home, they will not be humiliated and subjected to discrimination and indignity. Waldron explained it this way: "Each person . . . should be able to go about his or her business, with the assurance that there will be no need to face hostility, violence, discrimination or exclusion by others."[121] It is an implicit right to be protected from social harassment because, without these guarantees, the enjoyment of rights is impossible, and the social status conferred with citizenship is valueless.

Words are both instruments of communication and violence. The First Amendment functions as a smokescreen, the violence of speech obscured in the red, white, and blue haze of patriotic fervor. Only those with a sturdy constitution can avail themselves of this constitutional liberty. If speech came with disclaimer language, many patriotic citizens might choose silence. And for good reason. Law professor Richard Delgado observed that "mere words . . . can cause mental, emotional, or even physical harm to their target, especially if delivered in front of others or by a person in a position of authority."[122] And President Lyndon Johnson explained the moral necessity for the passage of the Civil Rights Act in 1964 by saying that "[a] man has a right not to be insulted in front of his children."[123]

# 14

# EUROPE'S FOCUS ON PRIVACY AND DIGNITY WITHOUT SACRIFICING SPEECH

*All sorts of protections exist to safeguard human dignity—even in societies that also value free speech. It is just that these nations do not overvalue free speech; they do not allow it to become a superseding right.*

AS COMPARED WITH Old World European values, where the private realm is sacred and the public face is something that still belongs to the individual, Americans show little regard for private lives and public dignity. Monica Lewinsky would absolutely have had a different experience in the public eye if she had interned for a French president. Moreover, an American candidate for president who found himself accused of a crime in France would never have been treated to a "perp walk" with all the fanfare that escorted Dominique Strauss-Kahn off a plane at JFK Airport on his way to an arraignment in a Manhattan courtroom. One of the reasons why the French were so appalled when they watched the spectacle of Strauss-Kahn—who at the time was the head of the International Monetary Fund and a prohibitive favorite to succeed as France's next president—handcuffed and removed from his first-class seat with photographers capturing every moment of his indignity is that such photo-ops are strictly forbidden in France. French law does not permit shame visited upon a potentially innocent person.

But what of freedom of the press and the right of the public to know about events as they unfold? Well, the French value privacy and personal dignity far more than the desire for immediate updates on the news of the day. News can wait; dignity cannot. The French are aware of the intrusions on privacy and invasion of personhood that our First Amendment allows. And they reject it. The European Union even has a "right to be forgotten," which permits individuals to file a legal action to remove embarrassing information that appears about them on the Internet.[124] In America, however, to make a spectacle out of someone else's indignity, especially if it is that of a famous person, is must-see TV.

Americans have priorities other than dignity. For instance, they place great value on the sanctity of private dwellings, which explains why warrantless government searches and seizures, eavesdropping, and home surveillance evokes such strong feelings of Fourth Amendment violation. It also explains why many American states have laws known as the Castle Doctrine, where men and women are truly the kings and queens of their castles. A homeowner is not required to retreat if threatened or attacked in one's own home. There is no legal duty to avoid a violent encounter during a home invasion. Indeed, in such cases, the homeowner is permitted to stand his or her ground and can even use deadly force for self-protection. The same allowance is not granted outside of one's home, however. On the street, most states place the burden on the victim to retreat.

As for Europeans, even though castles are far more common on their continent, they do not feel as entitled, nor are they legally permitted, to protect their homes with the same levels of vigilance. The better course of self-defense is to simply flee, and Europeans do not feel less chivalrous in doing so. Where they are far more sensitive—indignant, in fact—is over attempts by the press or private citizens to bring indignity to their public face.

To Europeans, *dignity is their castle*.

Europeans demand, and are granted, more control in protecting their public image. Sovereignty over the home is less important than sovereignty over the self. Americans, by contrast, seem to accept that the general public has claims on the private lives of their fellow citizens, especially the more famous ones. TV shows and tabloids exist for this very purpose—to track the movements and spread the gossip about the rich and famous. Venturing out into society exposes Americans to the elements, and to public scrutiny and ridicule.[125]

Europeans, generally, are not as fearful or skeptical of government involvement in their lives. Distrust of the government is America's obsession. "Don't Tread on Me" is a revolutionary slogan from Colonial times. Switching from a monarch to a president did not make Americans less cynical. The Bill of Rights, as discussed earlier, is a catalog of negative rights, drafted with a greater interest in placing checks on governmental overreach than in granting positive liberties to the people. Europeans are fixated on dignitary rights and are more than happy to empower the government to protect these rights with every means available.

All sorts of protections exist to safeguard human dignity—even in societies that *also* value free speech. It is just that these nations do not overvalue free speech; they do not allow it to become a *superseding* right. Rather, they see speech as yet another aspect of human dignity: One has a right to speak because a dignified person should possess such a liberty, but not if it means bringing shame and indignity to another human being. An attack on a person's dignity is tantamount to a breach of their peace and an invasion of their personal space—a far more vital plot of real estate than mere tangible property. In a society that regards protection of human dignity to be of no less importance than safeguarding the human body, such violations of personal honor undermine a citizen's right to personal security.

For instance, employees in Europe are protected under the law from being addressed disrespectfully, degraded, or even assigned humiliating tasks. In France, in a civil suit, employees prevailed over their employer who had required them to present a receipt proving that they had purchased the merchandise they were taking home with them. The court ruled that the employer's conduct exposed them to unnecessary indignity.[126] Anyone who has ever seen Martin's Scorsese's *The Wolf of Wall Street* will remember the disgraceful depiction of Wall Street "boiler-room" excesses where drunken stockbrokers tossed dwarves at targets as if they were mere darts. In France, such a game, even if played by a willing dwarf, is unlawful because it is an offense to the dignity of all dwarves, and it is undignified for a community to allow such a spectacle to even take place.[127]

Similarly, back in 2009, French president Nicolas Sarkozy was at the center of what in America would have been a politically incorrect scandal, in championing a ban against the wearing of the burka in French society. Two years later, such a law actually went into effect when the French Parliament passed such a measure, but its moral force had less to do with feminist philosophy than it did with general notions of human dignity. Some regarded the law as overly paternalistic, if not outright Islamophobic. The fact that some Muslim women may actually wish to be fully veiled in public, and depriving them of that right violated their religious liberty, was unconvincing to the French president. In his view, having their faces covered in public diminished their dignity regardless of their religious convictions. As an open society, France expected its citizens to be open to the liberty it affords and the dignity it demands. Addressing himself directly to Muslims, he said, "France was an old nation united around a certain idea of personal dignity, particularly women's dignity, and of life together. It's the fruit of centuries of efforts."[128]

While the law was provocative, it made sense to most citizens of France who, like the United States, fought a revolution to bring the values of the Enlightenment to the people. In France, religious freedom is not more important than human dignity. Neither is freedom of expression. A religion cannot cancel the dignitary rights of even its own adherents. And freedom of speech does not extend so heedlessly that it can cause an assault on dignity.

This is a familiar concept in other Western democracies, where free speech is equally guaranteed but not when it interferes with human dignity. Speakers, no matter what they have to say, no matter how important their purported ideas may be, are not entitled to quash the dignitary rights of others. Even the United Nations includes human dignity in many of its declarations and conventions. Indeed, its Universal Declaration of Human Rights is a valentine to human dignity, with the word appearing in five different provisions, each with a resounding commitment to dignity as a claim of right. The Universal Declaration of Human Rights begins with recognizing "the *inherent dignity* and . . . the equal and inalienable rights of all members of the human family." It declares that "[a]ll human beings are born free and *equal in dignity and rights*." Its preamble "reaffirm(s) . . . the *dignity and worth* of the human person."[129] Other international agreements follow the same standard and include the language of dignity. The Preamble to the UN's International Covenant on Civil and Political Rights guarantees that all human beings have "equal and inalienable rights derived from the *inherent dignity of the human person*."[130]

To Americans living in a dignity-phobic nation, this is a much harder sell. We have not exactly mastered the language of dignity even though the feelings of *indignity* are widely felt. In Europe, dignity is akin to mother's milk; in the United States, dignity is not even an acquired taste. What is it about these other democracies that recognize free speech as a fundamental human right but not at the expense of human dignity? What do they understand about the human condition that the United States somehow misses? Other practitioners of democratic self-government, some not from Europe, see no contradiction in guaranteeing free speech while criminalizing conduct that incites violence and causes harm to human dignity. Austria, Australia, Belgium, Brazil, Canada, Cyprus, Denmark, New Zealand, England, France, Germany, India, Ireland,

Israel, Italy, Sweden, and Switzerland all restrict hate speech, and do so for reasons that start with the protection of human dignity. A recent decision of the Australian appellate court imposed an obligation on democratic society to safeguard political pluralism by prohibiting insulting, humiliating, or intimidating statements that might cause emotional harm.[131]

Some nations go ever further by inserting a right to dignity into their founding documents. Namibia, Russia, Switzerland, South Africa, Ethiopia, Colombia, Poland, Hungary, Israel, and Germany include dignity as a constitutional right. Of the forty-five European states, thirty-two mention human dignity expressly in their Constitutions. Of the remaining thirteen, all are signatories to the European Convention for the Protection of Human Rights and Fundamental Freedom, in which human dignity is referred to as a constitutional value.[132]

There is nothing intrinsically wrong with one democratic nation going rogue on one specific value that other nations regard as sacrosanct. America is on a different continent, after all, although Canada, our continental neighbor, follows the dignitary lead of other democracies. Perhaps American exceptionalism entails a hardened spirit that has no need for any dignity reinforcement. The United States does not subscribe to the same international standards of civility that are fundamental to the self-identification of citizenship in other Western societies. In the end, that should not matter. The United States is not better off for rejecting the prevailing norms of dignity practiced by other nations. When harm comes to the dignity of individuals, damage done to pluralism is not far off. Criminalizing hate speech is a statement by a society that dignity is essential to citizenship. Law professor Martha Nussbaum has observed that these other nations regulate hate speech primarily to "secure for all citizens the prerequisites of a life worthy of human dignity."[133]

France is a good example. It guarantees protection for both free speech and artistic expression under its Declaration of the Rights of Man and of the Citizen, declaring that the "free communication of ideas and opinions to be one of the most precious of the rights of man."[134] It is no coincidence that France refers to rights as being owed to humankind as a whole and not just to individual citizens—a distinction that is more than semantics. It is a reminder that the purpose behind democratic liberty is to empower citizens with not just the passive receipt of rights. Individual citizens are also contracting parties with the state. They can make claims on that contract, and they have duties to perform under it, too.

Remember the earlier reference to the shock comedian Dieudonné M'bala M'bala and his many legal troubles? A French attorney in media rights, Mathieu Davy, explained why Dieudonné runs afoul of the law so frequently: "[T]here are clear limits in our legal system. I have the right to criticize an idea, a concept or a religion. I have the right to criticize the powers in my country. But I don't have the right to attack people and to incite hate."[135]

France recognizes the right but also prevents the abuse of freedom of expression. It sees no conflict regulating speech that detracts from democratic life. In fact, to address any confusion about the cultural and legal differences in how speech is treated in France, the government published an English language guide in 2015, which stated clearly that speech is one of France's highest values, "But this freedom has limits. . . . Racism, anti-Semitism, racial hatred and justification for terrorism are not opinions. They are offenses."[136]

As a nation, France has come to some collective understanding that protecting its liberal society, comprised of a multiethnic population, is more important than any truth that might arise from hostile, hateful speech. And it does not see why a speaker's right to freedom of expression, or the liberties taken by an artist, for that matter, should have more social or political value than another's right to dignity. If Dieudonné has something meaningful to contribute to the public discourse, he must say it in a manner that respects the pluralistic makeup of France. But whatever he may have to say as a citizen of France, he cannot blatantly degrade the dignity of others because doing so would violate their own rights of citizenship. Articles 10 and 11 of France's Declaration of Human and Civic Rights guarantees the freedom of holding and communicating one's opinion, but not if it "trouble[s] public order." The government always reserves the ability to regulate speech when the freedom is abused.[137]

Essentially, the French do not believe that it is too much to ask Dieudonné to refrain from making crude concentration camp and gas chamber jokes as an attack on French Jewry. The law he continues to violate is pretty straightforward. In France, "[c]rimes against humanity [are] defined as incitement to discrimination, hatred and violence."[138] That is how seriously the French judicial system takes Dieudonné's comic act—seeing in it not humor but as "crimes against humanity"—an indictment first made at the Nuremberg Trials, which, it must be remembered, also had to do with concentration camps and gas chambers. Moreover, under French law, the spread of false information is itself a crime. In addition to his assault on the humanity of Jews, his denial of the Holocaust demands punishment, too. For France, where the Holocaust also took place, it is imperative to defend objective truth from the purveyors of lies.

The United States sees it quite differently. In America, Holocaust denial is just another contentious "idea" that deserves an equal opportunity to compete in the marketplace of ideas. Serious-minded people are confident that there will be no takers for such mindless trash. But that requires an abundance of faith in discerning consumers, and we know that Holocaust denial is a trope for many in the alt-right community. One never knows what people can be led to believe—or desperately and fumingly want to believe.

A school principal in Boca Raton, Florida, in 2019, told a parent that the school would not be teaching the Holocaust because he was not in a position to confirm that it was "an actual, historical event."[139] Today, we hear from some in government that the press is the "enemy of the people." That "all Muslims are terrorists." That "immigrants are rapists." Tomorrow, who knows what will be unleashed at campaign rallies. The French are far more realistic about what the Parisian street would be willing to believe if made readily available and treated with the legitimacy of objective truth. Defending Holocaust denial is poisonous to the social fabric and collective goodwill of pluralistic societies. And some people might actually believe it—simply because it received a public airing.

Besides, what idea is being presented here that has a moral and objective claim to be reasonably and fairly rebutted? Must Holocaust survivors be required to produce evidence of their human existence and political legitimacy? The question itself is grotesque and inhumane; it is nothing but a denial of humanity itself. If the humanity of Holocaust survivors is being denied, then what does it mean to be a citizen in good standing?

Clearly this cannot be what the Founders had in mind for our first, or any other, amendment. The state's obligation under our Constitution, as embodied in the Fifth and Fourteenth Amendments, is to provide equality of access in the democratic process. Those rights are not conditional; they do not hinge on the free speech of others. Allowing citizens to deny the worth of fellow human beings gives them the power to set the terms of civic engagement.

Would we deny the Middle Passage or the scourge of slavery in the southern states? Is the Emancipation Proclamation still up for debate? Yet, being given the right under the First Amendment to burn a cross is tantamount to taunting African-Americans to step outside and debate those who insist that their race is illegitimate. It is even worse than that. The KKK is not seeking a rebuttal. They wish not for a debate, just the liberty to openly hate. That allows them to declare victory without having to hear from the other side.

# 15

# NOT EVERYTHING SHOULD BE OPEN FOR DEBATE

Other democratic nations around the world have a real-time appreciation of the cumulative impact of hateful propaganda and the challenges it presents to keeping the peace in multiethnic, pluralistic societies.

SOME MATTERS ARE simply never open to debate. For instance, humanity is a given; it does not come up for annual review. As a society, we should categorically state that we are not interested in what haters and harm producers have to say.

Our neighbor to the north, Canada, also has freedom of expression built into its Charter of Rights and Freedoms. Canada is democratic in its governance. But they see a higher purpose for free speech. In 1957, its Supreme Court recognized "[t]he right of free expression of opinion and of criticism, *upon matters of public policy and public administration*, and the right to discuss and debate such matters whether they be social, economic or political."[140] The rantings of Nazis, however, is not purposeful speech that informs the public on matters of common concern. Speech that merits protection must be positively directed toward the public good. The Canadians are right not to regard speech intended to cause emotional harm to minority groups as protected free speech.

When the Canadian Supreme Court ruled on a case where appellants distributed cards inviting people to dial a phone number and hear a recorded message denigrating Jews, it found the conduct to be deplorable and reaffirmed that "willfully promoting hatred" violated the Canadian Human Rights Act.[141] In the United States, the expressive intentions of the speaker—the viewpoint and content of the message—would have been the overriding concern for the Supreme Court. The speaker in the Canadian case wished to express his anti-Semitic views by leaving a recorded message for anyone who chose to dial a phone number. The country with whom we share a border has adopted many of our cultural traits, but we have something to learn from their humanistic impulses. In Canada, speech that does not advance social goals is unprotected under its Charter. Nazis need not apply. In Canada, free speech is a more conditional freedom.

In a stunning passage that speaks directly to why dignity matters, the Court wrote, "A person's sense of human dignity and belonging to the community at large is closely linked to the concern and respect accorded to the groups to which he or she belongs. The derision, hostility and abuse encouraged by the hate propaganda therefore have a severely negative impact on the individual's sense of self-worth and acceptance."[142]

In yet another case involving the use of telephonic communications to spread group hatred, the Supreme Court of Canada reiterated the serious threat to society that hateful propaganda presents. It wrote in 1990 that hate speech "contributes to disharmonious relations among various cultural and religious groups, as a result of eroding the tolerance and open-mindedness that must flourish in a multicultural society which is committed to the idea of equality."[143]

Canadians are far from alone in restricting speech that has as its objective not the transmission of valuable ideas but the discharging of harm to human dignity. Statutory language around the world invokes human dignity as a right no less worthy than free speech.

Article 30 of the Polish Constitution guarantees "the inherent and inalienable dignity of the person." The South African Constitution provides that "[e]veryone has inherent dignity and the right to have their dignity respected and protected."[144] Israel does not designate a formal right to free speech, yet the Israeli Supreme Court has incorporated free speech into the Human Dignity Clause of its Basic Laws. It reads: "All persons are entitled to protection of their life, body and dignity."[145] In a case that balanced the right to liberty and human dignity, the Israeli Supreme Court explained in 2002 that, "The rights of a person to his dignity, his liberty and his property are not absolute rights. They are relative rights. They may be restricted to uphold the rights of others . . . human rights are not the right of a person on a desert island. They are the rights of a person as a part of society . . . in a democracy."[146]

In the aftermath of the Holocaust, the Federal Republic of Germany, more so than any other nation, incorporated dignity as the primary value of human freedom that must be safeguarded by the state. Such a priority makes sense given how much dehumanization figured into the ethos of the Third Reich and how much the reconstituted Germany wished to redeem its moral honor and start anew. Article I of its Basic Law of 1949 subordinated all constitutional rights and values to human dignity, finding that "[t]he dignity of man is inviolable. . . . [It is] the supreme value [that] dominates the whole value system of fundamental rights. . . . Human dignity is thus a constituent part of humanity . . . the essence of the German social order . . . the highest legal value in Germany."[147] Article I imposes an affirmative obligation on the state to "respect and protect human dignity."[148] Article II of the Basic Law guarantees that "[e]very person has the right to the free development of his personality, insofar as he does not injure the rights of others."[149]

Dieudonné would not fare better if he headlined a comedy club in Berlin. The German criminal code specifically proscribes the use of intimidating hate speech that violates human dignity. Unlike zealotry around American free speech, German law is not conflicted about "balancing human dignity and freedom of expression," recognizing that dignity may even deserve more protection since the full exercise of free speech might leave vulnerable minorities exposed to contempt and derision.[150]

Given America's unbounded optimism in public discourse and its traumatic memories of King George III—a monarch with a low tolerance for sedition—the disparate treatment of free speech between the two continents becomes clearer. Unlike Europe, where the memories of Nazi Germany are easily recalled, the United States never fully owned up to its racist past, with its lingering remains still very much visible today. Other democratic nations around the world have a real-time appreciation of the cumulative impact of hateful propaganda and the challenges it presents to keeping the peace in multiethnic, pluralistic societies.

Inexplicably, few in the United States seem to be saying the obvious: Given that there was once slavery in this country and a civil war had to be fought in order to end it, surely the Klan cannot be granted a pulpit to antagonize and retraumatize African-Americans. There is something fundamentally indecent about still having to endure racist taunts in a nation that was once defined wholly by its racial divisions. That is what the Germans understand about neo-Nazis—never again can they be allowed to set the terms of public debate; never again should their agenda even *be* debated. In America, however, there is no sense of shame about allowing racism to take center stage in public life. And there is no consensus on the power of words to wound.

# 16.

# HATE LEADS TO VIOLENCE

Words have consequences, set in motion incrementally, perhaps, but in no way are those who voice them innocent and
inactive, oblivious to the effect they might have.

$S$ARA LIPTON, A historian, offered a reminder that the use of
hateful language and imagery toward Muslims, immigrants,
and abortionists may not intend a violent outcome, but that's
what is likely to result. In an opinion essay, she focused on the experience of Medieval Jewry. One thousand years of Christian theology that demonized Jews and Judaism for any number of cardinal
sins—from holding Jews responsible for the murder of Jesus Christ
to condemning Judaism as a debased religion, from the poisonous
residue of Passion plays to the libels against Jews as either blood-
thirsty Christian killers or rapacious money lenders—eventually
led to massacres throughout the Middle Ages. Spain expelled its
Jewish population in 1492, but the Inquisition would never have
come about without many years of preparatory propaganda—
anti-Semitism both feverish and pernicious, hysterical and surreal—combined with weekly Christian sermons that fomented
bigotry and hate. Such are the long-lasting consequences of dehumanization and the denial of human dignity even if it first shows

itself in seemingly innocuous ways—mild denunciations that call for no violence but foreshadow something much more severe as enmity hardens and empathy is lost.[151]

The same was true in Rwanda where radio broadcasts inciting violence against the Tutsi minority led to ethnic cleansing and mass killings with machetes by the Hutus. But it started with less bloody assaults against a rival population punctuated with name-calling and other acts of indignity. The genocide of Africans in Sudan and the Congo had similar origins. Palestinians are taught that Jews are pigs and monkeys and to hate Christians. Hamas and Hezbollah use school textbooks to disparage Jews and Christians. Crosses are still burned and swastikas painted in America, their meaning unmistakable, their intended targets equally well known. The Supreme Court in *Virginia v. Black* in 2003 finally spoke truth to cowardice in stating that cross-burning is historically linked to violence and intimidation and not truth-seeking. If one cannot find the words to express themselves and must resort to burning a cross to make their point—if a more civilized voice is too difficult to locate— then let us at least acknowledge that the expression has but one purpose: to intimidate another.[152]

On December 8, 2017, an Imam in Houston, Raed Salah Al-Rousan, preached a sermon that "Judgment Day will not come until the Muslims fight the Jews. The Muslims will kill the Jews." Several weeks later, a group of Muslim community leaders from Houston signed a statement stating that, among other things, "We understand that words can create fear and tension and . . . [we] reject any direct or perceived calls to violence."[153]

It is significant that the statement began with the recognition that "words can create fear and tension"—that words are not presumptively passive because they are merely spoken. Words have consequences, set in motion incrementally, perhaps, but in no way are those who voice them innocent and inactive, oblivious to the effect they might have. A glance at American history offers a tutorial on words that eventually took on more violent shapes, living beyond their original moments of conception with terrifying outcomes. African-Americans have been maligned as criminals, which inflamed racist stereotypes, influenced both the public's perception of black- and brown-skinned people, and poisoned the attitudes of law enforcement—fanning their own preexisting prejudices. Native Indian-Americans have been referred to as drunken and marauding savages—and, portrayed as such in Hollywood films, their likenesses and rituals misappropriated, have been turned into mascots for sports teams. Few recognize the damage that is done, the dignity denied, when these stereotypes become widely accepted, engrained in culture and unable to be overcome.[154]

The relationship between verbal indignity and future acts of violence is both well known and axiomatic. As psychologist Gordon W. Allport observed in 1979, "prolonged and intense verbal hostility always precedes a riot. . . . Although most barking (antilocution) does not lead to biting . . . there is never a bite without previous barking. Fully seventy years of political anti-Semitism of the verbal order preceded the discriminatory Nuremberg Laws passed by the Hitler regime. Soon after these laws were passed the violent program of extermination began."[155]

Those who perpetuate stereotypes and defame entire groups of people are not simply exercising their right to voice an opinion. They are engaged in the most pointedly anti-democratic of behavior—contributing to political inequality—denying the dignity of fellow citizens by eroding any of the inhibitions that keep incitement in check. These are acts of violence. Entire classes of people are rendered unworthy of equal treatment and become predisposed to harm. How is the First Amendment permitted to have veto power over the tranquility of those who do not wish to be forced into an exchange of weaponized words?

# 17

# WHERE DIGNITY IS ALREADY RECOGNIZED—A RIGHT TO PRIVACY AND DIGNITY

If Supreme Court justices and constitutional scholars believe that a right to privacy not only exists but includes rights to have an abortion and to marry a person of the same sex, then why should an American citizen not have a penumbral right to be treated with dignity and respect?

*I*N THE "BATTLE royale" of rights where speech vanquishes all, there has been some legal lip service paid to a recognition that dignity does, in fact, matter. Mostly this appears in dissenting Supreme Court opinions, but the language of dignity has also surfaced in lower court decisions. When "dignity" is invoked, it shows up in cases involving amendments to the Constitution other than the First—a tacit acknowledgment that limitless free speech and human dignity may be irreconcilable. Other constitutional rights, apparently, do not present the same problem. For instance, the "perp walk," which so offended the French people in the sexual assault investigation involving Dominique Strauss-Kahn (ironically in the same jurisdiction where Strauss-Kahn was indicted), was once referred to in a way consistent with the French values of protecting individual privacy. In *Laura v. Charles*, a federal appeals court in 2000 held that "perp walks" violate the dignity of the accused if no legitimate state interest is shown to justify such an otherwise personally humiliating affront to personal dignity.[156]

The Supreme Court has frequently drawn a connection between the Fourth Amendment, with its prohibitions on unreasonable and warrantless searches and seizures, and its effect on human dignity. The language of one such opinion stated that "unwarranted intrusion[s] by the state violated a person's privacy and dignity."[157] In the high court's iconic Fifth and Sixth Amendment cases that gave birth to the "Miranda warnings"—which were established to protect criminal suspects from making "self-incriminating" statements in the absence of legal counsel—the Supreme Court referred to the government's obligation to the "dignity and integrity of its citizens."[158] With respect to "cruel and unusual punishments," proscribed under the Eighth Amendment, the Supreme Court, in one of many cases over the years, invoked the "dignity of man" to justify why such punishments are unconstitutional.[159]

The Fourteenth Amendment's "due process" and "equal protection" clauses have, on occasion, inspired a justice on the Supreme Court to read into the amendment a dignitary value not expressly found anywhere in the language of the Constitution. After all, the Fourteenth Amendment was adopted after the Civil War, and it arose out of a period in which the legal transformation of former slaves into fully emancipated citizens required a reaffirmation of the liberty and equality that came with citizenship and could not be denied under the law to anyone without due process.

What is equal protection if it does not also preserve human dignity? More importantly, the abolition of slavery was a painful reminder of the suffering and indignity that African-Americans were forced to endure for nearly all of the first century of America's existence. Dignity goes unmentioned in the Fourteenth Amendment, but its presence is felt profoundly in the rights that the amendment has come to represent. Many of the Framers of the Constitution owned slaves. It took a civil war for a new generation of constitutional draftsmen to introduce language into America's founding document that imbued it with human dignity. This was surely the case in *Lawrence v. Texas*, the Supreme Court decision in

2003 that finally invalidated state statutes that criminalized homosexuality, and in *Hollingsworth v. Perry*, the decision in 2013 that legalized same-sex marriage.[160] The cases made sure to mention that these rights arise from the moral imperative of human dignity.

On rarer occasions, the Supreme Court will insert human dignity into a decision involving the Free Speech Clause of the First Amendment. In 1971, *Cohen v. California*, a protestor of the Vietnam War entered a public building wearing a jean jacket emblazoned with the words: "Fuck the Draft." Disturbing though this was to someone who happened to be present, the Supreme Court held that such conduct was protected speech under the First Amendment precisely because it involved a matter of public concern. Those words had the potential to create a more informed citizenry under "the premise of dignity and choice upon which our political system rests."[161] It is an amorphous statement, one that supports the dignity of the speaker. But what about the dignity of the listener? An offensive jean jacket may not present the right test case, but there are many examples where freedom of expression obliterates the dignity of a targeted listener.

Among the notable justices of the United States Supreme Court who presided during the first half of the twentieth century—Oliver Wendall Holmes, Louis Brandeis, and Benjamin Cardozo—the word *dignity*, as it related to self-respect and citizenship, never appeared in any of their written opinions or even their outside statements. Dignity enters the conversation of the First Amendment in the 1940s, thanks largely to the written opinions of Justice Frank Murphy. He may have had some assistance, or drawn inspiration, from the United Nations, which had only recently come into existence. As mentioned earlier, human dignity appears in five sections of the Universal Declaration of Human Rights, including its Preamble. Justice Murphy took the unusual step of speaking the language of dignity in ways unfamiliar to Supreme Court jurisprudence. In a dissenting opinion in 1945 where the majority ordered a new trial for a local sheriff who beat a black man to death,

Murphy wrote about the "fair treatment that befits the dignity of man, dignity that is recognized and guaranteed by the Constitution."[162] Where, precisely, dignity is both "recognized" and "guaranteed" in the Constitution, he failed to say. A year later in a concurring opinion, Justice Murphy impugned the scourge of racism because "[i]t renders impotent the ideal of the dignity of the human personality, destroying something of what is noble in our way of life."[163] Murphy's invocations of dignity sometimes inspired other judicial takers. Around this same time period, Justices Felix Frankfurter and Robert Jackson each identified human dignity as a virtue, as opposed to an actual right, that was protected under the Bill of Rights.[164]

Justice Murphy was the one reliable member of the Supreme Court who stood largely alone in recognizing human dignity as an unenumerated yet legally viable constitutional right. Dignity may be unmentioned in any of America's founding documents. But Murphy saw an implicit right, not unlike an offshoot of the right to privacy—another one of those penumbral rights that have been read into the Constitution as deriving from other rights but with equal force and entitlement.

A penumbra is a shadow of illumination, indefinite and yet present within the margins. When applied to constitutional interpretation, it embodies a group of rights that, while not explicitly expressed, nonetheless exist by way of inference, extrapolated from the meaning of other enumerated rights. Those rights are unified by a right that does not actually appear in the text. Penumbral legal reasoning is a holistic exercise. It requires a broader reading of an entire text and an open mind about the logical progression of rules. It does not fixate on literal meanings and dogmatic doctrine. And it is a nightmare for those who consider themselves to be strict constructionists of the Constitution.

The right to privacy, for instance, has given headaches to scholars of legal history who go by the name "Originalists." They are so named because they believe the Constitution must be understood and applied only according to its literal meaning—the original intentions of the Framers at the time of the Constitution's drafting.

Divining the intentions of the Framers has presented many challenges, however. The Constitution, after all, is a malleable document. It was meant to be subject to interpretation. Its amendments, and the rights listed in the Bill of Rights, are capable of suggesting multiple meanings and are most certainly not without ambiguity. It is a living document and was to a great extent intended to be adapted to the times in which it was being applied. A general right to privacy, which is not specified in the Constitution, has been imputed, which gave birth to a whole assortment of other privacy rights—from "abortion to homosexuality to same-sex marriage—none of which is expressly stated anywhere. Originalists have been left to wonder where in the Bill of Rights these privacy rights are to be found. Meanwhile, the right to privacy has continued to expand, slipping in as a loophole in the Constitution, where rights that do not appear in the text can be conveniently found to have always existed in the penumbras of other rights.

Dignity, too, is not explicitly mentioned in the Constitution. Perhaps this accounts for the reason why freedom of expression, which undeniably was part of the Framers' original thinking, is given priority over a dignitary right that the Founders never bothered to name outright. If Supreme Court justices and constitutional scholars believe that a right to privacy not only exists but includes rights to have an abortion and to marry a person of the same sex, then why should an American citizen not have a penumbral right to be treated with dignity and respect? After all, dignity, like the word penumbra itself, is but a shadow of the human personality. If any right should be read into the Constitution, one that preserves and protects dignity should be first among equals.

Perhaps that day in constitutional interpretation may someday arrive.

Curiously, it may come even sooner under state law.

While state constitutions within the United States mostly mirror their federal counterpart, there are three states—Montana, Illinois, and Louisiana—along with Puerto Rico, that treat dignity as a basis for a citizen's self-identification. The creators of our federal government left dignity in the margins, de-listed from the inventory of enumerated rights. Yet, a few states managed to expressly acknowledge the self-worth of individual personhood. In Montana, for instance, the language is emphatic: "The dignity of the human being is inviolable."[165]

Case law tells yet another story. Unlike the European model, American lawmakers and jurists have had an almost allergic reaction to formally integrating dignity into our constitutional framework. Since the enactment of the Constitution in 1789 until 2003, the word "dignity" has appeared in approximately nine hundred decisions. But very few of them use the word dignity in the context of the self-respect and intrinsic worth of a human being. Most speak of the dignity of the state or of the sovereign, or foreign countries, or even of the court itself.[166] Overall, it seems as if our laws—from the very beginning of the republic—resisted even mentioning dignity as a claim of right. More recently, however, yet another layer of ambiguity has been introduced that complicates the status of human dignity in American jurisprudence.

The American Declaration of the Rights and Duties of Man, drafted by the Organization of American States and adopted in 1948 right before the United Nations' Universal Declaration of Human Rights, now includes dignity as one of its granted rights. And the American Convention on Human Rights, which was adopted in 1969 (but not ratified by the United States), includes the language "respect for the inherent dignity of the human person." Were these newer iterations of American rights intended to compensate for the dearth of dignity language in the Constitution itself? Is their inclusion here only symbolic, or was it designed to remake American law so that it aligns better with the European model where dignity is the leading light of enlightened values? These new American declarations do not have the same force of law as the Constitution. And so, they dangle in the gravity of American democracy, their meaning elusive, a premonition of a more refined sense of citizenship still to come.

# 18

# THE JUSTICES FOR WHOM DIGNITY ALWAYS MATTERED

*The government's commitment to preserve a citizen's right to a dignified life is the essence of the social contract—and the Founders knew this and treated it as self-evident.*

ESPITE ALL OF the yin and yang of mixed signals, there have been a few Supreme Court justices, like Justice Murphy, who believe that a right to human dignity exists, even if it is only an implicit ideological value of the Constitution and not an enumerated right. Is personal dignity yet another emanation of the right to privacy—made explicit only through imaginative case law and not from a close reading of the text? A right to privacy, which brought sweeping progressive changes to all manner of personal autonomy—from marriage, sexual relations, and abortion—expanded the range of rights the Constitution guaranteed. Yet dignity, unlike privacy, does not need to be conjured from whole cloth. There is substantial evidence—in the form of historical letters, writings, and public debates—that the Founders saw human dignity as a natural right that this new nation should foster and protect.

For them it was inviolable: An attack on dignity is an assault against citizenship itself. This democratic nation arose from raucous debates and thundering clashes of personalities. Yet, the delegates to the First and Second Congressional Congress, and to the Constitutional Convention, expected to be treated with dignity and respect. Arriving at any consensus required it. Surely they believed in freedom of speech; democratic participation depended on it. But dignity and mutual respect was to be afforded all speakers. Healthy disagreement was very different from harmful abuse and running roughshod over the rights of others.

Having converted their natural rights into a Constitution, and forfeited the more tribal rules of man for the societal rule of law, these citizens expected the equal protection and security guarantees of citizenship. The government's commitment to preserve a citizen's right to a dignified life is the essence of the social contract, and the Founders knew this and treated it as self-evident.

In more recent times, the justices on the Supreme Court for whom dignity under the law has been most closely associated with their writings are William Brennan and the recently retired Anthony Kennedy.

All throughout his career on the high court, Brennan took human dignity seriously and said so eloquently. In 1978, *Paul v. Davis*, a right to privacy case, he wrote of how in a "free society [there is] the legitimate expectations of every person to *innate human dignity* and sense of worth."[167] In an Eighth Amendment case in 1972, he explained that "[t]he state, even as it punishes, must treat its members with respect for their intrinsic worth as human beings. A punishment is 'cruel and unusual,' therefore, if it does not comport with *human dignity*."[168]

Such a curious paradox in American law. At least one Supreme Court justice believed that death row inmates are deserving of human dignity, yet for nearly every other justice, an ordinary citizen assaulted by the sight of a swastika or a burning cross is inexplicably undeserving of the same dignity considerations.

In both of these opinions, Justice Brennan wrote in dissent. The majority of the Court believed otherwise, and human dignity went undiscussed. When it came to elevating human dignity as a right protected under the Constitution, Brennan always seemed to find himself in the minority.

Justice Kennedy, by contrast, often found himself in the majority—albeit as the fifth vote in one of his many swing-vote opinions—when he chose to invoke the language of dignity, implanting it into the Constitution as an offshoot of the right to privacy. In the landmark case in 2003 that invalidated a Texas sodomy statute, which ultimately legalized same-sex sexual activity in all of the states, Kennedy wrote that, "The liberty protected by the Constitution allows homosexual persons the right to choose to enter upon relationships in the confines of their homes and their own private lives and still retain their *dignity* as free persons."[169]

More famously, he became the architect of marriage equality on the Supreme Court, writing the majority opinions in two cases establishing a constitutional right to same-sex marriage. Kennedy noted in 2013 that the disparate treatment in denying benefits to same-sex couples places them in the "unstable position of being in a second-tier marriage. The differentiation demeans the couple, whose moral and sexual choices the Constitution protects . . . and whose relationship the State has sought to *dignify*." Kennedy went further in noting the humiliation felt by the children of same-sex couples in being treated differently from the offspring of opposite-sex marriages.[170] In the other marriage equality case, Justice Kennedy wrote in 2015 that, "*there is dignity in the bond* between two men or two women who seek to marry and in their autonomy to make such profound choices. . . . They ask for *equal dignity in the eyes of the law*. The Constitution grants them that right."[171]

Justice Kennedy also read dignity into the Constitution in determining whether the death penalty applied to offenders under the age of eighteen. In 2005, Kennedy wrote, "By protecting even those convicted of heinous crimes, the Eighth Amendment reaffirms the duty of the government to *respect the dignity of all persons*."[172] Even in his infamous unsigned majority opinion in *Bush v. Gore*, which put to an end the recount of the 2000 presidential election, he wrote of "the *equal dignity* owed to each voter."[173]

And yet, despite the words of human dignity invoked by Justices Brennan and Kennedy, while often lyrically stated, the legal significance of their pronouncements remains ambiguous. These invocations of dignity may be a stylish constitutional ornament without the color of law. Off the bench, Brennan spoke of dignity with the same moral conviction as an Immanuel Kant. He declaimed dignity as if it appeared in the Bill of Rights, stating in 1985 that "the Constitution is a sublime oration on the *dignity of man*, a bold commitment by a people to the ideal of libertarian *dignity* protected through law."[174] Is he speaking of dignity as an "ideal" rather than concrete reality—an "oration" on dignity rather than dignity itself? In 1954, in a speech delivered two years before he was elevated to the Court, he spoke of "the guarantees of justice and fair play and simple *human dignity* which have made our land what it is. . . . [A] system of government based upon the *dignity and inviolability of the individual soul*."[175]

Those latter words never made it into even one of his dissenting opinions. It is arguably par for the course, given the legal system's squeamishness about human dignity as a sound basis for *stare decisis*. Dignity has yet to receive its day in an American courtroom, although Justice Kennedy's retirement from the bench inspired quite a few commentators to note the lasting legacy of his jurisprudence on the recognition of dignitary rights.[176] Justice Kennedy's majority opinions, especially on the constitutional right to same-sex marriage, may be the strongest precedential legal authority for a general right of human dignity that we have under American law.

Nothing disqualifies dignity as a basis for constitutional interpretation. It could easily be read into the Constitution, as was the right to privacy. Instead, it only makes an occasional appearance in Supreme Court decisions. Aharon Barak, a former Israeli Supreme Court Justice, wrote that, in the United States, the "treatment of human dignity is fragmented and undeveloped. The Justices . . . do not explain what dignity is, [and] what it covers." Most especially, with respect to the First Amendment, there is "no discussion of the relationship between dignity . . . and a person's freedom of expression."[177]

Naturally, we wish to live in a society where human dignity is protected from harm. But the legal infrastructure does not yet exist in the United States where the dignity of a human being falls within the constellation of guaranteed rights. It could be accomplished with a constitutional amendment. Other constitutional democracies have such Basic Laws. But that would be unlikely. Hate speech statutes could be upheld should the Supreme Court interpret the Constitution to embody a right to dignity. The Supreme Court could expand the proscribed categories listed in *Chaplinsky* to include a speaker's assault on human dignity as yet another permissible restraint on speech. And a right to dignity could be asserted in civil suits for emotional distress by those harmed by weaponized speech. Trespass on private property is well-covered ground under the law. Trespass on mental peace is not. And surely not if it requires restricting the autonomy of a belligerent speaker.

Paradoxically, the whole point behind the tort of defamation is that speech can lower the tangible reputation that one has in the eyes of the community. Such an attack is treated as an intrinsic wrong, a tort against personality itself. Dignity denied is implicit in the tort of defamation because it diminishes the worth of the injured party. This is one area of the law where the rights of speakers are subordinated to the defamatory damages they cause. Damaged dignity plays no other role in restricting speech. Yet, there are far worse consequences to victims of malicious speakers—indignities that exceed defamatory harm. Wherever dignity is denied, a liability rule should be applied.

This search for dignity in the text of the Constitution has a history of its own. It makes sense that a liberal democracy would find human dignity to be essential. And yet a fulsome freedom of speech seems irreconcilable with dignity—like clashing liberties, negating magnetic fields, the Hatfields and McCoys of rights. In the United States, where speech is often a no-holds-barred, gladiatorial spectacle, harm can easily come from damaged dignity; vulnerable citizens learn firsthand the violence accomplished with words.

Nevertheless, speech can remain a liberty without it also being a license to do harm. Other democracies know that it is possible for speech and dignity to coexist in the same political ecosystem. Americans alone are tone deaf to more civil possibilities for speech. And yet, a society avowedly committed to pluralism should not permit free speech to interfere with other, no less important democratic values, such as a citizen's right to public safety and equality before the law. A legal system that privileges the speaker over the dignity rights of his or her target is neither fair nor equal. And the public square should not carry the same random risks as a drive-by shooting.

# 19.

# INCIVILITY AND ITS DISCONTENTS

*If everyone possesses autonomy over their own lives, then the freedom of any one individual cannot cancel out the autonomy enjoyed by others.*

HE DAMAGE TO dignity goes beyond the harm done to individuals. Incivility puts the lie to the pretense of an inclusive, democratic society. It makes equal protection a charade and calls into question the entire liberal ethos of our pluralistic culture. Assaults on dignity leave a stain on society itself. In explaining why he is in favor of some regulation on hate speech, Jeremy Waldron wrote in 2008 that, "[t]he restrictions on hate speech that I am interested in are not restrictions on thinking; they are restrictions on more tangible forms of message. The issue is publication and the harm done to individuals and groups through the disfiguring of our social environment by visible, public, and semi-permanent announcements to the effect that in the opinion of one group in the community, perhaps the majority, members of another group are not worthy of equal citizenship."[178]

Hate speech devalues human worth, and therefore its cost is too high—not just in the infliction of immediate injury but also in the consequences of allowing humiliation to harden, fester, and reconfigure into something more lethal. Thomas Hobbes wrote in *Levianthan* in 1651 about how the degrading of a fellow human being deals a lethal attack against his or her dignity and standing in the community.[179] Does not the state have an obligation to provide "security against soul-shivering humiliation"?[180]

Human dignity is not a secondary right, and it should not be treated as no right at all. Those who believe in absolutist notions of free speech often justify their position by arguing that the Framers were primarily interested in individual autonomy. The Declaration of Independence, with Jefferson's signature phrase, "life, liberty and the pursuit of happiness," modified from Locke's more generic "life, liberty and property," is a clarion call for personal autonomy and human perfectibility: freedom at all cost, with happiness as an attainable end. In many ways, it is as much a statement of narcissism as it is a quest for liberty. First Amendment absolutists believe that "life, liberty and the pursuit of happiness" is the guiding spirit behind free speech. The liberties enjoyed by others are not the concern of ordinary citizens engaged in their own autonomous pursuits. There is no rationing of liberty. Autonomy knows no limits with citizens each pursuing, often aggressively, lives of maximized liberty and happiness. It is the promise of autonomous freedom that turns ordinary, sensible speech into absolutist free speech that can terrify and torment vulnerable targets.

The Declaration of Independence, which preceded the Constitution by over eleven years, is merely a declaratory statement of aspirations. It is nothing but an unbinding wish. All that soaring Jeffersonian language has no actual legal effect. The Declaration of Independence is basically an ornament, a shiny precursor to the Bill of Rights. It should not be inciting Americans to run over each other with words. Moreover, autonomy does not have to be defined in such aggressively narcissistic ways. There is no evidence that America's Founders believed individual autonomy to be a Darwinian rumble. Lackluster pursuers of happiness are not disqualified from democratic participation.

To do otherwise is a misreading of America's political virtue. Autonomy has no democratic purpose if it is not shared equally throughout society. If everyone possesses autonomy over their own lives, then the freedom of any one individual cannot cancel out the autonomy enjoyed by others. "Burning a cross on a black family's lawn raises autonomy issues other than just those about the free speech of the actor," argued law professor Alexander Tsesis. "Hate speech engenders personal safety concerns in outgroup members, thereby inhibiting them from traveling in their own communities. Sometimes, fearing for their safety, minorities are forced to relocate. After a cross has been burned on their lawn, a black family is likely to be leery about approaching its own house. The spread of bigotry diminishes autonomy."[181]

Democracy is best served as a forum for treating individuals as "free and equal persons" in a system of governance that protects private "autonomous wills."[182] Autonomy is being exploited to excuse hate speech. Law professor Steven Heyman correctly observed that "[d]emocratic self-government is impossible in the absence of a minimal degree of civility and mutual respect among citizens."[183] Autonomy that approves of citizens perpetually at each other's throats is the very opposite of what the founding generation had in mind—and undermines the use of those throats for actual speech. Freedom was intended for citizens to coalesce around the shared democratic experiment and to arouse a spirit of cooperation, bringing out the very best in human enrichment. In more modern times, international human rights, as a movement, has recognized the value of dignity and its relationship to freedom. Freedom had no lesser meaning in the eighteenth century. Autonomy was never meant to undercut the aspirations toward public good. Democracy is not enhanced by autonomous selves seething with selfishness and antagonism.

# 20

# THE SOCIAL CONTRACT AND HUMAN DIGNITY

The communal gathering of civic-minded citizens imagined by James Madison and Alexander Hamilton has metasta-sized into something to be avoided at all cost. Better to stay home, bolt the doors, block out the noise, and wish for better days ahead.

*T*HE SOCIAL CONTRACT comes with a reasonable expecta-tion that the state is obligated to protect its citizens from violence. The natural rights that inspired the drafting of the Constitution included the right to personal security. The Fram-ers made no distinction between mind and body—a citizen had the right to feel secure in both. Protection of self-worth and peace of mind had a place at the table of these newly formed rights. Just as in Franklin Roosevelt's 1941 "Four Freedoms" speech, one is not truly free if he or she has unmet needs; one is not free if he or she has fears for personal safety. Citizens expect and demand freedom on meaningful terms.

As Heyman wrote in offering a Lockean perspective on natural rights, "My rights entail a correlative duty to respect the liberty and personality of others. . . . [T]he concept of freedom includes immunity from interference. If freedom is to exist, then it must be bounded by an obligation to refrain from interfering with the liberty of others. . . . . [F]ree speech is a right that is limited by the fundamental rights of other persons and the community."[184]

From the earliest days of the First Amendment, the natural rights of the speaker were always constrained by the fundamental rights of others. Indeed, at the time of its conception, the American legal system was more likely to be called upon to protect the rights of those who were being harmed by what the speaker had to say, or the manner in which he or she wished to say it, than to defend the right of free speech itself. The founding generation had a more developed understanding of the harm that words can bring. Thomas G. West wrote that, "[a]s for injurious speech, government not only may punish it, but it is obliged to do so . . . for the same reason that government is obliged to punish murder and rape."[185]

Harm from speech was never far from the Founders' minds. Free speech and civil society were envisioned as equal partners. Article 11 of the Massachusetts Constitution addressed injuries not just to person and property but also to character. Pennsylvania's Constitution of 1790 recognized the "right to speak, write or print on any subject, but citizens were held responsible for the abuse of that liberty."[186] Citizens were held accountable for injurious speech by laws that contemplated the prosecution of offenders. The Founders identified four categories of injurious speech: personal libel; seditious libel; speech that harms the moral foundations of society; and speech that brings about injurious conduct. Libel was regarded as a personal injury no less severe than an assault or rape. One who commits a libel "abuses his privilege, as unquestionably as if he were to plunge his sword into the bosom of a fellow citizen."[187] Chief Justice Thomas McKean of the Pennsylvania Supreme Court ruled in 1788 that "libelous speech was not unlike a personal injury and is ultimately more harmful than the criminal acts of an assassin or arsonist."[188]

The Founders also recognized that the abuse of freedom of expression could bring harm by undermining the moral foundations of society. Speech can have many victims when it tears away at public peace. In an important case before the Pennsylvania

Supreme Court in 1824, Judge Thomas Duncan wrote that "[L]icentiousness endangering the public peace, when tending to corrupt society, is considered a breach of the peace . . . [because] it is destructive of morality generally . . . [and] weakens the bonds by which society is held together. . . . [T]hese are not punished as sins or offenses against God, but crimes injurious to, and having a malignant influence on society."[189] In a case before the New York Supreme Court in 1811, Chief Justice James Kent wrote that speech and writings can be punishable when "they strike at the root of moral obligation, and weaken the security of the social ties."[190]

Clearly, speakers are not the only ones with rights. Listeners have them, too. *The First Amendment was never intended to favor the speaker over the listener.* In fact, among the basket of expressive freedoms contained in the First Amendment at the time of its creation, the one given the highest priority was the freedom of the press to criticize the government. The rights of individual speakers to do the same thing was secondary.

The original intention of the Founders has taken on a life of its own. The First Amendment is nearly always invoked to defend the speaker's right to overcome the government's attempt to silence the content of what is being said. Regulating speech is regarded as the kind of tyranny once reserved for prior restraints on the press, warrantless searches and seizures of homes, and cruel and unusual punishments. The protection of speakers, odious and reprehensible though they may be, is the signature sign of American freedom. Law professor Cass Sunstein was correct when he observed that, "[c]urrently American law protects much speech that ought not to be protected. It safeguards speech that has little or no connection with democratic aspirations and that produces serious social harm."[191] The captive listeners of harmful speech are left without a constitutional remedy—or even a soundproof booth in which to shield themselves from indignity and assault.

During the second half of the twentieth century, this idea of reasonable and sensible restraints placed upon freedom of expression as somehow being incompatible with American liberty was elevated to its own mythology. And it would surely have surprised the Founding Fathers for whom the right to speak freely was absolute as long as exercised responsibly. The Founders believed in more modesty around speech, imagining a nation that cultivated thoughtful, respectful orators rather than shameless blowhards. We have lost perspective on the limits of speech because we have forgotten how important speech was to the deliberations that led to the founding of this country. The Founders chose their words carefully. And they did not weaponize them either. Jurist St. George Tucker wrote in 1803 that, "Liberty and speech . . . consists in the absolute and uncontrollable right of speaking, writing and publishing, our opinions concerning any subject . . . without restraint, *except as to the injury of any other individual, in his person, property, or good name.*"[192] The Vermont jurist Nathaniel Chipman wrote in 1798 that, "Man has no right to pursue his own interest, or happiness, to the exclusion of that of his fellow men."[193] That principle applied as much to speech as to trespass—both could infringe on the rights of others.

The right of free speech always came with natural limits—even before Justice Murphy created categories of proscribed speech. The Founding Fathers never regarded free speech as a blank check, always payable under the full faith and credit of their new Constitution. As Thomas West astutely observed, "[t]he Founders protected liberty but not licentiousness. . . . Equal natural rights also imply equal natural duties. Your right to life and liberty means that I have a duty not to harm or enslave you."[194]

Even under the libertarian traditions of Locke, Jefferson, and Cato, the exercise of a given freedom, especially speech, was always understood to be contingent on the respect shown to the rights possessed by others. In the series of essays that inspired the American Revolution known as *Cato's Letters*, speech was recognized as a freedom provided that it "[i]njured neither the society, nor any of its members." Thomas Jefferson believed that natural rights, which represented the foundation of the Bill of Rights, were limited by a prohibition not to "commit aggression on the equal rights of another" and by "the natural duty of contributing to the necessities of the society."[195]

The philosophers of the Enlightenment took as an article of faith that all human beings were naturally endowed with both freedom and dignity. Freedom was never unlimited; and any claim to freedom was circumscribed by a reciprocal duty to respect the freedom of others and to refrain from interfering with their own equally shared liberties.[196] The essence of the social contract is not merely a grant of rights with the assurance of governmental protection of those rights. The "social" end of that contract carries with it the expectation that there are duties owed by individuals to the communities in which they were bound. It is the community, through the regulatory powers of the state, which is charged with the duty of keeping the peace, protecting the people from harm, and promoting of the common good.[197]

Heyman observed that there was always "wide agreement that, as natural rights, the freedoms of speech and press were limited by the rights of other individuals. . . . [M]ost Americans believed that those freedoms were also bounded by the rights of the community, such as the right to preserve the public peace."[198]

Curbing government excess has turned on itself, where the excess is committed by citizens drunk on liberty, distorting its original purpose and becoming perpetrators of an altogether different kind of tyranny—citizens against citizens. Much of the same argument can be made about the Second Amendment, where absolutists maintain a militia mentality that is more a mirage than an American right. The First Amendment was intended to empower citizens to speak out against their government. Now it has been misappropriated into a weapon aimed at fellow citizens.

Free speech was meant to draw people out into the public square where they would be made better informed, engaging in healthy debate, enticed to contribute their own ideas to the public discourse. But as law professor Robert Post observed, "the First

Amendment, in the name of democracy, suspends legal enforcement of the very civility rules that make rational deliberation possible."[199] The public square has become the private domain of those not with the better argument, but with the bigger bullhorn, tougher hide, and more aggressive tone. Why venture out of the house to exercise a fundamental right that is touted as a defender of neo-Nazis and white supremacists? The communal gathering of civic-minded citizens imagined by James Madison and Alexander Hamilton has metastasized into something to be avoided at all cost. Better to stay home, bolt the doors, block out the noise, and wish for better days ahead.

Physical violence that results in a harmful battery is addressed under both criminal and civil law because it violates both the criminal laws of the state and the civil laws in tort that protect and compensate individuals. A tort is a wrong committed against an individual; a crime is a wrong against the entire community. The duties owed to the community are not forfeited simply because an individual has an action in tort. These are two separate actions. A defendant owes debts to society and has a duty not to cause harm to individuals.

Yet, when it comes to speech, courts are reluctant to protect the public if it means interfering with the First Amendment rights of a speaker. Individuals remain free to pursue their civil remedies in tort. Why is the state deprived of a remedy against a speaker who may end up liable in tort?

A further paradox is that criminalizing violent acts against the body gives rise to tortious remedies that are seldom possible with speech. Offending personal dignity under tort law receives a better day in court than a similar assault from a speaker, which is more likely to go unpunished under criminal law.[200]

# 21

# TORT LAW TO THE
# RESCUE OF DIGNITY

When the floodgates to privacy are open, human dignity is drowned in the deluge. If privacy is constitutionally protected, so too, then, must dignity, because when one is treated with dignity, one possesses the respect afforded to a private life.

C RIMINAL LAWS FAVOR speech rights over dignitary rights. The law of torts offers much stronger legal protections for self-esteem and self-respect. For instance, the common law tort of battery can involve the nonconsensual indignity of spitting in another person's face. The physical harm of such an affront is minimal. But its assault on human dignity is immense. And because it is a battery, unlike common law negligence, harm is not even an element of the tort. The indignity itself is sufficient to create liability.

This very thing happened in 1872, in a case before the Supreme Court of Illinois. In a crowded courtroom, and in the presence of many onlookers, one party to the action deliberately spat in the face of the other. The court ruled that damages in the amount of $1,000 was not excessive, stating that the act "was one of pure malignity, done for the mere purpose of insult and *indignity*. An exasperated suitor has indulged the gratification of his malignant feelings in this despicable mode."[201]

Nearly a century later, this time in Texas, an African-American NASA scientist was about to make his selection at a luncheon buffet when a restaurant manager ripped his plate from his hands and announced to the assembled diners that the scientist would have to find some other place to eat on account of his race. No other physical contact or harm to his body had occurred. The court nonetheless found the restaurant manager liable for a battery, ruling that, "[p]ersonal *indignity* is the essence of an action for battery; and consequently, the defendant is liable not only for contacts which do actual physical harm, but also for those which are offensive and insulting."[202]

In neither of these cases had the plaintiffs been physically harmed. The injuries were to their human dignity alone. The personal humiliation and the contemptuous treatment was enough to trigger liability in tort. Both plaintiffs, under the aforementioned Talmudic principle, had been drained of their blood. Each had been deprived of his sense of security and personhood. Each court crystalized the tortious acts as harms to dignity—without any further showing of physical, tangible injury. Indignity was damage enough.

But, paradoxically, this is not the case with speech. The inner life of the human being somehow gets lost in any discussion about the First Amendment. All we seem to care about is the right of a speaker to blast his message acoustically. A parallel right to silence, private peace, and public security is ignored. This, despite precedent in tort to safeguard human dignity.

Spitting in someone's face; swiping a plate from the hands of a diner—both tortious acts. Burning a cross in front of an African-American—a perfectly lawful expressive act.

How can the legal system justify such disparate treatment? Either dignity matters, or it does not.

But it most assuredly does. A citizen's inner life should also be relevant under the First Amendment. And the maintenance of an inner life is a privacy right, which already exists under the law. After all, the right to personal dignity, which is so often incompatible with another's right to free speech, is itself a right to privacy. To maintain one's dignity against another's assault is to claim a privacy right in personhood and personality. A right to privacy, framed as responsible citizenship, would incorporate into the First Amendment the rights and protections the Framers imagined.

Before Louis Brandeis became a Supreme Court Justice, he coauthored, in 1890, a groundbreaking law review article that was the first to introduce a right to privacy that took account of the emotional life of a human being. In doing so, the article embraced human dignity as more than merely a value submerged within the Constitution. It made express what had been implied. Constitutional rights cannot ignore the privacy and dignity of citizens, which stand as checks against freewheeling liberty and overreach. Here in Brandeis' article was human dignity elevated to the status of a new tort—one that would eventually find itself applied to the Constitution itself. Human beings were entitled to "an inviolate personality"—the consolidated emotions, sensations, and thoughts that comprised an individual's inner world.[203]

Brandeis, like Kant, believed that the self-worth of a human being should not be used as an object for someone else's pleasure. Unwanted exposure to the public hijacks an individual's life and transforms it into a plaything. The personal is lost when a human being becomes an object for public viewing. What one wished to keep private was suddenly subject to public scrutiny and ridicule. The right to a private life entails the solitude and protection of being able to keep one's private affairs private.

The tort known as invasion of privacy recognizes the integrity of an individual's unique personality. Human dignity is so vital, a violation of personality can even take place without the victim's knowledge. Eavesdropping on another's conversations, for instance, or filming someone having sexual relations, violates a right to privacy. In 2016, an invasion of privacy lawsuit brought by the former professional wrestler known as Hulk Hogan body slammed the salacious online magazine *Gawker* right out of business (with some assistance from venture capitalist Peter Thiel, who financed the litigation), for having disseminated a sex tape of Hogan without his consent.[204] Many people wrongly concluded that the case was one of defamation. But Hogan had not been defamed. There was no untruth revealed by *Gawker*. He had sex with a married man's wife. That was true, but did *Gawker* have a First Amendment right to invade Hogan's privacy and publish a sex tape for all the world to see? A court said no. Hogan's dignity mattered more than *Gawker*'s freedom of the press.

The rule is clear: One is entitled to live a life with one's dignity intact. Yet this principle seems to fall apart once one enters the boisterous arena of the First Amendment, which serves as a legal loophole for assaults on human dignity cynically disguised as free speech.

Dignity is in danger when privacy is imperiled. When the floodgates to privacy are open, human dignity is drowned in the deluge. If privacy is constitutionally protected, so, too, then, must dignity, because when one is treated with dignity, one possesses the respect afforded to a private life. Brandeis and Warren explained the modern problem of the many ways in which the individual can have one's privacy invaded and the harm that immediately ensues. In one especially relevant passage focusing on harmful gossip, they wrote, "Each crop of unseemly gossip . . . becomes the seed of more, and . . . results in a lowering of social standards and of morality. Even gossip apparently harmless, when widely and persistently circulated, is potent for evil. It both belittles and perverts. It belittles by inverting the relative importance of things, thus dwarfing the thoughts and aspirations of people. When personal gossip attains the dignity of print, and crowd[s] the space available for matters of real interest to the community, what wonder that the ignorant and thoughtless mistake its relative importance."[205]

As the right to privacy in civil tort evolved, case law began to recognize four types of tortious behavior that constitute a violation of the right to maintain an inner life: the intrusion upon personal seclusion; appropriating someone's name or likeness; the public disclosure of private facts that is of no legitimate concern to the public at large; and the disclosure of private facts in such a way as to portray a victim in a "false light."[206] Each of these privacy claims, at their core, involves a violation of human dignity. In each context, a dignified life is severely compromised.

The logic then becomes: If invasions of the right to privacy constitute a tort, and if privacy and dignity occupy the same sphere of an individual's inner life, then any harm that comes to human dignity should command the same level of legal respect—whether in tort or as a criminal matter brought by the state.

Privacy and dignity are one and the same. The First Amendment is not a superseding right; it does not trump all other liberties or constitutional guarantees. Free speech exists, but it must coexist with other rights that preserve human dignity. *If speech cannot maintain its expressive power without causing harm to human dignity, then it must forfeit its constitutional protection until it learns how to play well with others.*

# 22

# SOME WORDS, BY "THEIR VERY UTTERANCE," LOSE THEIR FREE SPEECH PROTECTIONS

The Founders had fewer hang-ups about speech and possessed more common sense about it as well.

NDER EXISTING FIRST Amendment case law, some speech is permissibly restricted for categorical reasons. The Fighting Words Doctrine and its seminal case, *Chaplinsky v. New Hampshire*, is one such category. A civilized society is one that is not prone to casually hurling fighting words at each other. Civilization commands citizens to renounce dueling and honor killings and resolve their disputes through the apparatus of the state. Words that offend human dignity, therefore, expressly violate this legitimate objective of the state. In *Chaplinsky*, the Supreme Court made special mention of proscribed speech that is defined as the "insulting or 'fighting words'—those by which their very utterance inflict injury or tend to incite an immediate breach of the peace."[207]

Words by "their very utterance," and nothing more, can "inflict injury." Nothing else need occur. Merely by speaking them, injury is presumed. Its utterance is *per se* without First Amendment protection. The language of *Chaplinsky* is a very powerful statement that the First Amendment cannot operate independent of human dignity. Free speech can never be so free so as to allow certain words to inflict injury or instigate a fight. The Fighting Words Doctrine comes into play when the boundaries of civility have been crossed, injury caused by words is likely, and dignity and social status are under attack. Such hostile circumstances lose protection of the First Amendment.

Placing a limitation on free speech just to curtail physical violence is only half of the human story. Preventing harm to dignity is its own moral imperative.

The Supreme Court understood that some words, by their very utterance, directly cause injury even if they are not likely to instigate a retaliation. The injury they cause is in the form of dignitary harm. And that is injury enough. The Fighting Words Doctrine strips two categories of words that would otherwise receive First Amendment protection: those with the potential to incite a fight; and those that are an affront to human dignity. The Fighting Words Doctrine applies not just in circumstances where speech provokes a fight, or raises the specter of a breach of peace, but also to words that might make a reasonable person fear for his or her safety or violates his or her privacy rights by causing harm to personal dignity.

"Fighting Words" is a catchall phrase for all harm-producing speech. As Heyman pointed out, "It is precisely because fighting words 'inflict injury' that they 'tend to incite an immediate breach of the peace.' Fighting words injure others through aggression as well as through assaults on their dignity."[208]

The Founders had fewer hang-ups about speech and possessed more common sense about it as well. For instance, speech that was prohibited under the Sedition Act of 1798, such as malicious writing against the government "with the intent to defame, or bring either into contempt or disrepute," was widely accepted by most citizens. Today, such an overtly censorious measure by the government would not only be regarded as unconstitutional, it would start a riot.[209]

Those who align themselves ideologically with the originalist meaning of the Constitution might be surprised to learn that the Framers did not regard speech as the most important liberty within the panoply of First Amendment rights. Freedom of the press, actually, was arguably more fundamental. In fact, in earlier drafts of the Bill of Rights and the amendments to the Constitution, speech was separated from press, religion, and assembly. That's right: The Free Speech Clause was not originally even *in* the First Amendment, and it surely was not given carte blanche over other rights. The Founders believed speech to be a natural right, but they did not agree that the government was obligated to protect every kind of speech imaginable. If speech did not serve the public good, if it did not advance the aims of citizenship, it fell outside the operation of the First Amendment completely.

Law professor Jud Campbell argued in 2017 that, when it came to the Free Speech Clause of the First Amendment, the Founding Fathers were primarily interested in the "freedom to make well-intentioned statements of one's thoughts."[210] Speech was never intended to be a freedom without restriction, and the "First Amendment was not presumptively insulated from governmental regulation."[211]

In the context of the First Amendment, speaking, writing, and publishing could be restricted by laws that were intended to promote and protect the public good.[212] James Madison, for instance, granted the government authority to take actions to maximize the public good in the collective sense. The goal was to achieve the "safety and happiness of society" as a whole—for everyone, not just for narcissistic speakers.[213]

According to Campbell, the narrow private interests of a speaker's First Amendment protections were always meant to be subordinated to the interests of the whole society—the "common good, the Founders repeatedly implored, often required individual sacrifices."[214] Sometimes the rights of an individual must be sacrificed for a greater good.

The exercise of free speech loses its constitutional legitimacy once "well-intentioned statements" are revealed to be not so well intentioned—if they brought about "direct injury to others."[215] Writing in 1788, Pennsylvania jurist Thomas McKean defined the right to free speech as a liberty for "every man to publish his opinions, but it is due to the *peace and dignity of society* to enquire into the motives of such publications, and to distinguish between those which are meant for use and reformation, and with an eye solely to the public good, and those which are intended merely to delude and defame."[216]

Purposeful speech is free; injurious speech is too costly for all of society to bear. Cross- and flag-burnings, swastikas, gay bashing, and the indecent disruptions of funerals was surely not what they had in mind. In situations like these, when constitutional freedoms collide, it is helpful to deploy a little thought experiment and ask: What would George Washington do—or, even better, what would he have thought? Would he have believed that the First Amendment guaranteed the right to burn a flag in front of a family whose son gave his life fighting for American freedom?

Of course not. Surely one's discontent with the direction of American politics could be communicated in some other more dignified and mutually respectful fashion.

It is for the speaker to conform to the civilizing norms of society, to frame his speech in the language that captures the attention of listeners, rather than to drive them away in agony. Campbell wrote that "freedom of opinion did not encompass all expression. Individuals who joined together in a social contract . . . had no reason to immunize efforts to lie or mislead. Nor did they need to prevent the government from preserving norms of civility and morality. . . . [T]he Founders constantly mentioned that the inalienable right to speak was limited to those who spoke with decency and truth."[217]

That is because free speech had a purpose beyond simply advancing the antagonistic agenda of a hateful speaker. Free speech was necessary for the discovery of universal truths. What the Founding Fathers had in mind were town hall meetings where citizens gathered to debate matters of public concern. Robert H. Bork, many years before his scuttled nomination to the Supreme Court, famously wrote in 1971, "Constitutional protection should be accorded only to speech that is explicitly political. There is no basis for judicial intervention to protect any other form of expression."[218] Meiklejohn wrote of the fundamental belief in the First Amendment as the legal guardian of public, political debate, where "every citizen has . . . a right to . . . dignity—the dignity of men who govern themselves." This requires the mutual respect of "citizens engaged in 'a common enterprise.'"[219]

The right to free speech was never divorced from a companion obligation to do so with decency. Respecting the dignity of the intended audience was a condition of the free speech compact. In a session dedicated to revising Madison's proposed Bill of Rights, the committee decided that one of the natural rights that must be retained from the earlier drafts was the right of "[s]peaking writing and publishing . . . *with decency and freedom*."[220] Decency is never achieved by alienating and injuring an audience. And freedom assumes a maturity of mind and a mutuality of a shared liberty between speaker and listener.

Anything less makes no sense in a free society.

# 23

# "STICKS AND STONES" ARE NOT THE ONLY CAUSE OF SERIOUS HARM

The quality of the words spoken—and the manner in which they are delivered—is an important and permissible limitation on the First Amendment. Yes, quality—a standard of good intention, an aspiration of refinement, an invocation of seriousness, a seal of approval that what is being offered is worthy of entering the public sphere.

IF THERE IS one industry that knows something about broken bones, it is the National Football League. The thirty-two franchises of the NFL are stocked with gargantuan men who, as little boys, were undoubtedly once told during their more tearful moments of adolescence that "sticks and stones can break my bones, but names can never hurt me." (Of course, this all assumes that the future professional football player was at least once the victim of a schoolyard bully, and not the other way around.)

It is a wonderful nursery rhyme and probably an effective way to prevent a bloody nose by resolving a conflict with the turn of a childhood cheek. The problem, however, is that very few kids are gullible enough to buy it, and I imagine that even future gridiron greats of the NFL had thought the rhyme to be nonsense, too. Name-calling, and the humiliation that follows such torment, does hurt. While it may not involve the breaking of actual bones, it does result in the brokenness of spirit, with tangible physical consequences. The myth that emotional and physical harms are entirely distinct—and that the former is impossible to verify while the latter is demonstrably more damaging in degree—was always false. And now, thanks to advances in neuroscience and the imaging of the human brain, it is becoming much clearer that emotional injuries are not only verifiable, they produce physical consequences to both the human brain and body.

This medical confirmation that psychological harm is never trivial and that it leads to actual sickness was intuitively obvious, but the legal system was always hostile to intangible harm even though it never doubted that emotional and psychological injury was a reality of life. It was just not one that the law had an obligation to redress. Since the 1960s and the expansion of civil liberties, it has been particularly true that free speech was always privileged, even if it caused harm. Courts did not even bother to question whether words could actually wound. It was treated as a given. As law professor Frederick Schauer said in 2018, "[T]he claim that speech was harmless or casually inert was never true."[221]

But such injuries were not considered the business of the court. Priests and psychotherapists seemed better equipped to mollify these grievances. There was scant interest in affording mental peace the same respect as was routinely lavished on the body. Courts generally discredited the possibility that emotional harm could ever be as severe and scarring as physical scrapes that left tangible evidence. And, of course, it never occurred to juries and the judges who instructed them that emotional and psychological harm can actually bring about physical sickness and damage to the body.

Ironically, as technology advanced and society evolved, citizens were given more opportunities to harm one another with words. Today, thanks to the immediacy and reach of the Internet, a person can be attacked by anonymous, venomous trolls repeatedly without any means of self-defense. Reputations can be easily besmirched, if not outright libeled and defamed, resulting in concrete harm. The value of one's good name is dragged along the digital highway like a dangling muffler. Meanwhile, courts have exponentially expanded the free speech guarantees of the First Amendment, protecting offensive communications with ostensible political messages, while at the same time downplaying the harm these dubious claims to speech maliciously produced.

Not only did courts immunize violent speakers from government regulation, applying the First Amendment as a shield for thugs, it doubled down in the arena of civil actions, with wounded plaintiffs denied recovery for their injuries in tort. Tortious remedies for emotional harm mirrored the liberalized atmosphere for free speech in criminal cases: Whether the government tried to assert its regulatory powers in the interest of social peace or wounded individuals looked to tort to redress the personal, emotional harm they endured, the First Amendment got in the way, protecting the speaker over the one he or she injured. Moreover, should a plaintiff assert a claim for emotional injury in tort without showing physical evidence of that harm, his or her chances of recovery were limited still further. Yet, curiously, even though relief was denied, courts did not dispute that the hurt was real and that the psychological health of millions was being sacrificed to the cause of free speech.

Law professor David Goldberger acknowledged this legal paradox when he wrote, "One of the most puzzling aspects of the judiciary's stance protecting racially, ethnically and sexually offensive public speech is that it has rarely questioned the validity of the claims of harm. On the contrary, the judiciary has often conceded that offensive speech causes emotional harm while ruling that such speech, nonetheless, is entitled to constitutional protection."[222]

But now, after taking a time-out, let's get back to football.

A hard-hitting tackle can surely scramble a brain. The mere expression of words, however, strategically chosen, can bring on an altogether different configuration of cobwebs. Words intended and delivered to cause harm—verbal abuse, assaultive speech, bullying, and taunting—have a way of taking down even the giants among us. Constitutional scholar Alexander Bickel, writing decades ago, was aware that, "[t]here is such a thing as verbal violence, a kind of cursing assaultive speech that amounts to almost physical aggression, bullying that is no less punishing because it is simulated."[223]

The crushing nature of verbal violence proved to be particularly true for one NFL offensive lineman. One suspects he is not alone. It can happen to anyone. If words can topple a guard or tackle, the behemoths of their sport, then no position player is safe. After all, these men on the offensive line are blocks of granite. Their job is to protect quarterbacks from blindside blitzes and to plow holes through their genetic equals on the defensive line. And yet, despite all that muscle, their skin may not be thick enough to withstand the kind of emotional torment as that which former offensive lineman Jonathan Martin experienced and that led to his shortened professional career.

Indeed, Martin's aborted NFL legacy demonstrated just how vulnerable even the most imposing players can be to verbal abuse. Surely for most people, the NFL does not conjure a place of rampant workplace harassment. These are, after all, the most selective of jobs with the most specialized of physical requirements. Martin, for instance, who at the time played for the Miami Dolphins, stood six feet five inches tall and weighed 312 pounds. He had been an All-American at Stanford University before entering the professional ranks. All those natural talents, however, did not prepare him for a foe that ultimately chopped him down to size in 2013, shredding him of his dignity and stripping him of the confidence and will to play the game. He played only two more seasons, walking away from the sport not because of a physical injury, or even an illegal block, but on account of a bully who never outgrew the schoolyard and brought his dirty game with him to the NFL.

One of Martin's teammates, Richie Incognito, a self-styled friend, repeatedly texted and taunted Martin into an early retirement. These messages from a teammate were of such venomous, unremitting proportion, he lost interest in the game of football. He did not finish the season. Along the way, he probably also developed a new opinion about the so-called camaraderie among NFL players. (An investigative report commissioned by the NFL determined that two other teammates, John Jerry and Mike Pouncey, joined in along with Incognito as "equal-opportunity harassers.") Martin was first hospitalized. He then checked himself into a mental health facility. His tormentors were traded to other teams, and within a few years some were finished with professional football, too.

Among the many personal yet lethal texts he received and the verbal abuse he endured, unendingly delivered over several seasons, are these examples:

There were running jokes about shooting black people and about slavery (Martin is African-American.): "Hey, wassup, you half-nigger piece of shit. . . . [L]iberal mulatto bitch. [S]hine box."

There were some that included graphic, sexually explicit comments about Martin's sister: "We are going to run train on your sister. . . . I am going to fuck her without a condom and cum in her cunt. . . . I am going to bang the shit out of her and spit on her and treat her like shit."

Regardless of one's feelings about free speech, which does not apply to friendship, it is pretty clear that most people would not wish for their friends to speak so freely. Actually, they probably would wish for an entirely different set of friends. With friends like these, it is better to surround oneself with more civilized and buttoned-up enemies.

During this period when Martin was being tormented by his teammates, he acknowledged to his mother, in a text, that this was not the first time he had been bullied: "I used to get verbally bullied every day in middle school and high school, by kids that are half my size. I would never fight back. Just get sad & feel like no one wanted to be my friend."

The investigative report commissioned by the NFL stated, "The behavior that occurred here was harmful to the players, the team and the league. There are lines—even in a football locker room—that should not be crossed, as they were here."

The irony was that all of the players involved in this cruel excuse for sportsmanship were offensive linemen, whose job it is to provide protection for their own teammates. For some reason they felt less protective toward one another, at least when it came to the emotional health of one of their own.[224] To demonstrate the everlasting nature of psychological harm, long after broken bones are fully healed and the mind has well forgotten the sensation of ordinary, mendable breakage, the Martin case offers a poignant and unfortunate postscript of just how serious emotional injury can be. On February 23, 2018, years after Martin had retired and in the wake of a number of mass shootings at schools and places where large crowds gather, he was detained by police for posting a photo of himself on Instagram with a rifle and a message that read, "When you're a bully victim & a coward, your options are suicide, or revenge." Also included in his message was the name of the high school he had attended. The authorities decided to close the school on the day that Martin was questioned by the police.[225] Arguably, had Martin not been bullied in high school and even more so as a teammate with the Miami Dolphins, his playing days may very well have continued, and his mental health would likely have been as robust as his body.

This is just one example of the way words can wound. In the world that exists outside of classrooms and think tanks, where the stakes are much larger than the antics of faculty politics, people cannot afford to live under the received wisdom of nursery rhymes alone. Nor can they shield themselves from emotional turmoil by simply averting their eyes. If the pen is, indeed, mightier than the sword (another popular aphorism that probably is not true either), then the words that spill forth from both pens and mouths, composed and spewed for the purpose of causing harm, are how those blows are delivered. And they can lead to the same consequences that are generally outlawed when the damage is done in more overtly conventional and physical ways—when words are not elements of the crime.

In a case decided in the summer of 2017, a Massachusetts court ruled that words alone, without any "physical" conduct, can constitute the predicate act that causes a crime. On July 14, 2014, Michelle Carter texted her boyfriend, Conrad Roy III, urging him to commit suicide. Their relationship included regular texts and Facebook messages. Both were emotionally troubled. Roy contemplated suicide and, finally, on that fateful day, he pulled into a parking lot and connected a pump that brought carbon monoxide into the cabin of the car. Carter egged him on when he started to waver, when Roy, in fact, panicked and bolted from the car. She wrote, "I thought you wanted to do this. The time is right and you're ready, you just need to do it!" He regained his nerve, returned to the car, and soon died from asphyxiation. The court found Carter guilty of involuntary manslaughter, a pretty astonishing and highly unusual outcome. Most prosecutors in such a case would have pursued the far lesser charge of harassment. After all, the defendant was nowhere near the crime scene, and the blood on her hands was less apparent for a legal system that likes to see more bodily contact. Texting entreating words on a cell phone does not leave the obvious fingerprints of a murder.[226]

Many questioned whether the conviction violated Carter's First Amendment rights. After all, the scope of her entire conduct was limited to words—no other action took place. She was hardly an accomplice in the traditional sense—handing him pills, sharpening a knife, driving a getaway car. Did she not have the right to offer an opinion to her boyfriend, encouraging him to do what he had set out to do, provided she take no other independent physical action of her own? Here, the government regulated her speech simply because it did not agree with the content and viewpoint of what she had to say. Such interference with a speaker's point of view violates the First Amendment. Carter expressed an opinion, albeit not a political one, to a person who was a willing listener, and he regretfully acted upon it.

Of course, it is not clear that the Framers of the Constitution had these sets of facts in mind when they crafted the Free Speech Clause. They intended freedom of expression to furnish society with ideas that served the public good, not with advice on when to take one's life. Emboldening boyfriends to commit suicide surely was not on their list of essential liberties for a new nation. And Carter's text messages offered such "slight social value as a step to the truth," under the *Chaplinsky* doctrine, that it is not clear why this claim to freedom of speech is any less compelling than cross-burnings or marching neo-Nazis. Nazis were granted the right to march in Skokie under the full protection of the First Amendment. A troubled young woman could not rely on the same liberty when the legal system convicted her of sending a text to her boyfriend.

Constitutional scholar Lawrence Tribe made a distinction in 1978 between words that are expressed as "triggers of action" as opposed to words used as "keys of persuasion." The former is "not part of human discourse but weapons hurled in anger to inflict injury or invite retaliation." In such situations where words are being offered not in the spirit of debate but with the malice of bringing about harm, "[m]ore talk" won't "cure the injury."[227] Words used as "triggers of action," for instance, like the "incitement of imminent lawlessness," under *Brandenburg v. Ohio*, do not benefit from the safeguards of the First Amendment—nor should they, because they are delivered to provoke an action that will injure rather than persuade.[228] This makes sense if the original intent of the First Amendment was to create a climate of civilized debate where words are introduced as "keys to persuasion." In the case of Michelle Carter, her text messages can only be understood as "triggers of action," calculated to bring about her boyfriend's suicide. Perhaps that is why the court found no infringement of her speech in convicting her of involuntary manslaughter. Her words alone represented the overt act that both initiated and constituted the crime. Nothing else physical or tangible needed to occur. Cheerleading in such a deadly manner in cyberspace disqualified her from receiving the protection of the First Amendment.

In recognizing the violence that can arise from speech alone, *Commonwealth v. Carter* is simply ahead of its time in fully appreciating how words can lead to the manslaughter of another human being. Words alone can furnish all the elements necessary to complete a crime. In explaining the principles of *Chaplinsky*, law professor Hadley Arkes wrote in 1974 that, "certain forms of speech or expression may constitute an assault in themselves, even if they are not accompanied by overt acts that involve a physical assault." The overt act *is* the speech itself.[229] Recall that in *Chaplinsky*, the Supreme Court delivered what was arguably the most imaginative, if not provocative, phrase ever written in connection with the First Amendment: that there are some words "which by their very utterance inflict injury." The very utterance of the words creates the causal link between the act and the harm. Was that mere *dicta*, or is there real legal authority to this concept of *per se* injurious words?

Simply by speaking certain words—depending upon the context in which they are uttered, and to whom—harm can occur. This goes beyond the proscribed categories of speech that the First Amendment would not protect under *Chaplinsky*. Justice Murphy also introduced a concept of strict liability for certain utterances. They are regarded as vocal nullities, problematic exclamations, or verbal detritus, causing harm at their inception and alien to anything that qualifies as an idea. In explaining why such injurious speech should be barred from First Amendment safeguards, Murphy deemed these words as being without "ideas" or "social value." Some words simply and categorically serve "no essential part of the exposition of ideas" and are "of such slight social value as a step to the truth" that they undermine the preservation of civil society.[230]

Whatever value they might have is offset by the broader social interest in maintaining "order and morality." Injurious speech impedes the fostering of any climate of civility.[231] As law professor Rodney Smolla observed, "What makes *Chaplinsky* quite remarkable . . . is the suggestion that there are occasions when *words alone* may inflict injury that society may redress without abridging the guarantees of the First Amendment, including injury to society's *moral* fabric."[232]

The quality of the words spoken—and the manner in which they are delivered—is an important and permissible limitation on the First Amendment. Yes, quality—a standard of good intention, an aspiration of refinement, an invocation of seriousness, a seal of approval that what is being offered is worthy of entering the public sphere. What degrades the quality of speech and causes it to miss the mark of acceptable discourse is any intent to bring harm to the audience. In the permissive atmosphere of free speech absolutism, where the government's role is only in safeguarding speech, there is little thought given to protecting society from unsafe speech. This imbalance demonstrates how far we have deviated from a commonsense understanding of the First Amendment. Words should not be so casually introduced into the mainstream without sufficient attention to quality control and warranties of fitness. Like food and drugs, there is spoilage in speech that can be dangerous in the wrong dosage. *Commonwealth v. Carter* is an example of how words can be part of the chain of events that result in manslaughter.

A subcategory of murder is one thing, but what of the more bloodless emotional injury? A foundational question must first be introduced: Should damaged dignity and psychological harm even be addressed under the law? These are areas that continue to bedevil the legal system. In the ever-narrowing formulations of legal analysis—the dicing and slicing of court precedents—redressing emotional pain, especially when it was brought about by words, is a conundrum without a clue.

# 24

# ENTER SCIENCE—
# PUTTING THE MICROSCOPE
# TO WOUNDING WORDS

Pain has a shared circuitry in the human brain, and it makes
no distinction between being hit in the face and losing face
(or having a broken heart) as a result of bereavement, betrayal, social exclusion, and grave insult.

O N THE WEAPONIZATION of words, the law has woefully
lagged behind the sciences—specifically neuroscience
and cognitive psychology—which have proven the existence of psychological injury that is both real and verifiable. For
instance, we now know for certain that words can cause both emotional and physical harm. Studies conducted at such universities as
Purdue, UCLA, Michigan, Toronto, Arizona, Maryland, and New
South Wales show, among other things, through brain scans and
controlled studies with participants who were subjected to both
physical and emotional pain, that psychological harm is equal in
intensity to that experienced by the body and is even more
long-lasting and traumatic. Physical pain can subside; emotional
pain, when recalled, is relived.

Pain has a shared circuitry in the human brain, and it makes no
distinction between being hit in the face and losing face (or having
a broken heart) as a result of bereavement, betrayal, social exclusion, and grave insult. Indeed, research has shown that pain relief

medication can work equally well for both physical and emotional injury.

Of course, everyone, to some degree, has experienced the debilitating effects of emotional harm. What these studies have made empirical and undeniable have always been intuitive to most people. The legal system, however, remains stuck in a prehistoric era of mind-body polarity, clouded further by an empty-headed misapprehension of the true consequences of assaultive speech. Brain damage is thought to be impossible without blunt instruments and brain-scrambling concussions. Untangling the mysteries of the mind, and the vagaries of human emotion, has always been regarded as the legal equivalent of crossing the Rubicon. There are endless doubts about the veracity of emotional distress claims. Such injuries are believed to be impossible to evaluate, given that they are entirely subjective. Without the objective evidence of bruises, breaks, or visible wounds, how is a court to judge? How can a jury actually know the extent, no less the truthfulness, of the claimed injury? Claimants themselves are unreliable, overly emotional, ill-suited to the decorum of courtrooms. They are all individuated human puzzles, their secrets under lock and key, each harboring his or her own Rosebuds, to borrow the interior mystery of Charles Foster Kane in *Citizen Kane*. The very idea of psychological harm has always been anathema to the cool rationality of the law. Finding facts amid such a mess of emotions, and the general unknowability of the human brain, is thought to be beyond the competence of the law. Physical injuries, after all, can be measured; emotional harm has been difficult to determine and can also be feigned.

For decades, the perceived unreliability of the evidence and the mysteries of the cognitive world caused the legal system to regard such claims as headaches. The mind was confounded by each one of the few efforts the legal system made to embrace emotion and the workings of the human brain. This was true not just for psychological harm, but also for mental disease. What is the proper test for determining temporary insanity? A defendant operating under a mental impairment, as a matter of law, cancelled out the necessary guilty mind, *mens rea*, to establish the crime. He or she did not have the mental capacity to meet the threshold cognitive standard.

Civil cases presented their own mental gymnastics. How to know whether the plaintiff actually suffered from emotional distress due to the intentionally outrageous actions of the defendant? For First Amendment purposes, courts sought to avoid the infernal ambiguities of the human psyche altogether. The easiest way to accomplish that was to simply favor the prerogatives of speakers over the harms they may have caused their targets. Emotional injuries in tort were subjected to onerous evidentiary requirements that made obtaining a legal recovery for psychological harm, absent evidence of accompanying physical injury, a rare occurrence. Meanwhile, nearly anyone who purported to make a political statement or to profess even an inkling of an idea was awarded a public airing, all courtesy of the First Amendment—regardless of the consequences or harm that lingered long after that speech had subsided.

Why this blatant prejudice against the emotional world? It cannot be solely because proving damages was always thought to be more difficult. Doubt and skepticism about actual injury, after all, exists in the physical realm, as well. Rarely is it the case that the severity and degree of the physical injury is beyond reproach. Physical harm has its own doubters, no less or more than what people believe about the emotional sphere. Besides, the unknowability of emotional injury was always exaggerated. Everyone can distinguish mere insults and slight offenses from true emotional assaults calculated to bring about a severe emotional disturbance. The *Restatement of Torts* even accounts for this distinction between an ordinary insult and the devastation of emotional well-being—which is tantamount to an assault without battery. For the purposes of satisfying the "extreme and outrageous" element in a claim for the intentional infliction of emotional distress, section

46 of the *Restatement* states that "liability does not extend to mere insults, indignities, . . . annoyances, petty oppressions, or other trivialities."[233] There was already language in the law that distinguished a range of emotional responses that seemingly rattled the brains of judges.

Most people know what "outrageousness" looks like when they see or hear about it. In *Knierim v. Izzo*, a 1961 case originating in Illinois, a woman was awarded damages for the intentional infliction of emotional distress against a man who threatened to kill her husband. The court ruled that "a line can be drawn between slight hurts which are the price of a complex society and the severe mental disturbances inflicted by intentional actions wholly lacking in social utility."[234] There was nothing ambiguous about the defendant's threat. He was clear in his intent, and she had every reason to take him seriously. And such a fear instilled in a spouse could reasonably result in emotional distress without any other overt act taking place.

Juries are often faced with more ambiguity in the physical realm. Finding the necessary facts and assigning the appropriate blame, then awarding damages, presents its own evidentiary challenges. In many of these cases, no one knows for certain whether the plaintiff wearing a neck brace cannot actually run the New York Marathon. One expert is called in to testify that the plaintiff will never again lead a normal life. Another expert, equally well credentialed, testifies on behalf of the defendant and offers a completely contradictory opinion: The plaintiff is a picture of perfect health. The jury is left with insurmountably conflicting questions to resolve. Courts do not refuse to entertain tortious claims for relief simply because the extent of the physical injury is ultimately unknowable—despite expert witnesses and hospital records. Juries do the best they can to discover the facts and determine guilt in criminal cases, and assign fault in civil ones.

Given these acknowledged imperfections in the justice system, the difficulties of deciding hard cases and how they are ultimately reconciled, there is no reason why emotional damage should render the legal system so paralyzed. We tolerate the fake slip and fall—the wheelchair more prop than permanent sign of handicap—but we feel absolutely helpless in evaluating whether words and gestures intended to harm actually do cause harm. Jurors may be as capable of working through the uncertainties of emotional injury as they are in uncovering the circumstances and assessing the damages that occur with bodily harm. Hadley Arkes is correct when he observed that, "[t]he meaning of words cannot be so arbitrary and subjective. They may, of course, be borderline cases that are difficult to judge. But there are borderline judgments to be made in all kinds of cases, including murder, assault, and rape. These situations may pose a dilemma as 'slippery' and 'subjective' as anything one is likely to encounter in cases of speech or verbal assault. . . . Our standards for recognizing a verbal assault or an act of defamation are no more uncertain than the standards we have for the recognizing of other kinds of assaults. . . . The fact that mistakes may be made at times in judging matters of speech can no more stand as an argument against the law than the mistakes made by juries in cases of murder and assault."[235]

Indeed, it may, in fact, be easier for lay juries to actually judge the severity of violent, assaultive speech than it is to evaluate the wreckage of physical damage. After all, jurors are routinely instructed to find the facts that can establish what actually happened in devastating car accidents. Yet, most people, fortunately, have never been involved in any kind of collision beyond fender benders or rear-end dustups. They sit on juries glancing at trial exhibits with glazed eyes and hearing from jargon-spouting expert witnesses—those professionals who study the physics of physical harm—and on what basis of personal experiences are they equipped to comprehend the extent of the damage? Yet, there are no such barriers to common understanding when it comes to emotional harm. In the world of emotions, we are all experts and geniuses. Even the emotionally crippled and empathically deficient know what it feels like to be humiliated. We all understand the contours of emotional hurt. Our minds are filled with such memories of indignity and pain. Each of us knows something about the trauma of human loss. Everyone has experienced some manner of betrayal and abandonment. In the dark recesses of emotional injury, we all know the difference between an insignificant insult and psychological ruin.

These kinds of emotional assessments are not rocket science. Is the legal system willing to accept that damage done to the human spirit is equal, if not even more severe, than anything that can be done to the human body? If it can, it will finally begin to redress the full sweep of human experience.

And it will add an entirely new dimension to our understanding of the First Amendment.

It is time to stop living with an exaggerated fear of slippery slopes and doomsday prophesies about the death of free speech. The First Amendment is grounded in both law and justice. And there is nothing legally just in a constitutional amendment that enables one group of citizens to make life miserable for vulnerable minorities who are guaranteed equal treatment under the law. Words do cause harm. The First Amendment will surely survive some modest and sensible regulation of speech in order to live up to the promise made to citizens that, by their signing of the social contract, the state will protect them from other citizens who take liberties with their own rights. Assaultive speech is non-speech precisely because there is no meaningful communication taking place. Arkes dismissed the central argument against hate speech in stating that, "it is hard to believe that we would lose our character as a constitutional democracy if a number of cities and towns suddenly took a harder line on the matter of racial and religious defamation. . . . [W]e could survive those mistakes more easily than we could survive the consequences of making no judgments at all, or professing no recognition of any standards by which one could ever hope to judge."[236]

Free speech should not stand in the way of common decency. No right should be so freely and recklessly exercised that it becomes an impediment to civil society, making it so that others are made to feel less free, their private space and peace invaded, their sensitivities cruelly trampled upon.

And it is especially true now, when neuroscience is providing a much clearer picture of the brain at work, of the relationship between psychological harm and physical decline, and the human mind's cognitive and emotional properties. What brain scans reveal is that emotional harm is not trivial. The damage done from violent speech cannot simply be shrugged off, casually allowed to slide off our backs as the platitude "sticks and stones" falsely reassures— surely the least effective self-defense to psychological harm ever known to humankind.

# 25

# THE PHYSICAL AND THE EMOTIONAL: ONE AND THE SAME IN THE HUMAN BRAIN

A human being who faces perpetual fear and chronic stress is well on the way to brain damage. Given the overlapping symptoms of mind and body, physical decline is not far behind a mind that is in the throes of distress.

*A*LL OF THE hesitations about granting recovery for emotional injury—the fraudulent claims, the doubts surrounding their subjective, unprovable nature, the risk of allowing hypersensitivities to trap us all in a police state where every errant, innocuous word could lead to a jail sentence—are mollified given what we now know about the real effects of harmful speech. Intentionally assaultive words cause stress, and prolonged stress leads to physical harm—quite apart from the more obvious and direct psychological damage. Recent neuroscientific discoveries provide medical confirmation that speech can be a form of violence.

Psychologist and scholar Lisa Feldman Barrett has been at the forefront of research discoveries related to the study of emotion. In her recent book, *How Emotions Are Made*, published in 2017, she addressed specifically the false dichotomy under the law between physical injury and emotional harm. The danger that emanates from words is an open secret with serious consequences. And the failure to have acknowledged this obvious truth has had all the staying power of an urban myth that everyone mystifyingly believes. Barrett states that "emotional harm can do more serious damage, last longer, and cause more future harm than breaking a bone. This means the legal system might be misguided when it comes to understanding and gauging the degree of lasting injury that can come from emotional harm. Chronic stress manifested in psychological illness doesn't stop merely with the brain. It eventually has the potential to lead to physical illness and injury. Rather than dismissing the consequences of emotional harm, it is time for the legal system to recognize that emotional damage can shorten a life."[237]

The human brain, apparently, does not compartmentalize injury in the same way as courts do. When the brain is activated from the neural sensations of pain, it apparently cares little for how it got there—whether the body received a jolt or whether the pain struck below the surface of the skin. The mind is blind to external bruising, whereas the legal system believes that it has no role in resolving disputes unless a tangible, material, visible mark is created from a human interaction gone wrong. In the workings of the human brain, chronic pain, stress, anxiety, and depression are all constructed in the same manner as how emotions are made. External physical pain and interior emotional hurt are not opposite human reactions. They are twin expressions of damage.[238] In fact, there is even a placebo test that can prove their symbiotic relationship, which is called a nocebo. In a routine injection, before the needle even touches the arm, the brain can actually simulate the feeling of physical pain. The physical pain was felt without there being an external incident to justify the sensation. It was all in the head. The mind did all the work.[239]

The irony of this phenomenon should not be lost on the legal system. Given all the efforts to separate physical from emotional injury, the bruising of the body, and the swelling and inflammation it causes, has its own analog in the brain, which is not without deleterious effects on the emotions, as well. The legal system has continually bought into an anatomical falsehood: The human brain is inactive when the body endures and registers physical injury. Wholly untrue. Physical injury is chronicled in the brain just as severely.

Whenever there is injury or illness, cells secrete cytokines, which are proteins that produce inflammation. Blood surges to the affected region, raising the temperature around its source, and causes swelling. In response to chronic stress or fear, social rejection and loneliness, even the worry that comes from persistent poverty, the body releases too much cortisol. The body can actually become flooded with cortisol and cytokines, to its considerable detriment. The consequences of having too much cortisol in the bloodstream is an increase in inflammation, due to the presence of so many proinflammatory cytokines. Neurobiologist Amy Arnsten at Yale University conducted studies demonstrating the significance of increased chronic stress and its flooding of the body with cortisol. Cortisol is a stress hormone, which, among other things, manages the flight or fight impulse of a human being. Taxing the mind with this existential decision—whether to flee or fight in response to a physical threat or verbal humiliation—releases a hormone that, in excess, is dangerous to one's health. Cortisol can damage the cells in the hippocampus, overwhelming the brain with enzyme kinase C, which breaks down the dendritic spines of neurons in the prefrontal cortex of the brain.[240]

A human being who faces perpetual fear and chronic stress is well on the way to brain damage. Given the overlapping symptoms of mind and body, physical decline is not far behind a mind that is in the throes of distress.

Professor David Alexander, director of the Aberdeen Center for Trauma Research, has conducted extensive work with survivors of disasters—the Asian tsunami, an earthquake in Pakistan, the war in Iraq, the Piper Alpha oil-rig disaster, and others. Of his many discoveries is the link between physical and emotional pain.

Whether it derives from a physical or emotional setback, pain is activated in the anterior cingulate cortex of the brain. The triggering of pain makes little distinction between its original source—interior emotion or external body are equally prickly; the mind plays no favorites for pain purposes. The grief-stricken from bereavement are vulnerable to heart attacks and strokes. Humans can actually die of a broken heart. The hormones involved in managing the stress of bereavement leave a lasting imprint—on the mind and body. Alexander noted that if one listens to people who are damaged emotionally, they will refer to their pain by using physical descriptions: "'My head is bursting, my guts are aching' and so on. The parallel is very strong."[241]

According to Feldman Barrett, inflammation is problematic everywhere, but especially in the brain. A chronic condition of inflammation irreparably damages an immune system and causes illnesses such as diabetes, obesity, heart disease, depression, premature aging, mental illness, and dementia.[242] And one particularly toxic culprit of inflammation is assaultive speech. Wounding words, too freely spoken, bring about sickness, alter the brain, destroy neurons, and shorten lives. Speech that torments a human being, and instills a sense of perpetual fear, is a form of violence no less destructive of brain cells than an actual head injury. One might as well ride a motorcycle without a helmet on black ice at top speed rather than expose that same head to unremitting torment.[243]

The legal system has always had it wrong. Treating words as if they are ultimately harmless, mere slights that should be ignored, annoyances that can be dispatched with a shrug, has no basis in medicine or science. Courts simply choose to avoid taking emotional injuries seriously, largely for reasons of laziness—not wishing to introduce yet another category of legal relief—and on account of some stiff-upper-lip Anglo-ethos that owes its allegiance to a bygone Victorian era. There is also an exaggerated, misguided notion that America is the land of free speech, where the rights of speakers always prevail. But there is no legal or moral principle that justifies a government ignoring overt acts of violence against fellow citizens and its contribution to social instability—especially when the violence causes such severe injury. Assaults that are manifested in bodily harm, and assaultive speech that takes aim at the emotions, are at least equally hazardous to the individual. And both are disruptive of social peace. Arkes noted that there is "something in the nature of the words themselves that constitutes an assault. No government that would call itself a decent government would fail to intervene in these cases and disperse the crowd."[244]

Seen in this way, chronic stress, which is widely dismissed as a weak-willed problem only experienced by perpetual head cases, ultimately damages one's physical health by, among other things, remodeling the brain and rewiring its circuitry. Feldman Barrett wryly concluded, "So much for the classical division between mental and physical illness."[245]

And this is even more true when it takes the form of racial prejudice, in which many different occurrences of bigotry accumulate, leading to both psychological harm and physical decline. In the 1954 landmark civil rights case, *Brown v. Board of Education*, which effectively put an end to racial segregation in public schools, the Supreme Court implicitly recognized, wholly apart from the constitutional issue, that "segregation caused psychological harm, which was important enough to rise to a constitutional issue." Psychological harm *is* harm worthy of a legal remedy. Over longer periods of time, even lesser incidents take their toll. Wearing a person down with indignities leads to cumulative damage and makes them vulnerable to poor health.[246]

Should anyone now doubt that free speech, while a perfectly fine liberty and the essence of self-government, is not without serious transaction costs? Not only does free speech not guarantee valuable ideas, when wholly unregulated, unmoderated, reckless, and maliciously exercised, it may actually be bad for one's health. Not unlike the consequences of heedless smoking or immoderate overeating, the irresponsible, self-centered gluttonous practice of harmful speech can shorten a life. The difference here, however, is that the speaker is not bringing harm to him or herself. Violent speakers are not engaged in the verbal equivalent of secondhand smoke. The damage done to others is neither incidental nor ancillary; it is primary. And the foulness of their own speech has no consequences to them. Smokers, alcoholics, or reckless drivers at least know that an assumption of risk accompanies their habits. Speakers are not operating under the same warning labels. No such death wish befalls assaultive speakers. Indeed, it is the targets of their injurious speech who are consigned to suffer the consequences of their indulgent misuse of this liberty. The cost of violent speech is born entirely by innocent bystanders, minding their own business until someone decides to unleash his or her venomous First Amendment freedom at another's expense.

Another difference, of course, is that we can no longer plead innocence as to the harm that speech can cause. We now know how destructive words can be. We can glimpse the final bill, and the sticker shock should be unsettling. It is time to finally address the collateral damage of speech. Our collective neglect will end up producing its own anxieties. And we know that it is dangerous. For instance, children who have been victims of verbal abuse and emotional bullying have shown low-grade inflammation that stays with them as they grow older and predisposes them to psychiatric and physical disease. Feldman Barrett noted the absurdity that "[i]t's perfectly legal for a high school bully to insult, torment, and humiliate your children even though this will shorten their telomeres [which protect the ends of chromosomes] and potentially their lifespans. . . . Most kids are unaware that the mental anguish they inflict can translate into physical illness, atrophied brain tissue, reduced IQ, and shortened telomeres."[247]

26.

# FIRST AND SECOND
# AMENDMENT CRAZIES

The First and Second Amendments are interpreted as though there are no reciprocal, mutually reinforcing rights enjoyed by those who are being asked to take a bullet, so to speak, for the unchecked liberty of others.

T̲RY HAVING THIS type of a conversation and sharing these discoveries about the harm of assaultive speech with free speech absolutists. They would be no more willing to part with any participle of free speech than would a zealous gun owner voluntarily surrender his or her purported right to own an AR-15 semiautomatic assault rifle. The argument would devolve quickly into the zero-sum, black-hole category of: "It's a free country, and I am allowed to say whatever I want!"

As a nation, we have failed to undertake a serious and honest conversation about the consequences of unrestricted gun ownership. Second Amendment absolutists simplify the issue as the inalienable right of citizens to bear arms. It is a right they are unwilling to limit or modify in any way. Similarly, First Amendment absolutists outline their case for unrestricted speech as a matter of constitutional right. And they display a similar uncompromising nature when it comes to placing limitations on free speech.

The violence that emanates from the exercise of rights—side effects of both the First and Second Amendments—is justified as the price of citizenship. The Constitution is being asserted as a defense to both the physical and moral killing of fellow citizens. Pick your poison, the dark truths of liberty run amok: gunned down in a hailstorm of bullets; or laid to waste from the indignity and ruin of assaultive speech. No one can supply a ready and reasonable answer as to why the first two constitutional amendments are one-way liberties—enjoyed only by those who exercise them. The First and Second Amendments are interpreted as though there are no reciprocal, mutually reinforcing rights enjoyed by those who are being asked to take a bullet, so to speak, for the unchecked liberty of others. They are negative rights, insomuch as they are defenses against government action, but they are most decidedly being deployed as offensive weapons. The rights possessed by the victims of First and Second Amendment abuses do not seem to count for much.

If true, this is patriotism that has lost its unifying national perspective—a patriotism personified by smugness, vanity, and false glory. And, yet again, it is a patriotism that would have confused the Founding Fathers. The Framers were obsessed with the general welfare and the public good. They also wanted to retain rights for the people, but for a specific purpose. The First Amendment allowed the people to speak out against the government should the occasion require it. The Second Amendment empowered them with the right to possess weapons and arm militias in the event circumstances proved perilous and defending themselves against that very same government became urgent and necessary. The First Amendment says nothing about citizens attacking each other with harmful speech; and the Second Amendment is silent on the subject of citizens possessing guns so they can kill each other.

Our first two amendments to our founding document are being misapplied in the service of selfishly violent ends. The First and Second Amendments, unlike the remaining Bill of Rights, are responsible for America's outlier status among other liberal democracies. The Second Amendment is becoming better known around the world for providing psychotic and murderous Americans with the legal armature to commit school shootings. Meanwhile, our First Amendment, in a fit of aberrational excess, protects the free speech of neo-Nazis, gay bashers, Islamophobes, and white supremacists. Like our obsession with firearms, other democratic nations see American free speech as permitting violence that is completely outlawed in their equally free societies. They will not stand for it, and they do not feel less free on account of it. It is plainly wrong and harmful, and unbecoming of modern, pluralistic societies. Feldman Barrett described our First Amendment culture as "a political climate in which groups of people endlessly hurl hateful words at one another, and of rampant bullying in school or on social media. A culture of constant, casual brutality is toxic to the body, and we suffer for it."[248]

The answer vacillates around leaving well enough alone. Some would argue that restricting AR-15s is the slippery slope that leads to the confiscation of small handguns. So, too, does curtailing free speech have its line-drawing apprehensions. The subjective nature of speech, and the hypersensitivity that many have to insult, only heightens these alarms. How is one ever to know whether what they are about to say may actually bring about harm to their listeners, and therefore legal consequences to the speaker? Such arbitrary rules applied to every casual passing remark is intolerable. Greg Lukianoff, the president and CEO of the Foundation for Individual Rights in Education ("FIRE"), wrote in 2015 that "[i]t is impossible and ultimately counterproductive to regulate speech based on subjective emotional harm." He fears that speakers will be held hostage to the wounded feelings of the most sensitive among us. Speakers will be punished based on "constantly changing and unknowable standard[s]."[249]

Is it not better to just place the burden on listeners to develop a tougher hide than to expose speakers to the dark mysteries of another's psyche, potentially a person whose feelings are always on the verge of bursting some inner dam? Under common law, both in criminal and civil cases, a wrongdoer takes his victim as he finds him, meaning that he or she always assumes the risk that his victim possesses an eggshell skull. The unexpected fragility of an injured victim is not a valid defense. In a case brought before a court in the United Kingdom in 1996, *Page v. Smith*, Lord Lloyd dispensed with the argument that someone suffering from emotional harm should buck up, demonstrate more spine and internal toughness, and not be so supersensitive. "In the case of physical injury," Lord Lloyd wrote, "there is no such [normal fortitude] requirement. The negligent defendant . . . takes his victim as he finds him. The same should apply in the case of psychiatric injury. There is no difference in principle . . . between an eggshell skull and an eggshell personality."[250]

The government does not want the task of wielding its own sword in punishing those who say the wrong thing in the presence of someone who takes offense too easily. But perspective matters, and proportion is possible. Just as there is a bright-line distinction between a single-shot hunting rifle and a machine gun that dispenses a fuselage of bullets, so, too, is it possible to separate merely offensive statements from those that are truly damaging. Offensive is not dangerous to either body or brain. The human nervous system, fashioned from evolution to adjust to a wide range of human encounters, was designed to cope with mere slights. Humankind knows better that "loving thy neighbor" is a nice but largely unpracticed religious ritual. We have come to expect encounters with mean girls and boys. And the law has always accounted for such unpleasant interactions in the ordinary course. The *Restatement of Torts*, for instance, acknowledges that "some minor or modest emotional harm is endemic to living in society and individuals must learn to accept and cope with such harm."[251] There is a difference between the momentary breach that leads to hurt feelings and protracted experiences with fear, stress, and intimidation where words are used to rob citizens of the tranquility so fundamental to meaningful citizenship. The *Restatement of Torts* even defines emotional harm as an impairment or injury done to "emotional tranquility."[252]

In the modern era, psychological harm can present itself in many different forms: emotional distress, privacy intrusions, reputational damage, incitement to violence, revenge porn, cyberbullying, and, of course, harassment over the Internet. No matter how it occurs or the form that the emotional injury takes, the extent of the injuries is now fully verifiable. Harmful speech no longer exists only as self-serving declarations of hurt feelings. Thanks to neuroimaging and diagnostic techniques in examining the brain, emotional harm is no longer an enigma. With the aid of brain-scanning technology, neuroscientists are able to prove that emotional injuries, like physical injuries, have a psychological basis that can be measured.

# 27

# WHAT BRAIN SCANS SHOW AND WHAT SOME LEGAL DECISIONS SAY

The skepticism over feigned emotional injury is no longer a reason to dispute claims for emotional distress. Emotional harm now has a physiological component.

ACCORDING TO LAW professor Betsy Grey, brain scan imaging produces specific findings that eliminate concerns of pure subjectivity in emotional perceptions. Specifically, functional magnetic resonance imaging (fMRI) takes a live photograph of the mind at work and measures the neural impact of various types of psychological harm. The incidence of emotional harm activates certain sectors of the brain in responding to painful stimuli—a derogatory word, a sign or poster that evidences social exclusion. This requires more oxygen to be pumped to the brain. The increase in oxygen consumption expands the blood flow of active neurons. Other types of scans, such as positron emission tomography (PET), employ radioactive isotopes to detect energy metabolism. Both scans measure and make visual the flow of blood to the brain. The reason behind all that racing blood is a neural response to outside forces that manifests itself as changes to brain function.[253]

One thing is for sure: The skepticism over feigned emotional injury is no longer a reason to dispute claims for emotional distress.

Emotional harm now has a physiological component. Objective standards of reasonableness can be employed to evaluate a plaintiff's claim of emotional injury. Indeed, the very same Reasonable Person Test, which is applied in cases of physical harm, can be used to standardize the extent of emotional harm. Charting the brain scans of a critical mass of people in a given community and observing how they react to certain situations—the flow of blood to designated sectors in the brain that light up in response to fear and intimidation—allows medical experts to quantify the levels of emotional pain.[254]

Once armed with objective evidence, courts no longer need to flail when faced with psychological harm, treating emotional injuries as a second-class category in the doctrines of tort law. Psychiatric disorder is not only knowable, it is tantamount to bodily harm. In *Allen v. Bloomfield Hills School District*, a 2008 tort action in Michigan, a train operator spotted a school bus that negligently maneuvered around a crossing gate instead of waiting for the train to pass and the gate to open. The train operator attempted to avoid crashing into the school bus, but failed to do so, causing him to witness the train ram through the bus. (Fortunately, the bus was empty of children.) As the plaintiff in the action against the school district, he was diagnosed with PTSD, and no other bodily harm. He sued for the negligent operation of the school bus. Surprisingly, the court permitted him to recover for "bodily injury" on the theory that the accident caused actual physical brain damage. PTSD constituted bodily injury to his brain, evidenced by a PET scan. The court noted that the brain scan presented "objective medical evidence that a mental or emotional trauma can indeed result in physical changes to the brain." In reaching this conclusion, the court allowed expert testimony showing that PTSD "causes significant changes in brain chemistry, brain function, and brain structure. The brain becomes 're-wired' to over-respond to circumstances that are similar to the traumatic experience."[255]

These are all steps in the right direction. And it mirrors the way legal rules apply to emotional injury in the United Kingdom.

In England, courts do not make distinctions between emotional and physical harm. Like the court in *Bloomfield Hills School District*, psychiatric illness is treated as bodily harm. All illnesses, after all, affect the body—in their own way. It is an extreme leap of metaphysics to believe that damage to the human mind has no repercussions on the physical body. Emotional harm *is* bodily harm. Under the English system of tort law, if an injury establishes a recognized psychiatric disorder—depression, PTSD, severe grief— then for liability purposes, it is tantamount to bodily harm.[256]

Even in the United States, there has been a movement to ensure that health insurance plans treat with parity their coverages for psychological and physical harm. As House Speaker Nancy Pelosi declared in 2008, "illness of the brain must be treated just like illness anywhere in the body."[257]

All of this represents a more complex understanding of the ways in which the mind works. Emotional injuries cause structural changes to the brain. The regions of the brain most associated with emotional trauma are the medial prefrontal cortex, orbitofrontal cortex, anterior cingulated, insular cortices, the amygdala, and the hippocampus—all of which are involved in processing emotions.[258] Emotional harm rewires the processes in these sectors of the brain, causing overload quite apart from the toll taken from physical injury. The full effect from both emotional and physical injury is to bring about dysfunction in brain circuitry.[259]

Even a single exposure to a traumatic event can create permanent cellular changes in the amygdala, the sector of the brain that is activated in response to anxiety and the recollection of painful memories—often known as the "emotion center" of the brain, the "arousal system" stimulated from trauma and stress.[260] When this happens, brain circuitry is disrupted, and anxiety sets in. Prolonged stress, and its effect on creating inflammation in the body, starts out by impairing the functioning of the prefrontal cortex, which would otherwise smooth out the emotions emanating from the amygdala. When the prefrontal cortex is exposed to stress, fear, and intimidation, the amygdala is left without regulatory balance, which is why people oftentimes describe themselves as "feeling out of control." Their perception of reality is altered. Clear thinking is lost. Those who have experienced PTSD from prior traumas, or those who are easily anxious, will overreact through no fault of their own. Their amygdalae are always on high alert, supersensitive and hyperactive, and fully inflamed.[261]

In the past, it was easy to misread what was happening in the brain. When symptoms suggested that an individual was responding emotionally, the immediate conclusion was that he or she had fallen into a disoriented, altered state of cognition. Only God knew what was really going on. Setting a broken bone was a picnic by comparison. But what was really occurring was not nearly that mysterious. It was simply a breakdown in the neural networks, especially in the prefrontal cortex, which otherwise regulates fear, stress, and memory. Over time, traumatic experiences cause physiological changes in the brain. Today they are easily identified through neuroimaging.[262] Neuroscience can show a connection between traumatic experiences and cognitive disorders. In time they manifest as neurological conditions. Once that sets in, the neural system is unable to regulate the emotions emanating from the amygdala. It is like a remote control that cannot seem to connect with the TV—a looping slide show of channels without end. With each exposure to stress and fear, the greater the neural dysfunction. Subjective emotional injury is no longer legally suspect, with clashing experts hawking different diagnoses and claimants delivering Oscar-worthy performances. Damage to the brain can be as conclusively and objectively verified as bodily harm. Neuroscientist Joseph E. LeDoux summed up the new diagnostic climate in 2000 by stating that, "brain researchers need to be more savvy about the nature of emotions, rather than simply relying on common sense beliefs about emotions as subjective feeling states."[263]

It is for this reason that the legal system should stop treating the intentional infliction of emotional distress as a token tort that rarely receives legal relief on its own. The general rule under common law, which was codified in the 1965 *Restatement of Torts*, was that: "One who by *extreme* and *outrageous* conduct intentionally or recklessly causes *severe emotional distress* to another is subject to liability for such emotional distress."[264] In the follow-up *Restatement*, the "extreme" and "outrageous" prongs received an additional element to establish the tort. To be recoverable, the action must "exceed all permissible bounds of civilized society."[265] With such a high burden of required evidentiary proof, in which the tortious act must fall into a largely undefinable category of *outrageousness*, no wonder that recovery for the intentional infliction of emotional distress arises, if at all, only in cases where it can be an add-on to another tort that has a physical, tangible damage component. The body becomes the controlling canvas for legal relief. Disfigure the body with bruises, and the legal system mobilizes into high alert. Emotional distress, absent bodily injury, is a much lonelier road to recovery, in part because such claims are so widely dismissed and disbelieved, as is the case with the recognition and treatment of many forms of mental illness.

Emotional distress claims without the *mens rea* component, however, as in the negligent infliction of emotional distress, are far easier to prove. It requires neither the extremity nor outrageousness elements that must be met when the tort is framed as an intentional harm. Negligent infliction focuses entirely on the harm that arose from the negligence itself—and dispenses with any burden to establish either the intent of the act or the outrageousness of the conduct. All that has to have occurred is the breach of a standard duty of care, causally connected to an action of a tortfeasor, and a showing of harm.

The *Restatement of Torts* defines emotional harm caused by a negligent actor as one who placed the plaintiff in "immediate danger of bodily harm," and whose negligent conduct is likely to cause a serious emotional disturbance.[266] Today, with the aid of neuroscience, treating emotional harm as an ordinary negligence claim is a much simpler evidentiary burden to meet. The harm is revealed not entirely through subjective testimony but through brain scans showing the link between emotional damage and bodily sickness. Law professor Deanna Pollard Sacks is among several academics who have argued in favor of using ordinary principles of negligence to establish liability in tort for unreasonably dangerous speech. Causing emotional distress in another constitutes a tort in negligence and such an action can be brought by the injured party. The government need not initiate any proceeding against the speaker for violating a criminal law statute or an ordinance barring certain behavior in public—such as a protest or march. Civil claims in tort under state law provide a clear pathway to respond to the injurious nature of assaultive, violent speech, especially in situations where there is the "likelihood and gravity of public risk, and . . . [when] the risks are sufficiently foreseeable to warrant punishment."[267]

Neuroscience is not the only way we have come to learn more about the human brain and its processing of emotional injury. Many studies have been undertaken in the past few years that establish just how harmful emotional injury can be—especially harm that originates with speech. For instance, talk radio and podcasts, which often include an unhealthy dose of hate speech targeting vulnerable groups, have been found to increase a stress-related hormone in whomever happens to be listening to the message—and regardless of the race, ethnicity, nationality, or ideological alignment of the listener. This means that hate speech over the airways harms not just the intended targets but also anyone who has unwittingly tuned in. One study in 2002 found a correlation in the symptoms of clinical anxiety, the production of salivary cortisol in the body, and the onset of chronic inflammatory diseases, which can lead to cancer—all on account of listening to hate speech. Alex Nogales of the National Hispanic Media Coalition, which commissioned the study with the assistance of researchers at the UCLA Chicano Studies Research Center, observed the paradox that, "[t]his study demonstrates that harm is not isolated to targeted groups and that it could . . . even harm the physical health of those that are ideologically aligned with the haters."[268]

A similar finding arose out of a 2012 study in Boston where researchers discovered that not only were victims of hate crimes three times more likely to be hospitalized but (not unlike the findings in the UCLA study) those who heard the hate speech directed at vulnerable minorities also experienced an increase in salivary cortisol with its chronic inflammation and connection to cancer. Once again, the ethnicity or race of the listeners is irrelevant for the risk to be present. Moreover, the listener need not be sympathetic to the victim. Exposure to the hate, even from a fellow bigot, is enough to bring about this physiological enigma.[269]

In response to Germany's new online hate speech law, which went into effect in 2018, social media networks such as Facebook and Twitter—faced with severe fines for failing to remove illegal content from their sites within one day of notification—took affirmative steps to monitor their own platforms. They stepped up what were once lackadaisical deletion centers that had been charged with removing content that incited hatred. Thousands of content moderators work in such facilities across Europe. On any given day they might each have to examine 1,500 reports of online hate speech and the posting of unlawful content. It can be devastatingly nightmarish work. "Every so often someone breaks down. A mother recently left her desk in tears after watching a video of a child being sexually abused. A young man felt physically sick after seeing a video of a dog being sexually tortured. The agents watch teenagers self-mutilating and girls recounting rape."[270] Harm comes even to those who simply come into contact with these horrific acts of self-expression. The viewer does not have to be the intended target to feel the residual effects of the harmful speech.

28.

# THE MIND'S RECALL OF PAIN

The human brain exhibits amnesia when called upon to reexperience the blows from sticks and stones. With humiliation and indignity, however, the brain is a steel trap of merciless memory.

IT SHOULD COME as no surprise that victims of hate crimes suffer greater emotional distress and cumulative psychological harm than victims of non-bias-motivated crimes. Indeed, five years after the traumatic encounters, they experience greater levels of depression and anxiety than other crime victims. The impact to both mind and body lingers much longer. The incidence of severe trauma from hate crimes requires a lengthier recovery period—if recovery is even possible at all.[271] Similarly, hate crime victims report that their reintegration into society is much more difficult to achieve. Deprived of self-respect after experiencing ordeals of indignity, victims of hate speech struggle with the everyday tasks of socialization. One obvious outcome is in "trying to be less visible," which the hate crime victim achieves by moving to an entirely different environment.[272] In this way, hate speech serves to undermine free speech itself precisely because it silences the targeted group, compelling them to disappear socially.[273]

Moreover, even watching someone else experiencing pain can create greater sensitivity in one's own pain perception. So finely calibrated is the processing of emotions in the human brain, it turns out that showing empathy to a fellow human being carries some emotional risk. In a 2009 study conducted simultaneously at the universities of Arizona and Maryland, researchers discovered that the anterior cingulate cortex, the region of the brain that regulates emotional reactions, responds to an emotional insult by unleashing a wide variety of physical responses—stress-induced sensations in the chest, muscle tightness, an increased heart rate, and stomach pains—all triggered from the same sector of the brain. Another study undertaken by two professors from the University of Virginia in 2006 supported the finding that activation in the anterior cingulate cortex coincides with the onset of chest pains. The researchers concluded that "emotional pain involves the same brain regions as physical pain, suggesting that the two are inextricably linked."[274]

In fact, medical evidence abounds showing how emotion and physical harm share the same circuitry in the human brain. The *New England Journal of Medicine* published a research study in 2013 on how subjects experienced both physical and emotional pain by looking at a photo of a cherished person who died. Brain scans indicated the same neural activity when a subject was exposed to heat on his or her forearm as when shown a photo of a lost loved one. Experiencing physical pain did not yield a separate neural response that was distinguishable from emotional pain. A burned forearm and an aggrieved heart elicited identical neural reactions. One of the researchers on the study, Tor Wagner, a professor of neuroscience at the University of Colorado in Boulder, explained the reasons for this unexpected outcome, stating "[t]hat may be why social pain is so painful: every time you remember it, you feel it all over again and that is not true for physical pain. Of all the things I've observed in the brain, nothing is more similar to physical pain than social pain."[275]

And the consequences of "social pain" are even more severe. The pain from social exclusion and indignity, which begins with emotional distress, ends up rendering a person physically sick. The two regions of the brain once thought to be the epicenter for the processing of physical pain show similar patterns of neural activity when the mind focuses on a photograph reminiscent of rejection or loss. A research team from the University of Kentucky set out to demonstrate this neural overlap between social and physical pain systems. Apparently, the same behavioral and neural mechanisms are at work in processing what many would believe to be disparate manifestations of pain. Psychology professor C. Nathan DeWall explained the significance of his team's findings in 2009: "Social pain, such as chronic loneliness, damages health as much as smoking and obesity. We hope our findings can pave the way for interventions designed to reduce the pain of social rejection."[276] He also speculated about the reasons why the human brain evolved in this manner. "Instead of creating an entirely new system to respond to social hurt," he said, "evolution piggybacked the system for emotional pain onto that for physical pain." The evolution of the human brain allowed emotional injury to take a free ride on the circuitry associated with physical pain.

And not surprisingly, when it comes to hate crimes and their origins in racial bigotry, the overall bodily damage arising from such injurious speech tends to be even worse. Law professor Richard Delgado noted that, "[i]n addition to these long-term psychological harms of racial labeling, the stresses of racial abuse may have physical consequences. There is evidence that high blood pressure is associated with inhibited, constrained or restricted anger . . . American blacks have higher blood pressure levels, and higher morbidity and mortality rates from hypertension, hyper-intensive disease, and stroke than do white counterparts. Further, there exists a strong correlation between degree of darkness of skin for blacks and level of stress felt, a correlation that may be caused by the greater discrimination experienced by dark-skinned people."[277]

Psychology professor Geoff MacDonald, from the University of Toronto, has charted the trajectory of bodily and psychological harm caused by social insult. He noted that, not unlike damage done to the body, the initial sensation of emotional hurt produces a surge of stress hormones. In the context of a physical injury, the purpose of this hormone is to brace the body for yet another attack. It provides confidence to both body and mind that the individual can actually take and survive a punch. The release of these stress hormones accounts for why a person can actually walk away on a broken leg or manage to speak despite having a shattered skull. After the surge of this energy dissipates, the pain ensues. The same release of stress hormones occurs when a person faces severe emotional, social pain. Proving the Talmudic injunction not to humiliate a fellow human being because it is tantamount to draining him of his blood, neuroscience can now account for how the ancients knew something about what happens, physiologically, to human beings who have experienced severe indignity. The brain discharges a sufficient amount of stress hormones to handle the first blow. When the damage is done and the insult has subsided, the body will begin the process of dissipating the pain, and the blood flows away from the afflicted area.[278]

The difference, however, is that, unlike physical pain, where bones will ultimately heal, and the pain of the experience will become wholly forgotten, social pain can be—and often is—relived over and over again. The sensation of the pain is instantly recalled and reexperienced. This is the consequence of how our memories cope with traumatic stress, resulting in a cruel admixture of the mind. Physical pain, by contrast, can be remembered as once being painful, but the pain itself cannot be reclaimed. The human brain exhibits amnesia when called upon to reexperience the blows from sticks and stones. With humiliation and indignity, however, the brain is a steel trap of merciless memory.

With sets of patients who had experienced physical injury and another group that suffered from emotional harm, researchers at

Purdue University did a five-year study and checked back in with the participants each year after the incidents that caused them such pain. The focus of the study was to determine how they felt about what they had experienced five years earlier. The results, published in 2008, were not surprising to neuroscientists but surely would be perplexing to emotionally adverse judges. Those participants who had experienced emotional injury reported higher levels of pain than participants who experienced physical harm. They were still feeling the emotional effects of the harm. Psychology professor Kip Williams of Purdue stated that, "While both types of pain can hurt very much at the time they occur, social pain has the unique ability to come back over and over again, whereas physical pain lingers only as an awareness that it was indeed at one time painful."[279] A few law professors had been making similar points over the years, with much skepticism from their colleagues and the courts. It must have just seemed intuitively obvious. Arkes, for instance, once presciently wrote during the Stone Age of such speculations (in 1974), "There is in fact such a thing as a psychological injury, which may be quite grave . . . as an assault on one's body or a broken leg."[280]

Heresy and constitutional apostasy at the same time.

Today, there is research showing that something far less than a hate crime—say, perhaps, an emotional injury that might arise from social exclusion—can cause chronic pain disorders such as fibromyalgia. Psychology professor Ethan Kross, a lead researcher in yet another study—this one from the University of Michigan—explained just how damaging emotional trauma can be on both the human brain and body: "What's exciting about these findings," Kross said in 2011, "is that they outline the direct way in which emotional experiences can be linked to the body." The study demonstrated that the same sectors in the brain that are activated when experiencing physical pain—dorsal posterior insula and the secondary somatosensory cortex—overlap with the network of brain regions involved in processing emotional pain. Kross' team compared MRI brain scans with a database of five hundred published studies and were able to establish positive predictive values up to 88 percent. The brain is a pinball machine with bells ringing and pain pulsating regardless of whether the pain originated from a blow to the body or the heart. Sickness eventually emanates from either.[281]

Apparently, heart*aches* and *painful* breakups are "more than just metaphors," Kross concluded. Feelings of rejection, indignity, and emotional trauma are direct causes in the development of chronic pain disorders.[282] In conducting research on the neural responses to social rejection, Jonathan Rottenberg, Professor of Psychology at the University of South Florida where he directs the Mood and Emotion Laboratory, concluded in 2009 what now seems to be obvious among the neuroscientific community in their search for how emotion is processed in the human brain. He stated that, "in interviewing depressed people, I've often been struck by the tremendous blurring between physical and emotional pain. In depression, *everything* hurts."[283]

We now also know that pain medication, in the form of aspirin or acetaminophen, works equally well for emotional pain. The same pill that provides medical relief for a headache can also work miracles for heartache. Pain relief and dissipating inflammation works the same in both cases. As reported in *Psychological Science* in 2011, the participants in a study undertaken at the University of Kentucky were given pain medication—like acetaminophen—as a remedy for the emotional pain they were all experiencing. And just like the dissipation of a throbbing headache, the ache caused by a wounded heart was given temporary relief.

In spite of a long-standing nursery rhyme that reassures us that we have nothing to fear from name-calling, we now know that "words alone are capable of activating our pain matrix. Even verbal stimuli lead to reactions in certain areas of the brain," confirms Thomas Weiss, a professor at Friedrich-Schiller University Jena in Germany. In a study published in *Pain* in 2010, healthy people whose brains were scanned were each asked to listen to words associated with pain—such as "excruciating," "tormenting," "terrifying," or "grueling." In every instance, the processing center of the brains of each participant evidenced significant neural activity simply after hearing a word associated with pain. So powerful are words, they are not only suggestive, they actually trigger neural reactions that cause physical pain—remarkably, even if the individual has experienced no pain at all.[284]

And unlike physical pain, emotional injury leaves an imprint on the mind that digs deeper than any scar permanently etched on the skin. Neuroscientist Martin Teicher from the Harvard Medical School published a study in 2010 of brain imaging in the *American Journal of Psychiatry* on the lingering effects of taunting and other verbal abuse.[285] The participants, age eighteen to twenty-five, had been exposed to verbal abuse from their peers since middle school. The brain scans revealed less developed neural connections between the left and right sides of the brain and a detrimental buildup of fibers—called corpus callosum—connecting the two sides. Verbal abuse causes more than emotional trauma. It inflicts lasting physical effects on the structure of the brain itself, along with higher levels of anxiety, depression, hostility, and drug abuse. From this study, Professor Teicher was able to conclude that verbal harassment causes more than just emotional harm. More alarmingly, it can change the physical structure of the human brain, compromising its actual development. The brain scans he examined noted a reduction in the size of the hippocampus. Traumatic and highly stressful experiences produce long-term effects on the structure and functioning of the brain at the very point where the prefrontal cortex—the section of the brain where the emotions are centered—and the sector of the brain burdened with human survival converge.[286]

# 29

# THE CONSEQUENCES OF FREE SPEECH TAKEN SERIOUSLY

*The chronic injuries from weaponized words do not go away. Emotional trauma is forever recurring and easily renewable, scarcely avoidable, and, in whatever form it takes, never trivial.*

BSOLUTIST ENTITLEMENTS TO speech on demand, regardless of who gets hurt, should not overshadow the burdens that the First Amendment imposes on the targets of speech. Among other scholars, law professor Erica Goldberg has focused her attention on the academically heretical notion that free speech has consequences that should not be so casually ignored.

"Free speech consequentialism" begins with the idea that harms caused by speech should be treated no differently from harms that arise from overt physical acts and conduct. Courts should neither ignore the harms caused by speech nor pretend to be unaware of the harmful consequences of speech—especially when we know the potential consequences of speech to the mind and body. The chronic injuries from weaponized words do not go away. Emotional trauma is forever recurring and easily renewable, scarcely avoidable, and, in whatever form it takes, never trivial.[287] Goldberg wrote in 2015, "People might rather be punched in the face than lose their jobs, or break an arm rather than have their heart broken. Often our emotional health dictates our happiness and productivity far more than our physical capacities."[288] Professor Lawrence surmised that "psychic injury is no less an injury than being struck in the face, and it often is far more severe."[289]

Recognizing the consequences of free speech and introducing a harm principle into First Amendment law is not a first step toward censoring speech. It is merely a long overdue acknowledgment that speech that causes harm must be regulated rather than be given a free pass. And reasonable regulation should not present a problem of content- or viewpoint-based discrimination. It is not solely a matter of rejecting disfavored speech. Speech that denigrates and defames is debilitating by nature and design. Nothing but hate crimes can come from it. Those who peddle such speech seek nothing but to foment hate. The reason to take a harder, more restrictive stance is wholly on account of the harm. The viewpoint, such that there is one, is not being rejected. Viewpoint, in cases like this, should not be considered at all. The speaker forfeits the right to have his message examined for meaning because of the violence he is causing by voicing it.

With such a regulatory role, the government would not be targeting the message; its sole purpose would be to protect those who are, themselves, the targets of harmful speech. The Supreme Court, however, continues to downplay the potential consequences of free speech. It could expand the list of proscribed categories in *Chaplinsky* to include some variant of harmful speech—whether it be called hate speech or designated by some other name. And it could modify the existing categories from the original list, such as "fighting words," to include weaponized words. But the Court seems resistant to any expansion or modification of the proscribed categories in *Chaplinsky* that might incorporate a hate speech agenda.

The most recent First Amendment case in which such an expansion could have occurred came in *Stevens v. United States* in 2010, which involved a federal statute outlawing films depicting cruelty to animals. The Court deemed the statute to have violated the First Amendment precisely because it would have cancelled the free speech rights of those who make such detestable films, deeming them excluded from First Amendment protection, like libel, obscenity, and "fighting words."[290] By a majority vote of eight to one, the Supreme Court ruled that the statute was overbroad, and, in invalidating it, inexplicably favored the rights of those who make "crush videos" to satisfy the sexual fetishes of their audience over the rights of animals to be free from such cruelty. *Stevens* is a disturbing example of just how far the Supreme Court will go to protect the right of personal expression and to limit the scope of *Chaplinsky*'s categorical list of unprotected speech. It is difficult to imagine what the Founding Fathers, even those who were not animal lovers, would have said about that.

# 30

# THE *CHAPLINSKY* LIST AND A HARM-BASED ANALYSIS

The Supreme Court pivoted away from the dignity and privacy rights of the targets of speech. And few courts have been willing to walk the First Amendment back to those values.

*HAPLINSKY* IS STILL good, although largely dormant, law. Since 1942, when it created the Fighting Words Doctrine, the Supreme Court has never once applied the doctrine to strip First Amendment protection for "fighting words" or other words that caused harm. It is as if the Court is afraid to deploy its own doctrine if done in the service of limiting free speech. As law professor Rebecca Brown observed, "[A]s the Court in time became more inclined to protect speech, it narrowed several of the categories of speech on the list. . . . The list slowly . . . took on the character of exclusivity, such that if not on the 1942 list, then a kind of speech was not subject to any kind of content-regulation."[291]

That does not mean that the *Chaplinsky* Court was unmindful of the harm that can arise from speech. It also does not suggest that the justices on the Court at the time of the *Chaplinsky* decision believed the categories to be forever fixed and exclusive. Justice Murphy's opinion clearly benefited from the thinking of constitutional scholar Zechariah Chafee in his seminal mid-twentieth-century work, published one year before *Chaplinsky* was decided. The language in *Chaplinsky*, and the impetus for creating the proscribed categories, are similar to what Chafee had proposed in his own book. He wrote, specifically, that "the law also punishes a few classes of words like obscenity, profanity, and gross libels upon individuals, because the *very utterance of such words* is considered to *inflict a present injury upon listeners*, readers, or those defamed, or else to render highly probable an *immediate breach of the peace*. This is a very different matter from punishing words because they express ideas which are thought to cause a future danger to the State."[292]

The language is notably familiar. He went on to explain that "the existence of a *verbal crime* at common law [is justified because such words] . . . *do not form an essential part of any exposition of ideas*, have a slight social value as a step to the truth, which is clearly outweighed by the *social interest in order, morality* . . . and *the peace of mind of those who hear and see*. . . . The harm is done as soon as [the words] are communicated, or is liable to follow almost immediately in the form of retaliatory violence. . . . [T]he words are criminal, not because of the ideas they communicate, but like acts because of their immediate consequences to the five senses. . . . When A urges B to kill C and tells him how he can do it, this has nothing to do with the attainment and dissemination of truth."[293]

Justice Murphy was clearly influenced by Chafee's understanding of the existence of a distinctly *verbal* crime under common law. Essentially, Chafee recognized a harm-based principle that should not be ignored under the First Amendment—although we have been ignoring it since the 1960s, which has resulted in a free speech absolutist bonanza ever since, and an utter failure to appreciate some of the high costs of free speech. Chafee did not concern himself so much with the low value of certain speech, which, as discussed earlier, is awarded lesser First Amendment protection. But he did focus on the imminent harm that certain words can produce in the emotional life of listeners. He did not fear that reasonable restrictions would amount to the censoring of speech or the stifling of ideas. Instead, he took aim at the avoidance of harm—surely enough of a reason to curtail speech on its own. Whether it be of high or low value, speech should not be used as a weapon that causes harm.

Since then, however, the Supreme Court has distanced itself from the dignity-enhancing, harm-identifying features of *Chaplinsky*. Harm is still not a First Amendment consideration. The presumption that speech produces mostly ideas and nothing else still prevails. Stanley Fish wryly observed in 1994 that, "First Amendment jurisprudence works only if you assume that mental activities, even when they emerge into speech, remain safely quarantined in the cortex and do not spill over into the real world, where they can inflict harm."[294] No new proscribed categories have been added to the original list. And a true "fighting words" case was never again upheld. *Chaplinsky* has fallen into a netherworld of uncertain legal authority. The Supreme Court pivoted away from the dignity and privacy rights of the targets of speech. And few courts have been willing to walk the First Amendment back to those values. As Arkes observed, "Gone was the sense that came out of *Chaplinsky* that one had some right to be protected against a verbal assault or the knowing infliction of a psychological shock when one entered a public place."[295]

# 31

# AND THEN THE SUPREME COURT GOT EVEN MORE FREE SPEECH CRAZY

Stopping a church group from torpedoing a military funeral is not an outright ban on making their opinions known. It merely required them to choose another venue and another manner of speaking—and in an acceptably civilized tone.

*C*HAPLINSKY COULD STILL easily serve as legal authority for un-shielding assaultive speech from protection and setting more sensible limits on the First Amendment. But *Snyder v. Phelps* hit a new low of moral debasement on the matter of free speech. It is certainly a case that would have sickened the Framers of the Constitution and kept Justice Murphy up at night wondering how his opinion in *Chaplinsky* could have been so woefully ignored.

Decided in 2011, the Supreme Court, in *Snyder*, upheld the Fourth Circuit's ruling, which had overturned a jury verdict awarding $5 million in both compensatory and punitive damages to the plaintiff—the father of a deceased marine—for the intentional infliction of emotional distress. At his son's funeral, a church group that had obtained a permit conducted a protest from a distance of a thousand feet that included placards objecting to homosexuals serving in the military and other matters related to gay life.[296] Snyder's son was not gay, and the protesters from the Westboro Baptist Church did not care about this marine's sexual orientation. Their presence at his funeral was not unlike many others they had attended and disrupted across the country without regard to the specific sexual identity of the deceased. All that mattered was that the servicemen had died in action, and that the church despised homosexuals, especially when they wore a military uniform.

Justice Roberts' majority opinion, joined by seven other justices, focused entirely on Westboro's First Amendment rights. The jury's verdict, which found that the church's conduct was "outrageous" for the purposes of establishing a claim for the intentional infliction of emotional distress, seemingly had little value to the Court and was indifferently set aside. Justice Roberts saw the state court's remedy as stifling the church's free speech guarantees under the First Amendment. Gays serving in the military is a political matter. Westboro's opposition earned them free speech protection. A father's right to bury a son without the ceremony being turned into a protest rally fit nowhere within the Bill of Rights.

The opinion did not even attempt to support the claim for emotional distress. Nor did it grant much weight to the fact that a grieving father should have a reasonable expectation of privacy when laying his son to rest. Snyder and his family were targeted as individuals even though the church's dispute was, arguably, public in nature and against the federal government. What Justice Roberts found dispositive was a political matter of public concern— the tolerance, or intolerance, of gay life in American society. Westboro delivered its message on public property and in accordance with the necessary local permits. The Supreme Court invalidated the jury verdict for the intentional infliction of emotional distress and barred the claim on First Amendment grounds.

Justice Roberts summed up his general feeling about the substance of the case by writing that, "[s]peech is powerful. It can stir people to action, move them to tears of both joy and sorrow, and—as it did here—*inflict great pain*. On the facts before us, we cannot react to that pain by punishing the speaker."[297] It was a heartless ruling, for sure. Eight justices of the Supreme Court joined an opinion in which the Chief Justice conceded that the actions of the Westboro Church inflicted "great pain" upon a family attempting to say goodbye to a son and brother killed while serving his country. The pain was acknowledged but discounted; the speech, such that it was, was grossly overvalued. What did the church members need to say that required such a malicious and indecent disruption of a funeral? What made the exercise of their free speech right so vital to the health of our democracy? The posters read: "Thank God for Dead Soldiers," "Fags Doom Nations," "Thank God for 9/11," "You're Going to Hell," "God Hates You," and "God Hates Fags." These artless and heartless efforts at speech were deemed more important than the privacy right of a father to properly mourn the loss of his son.

Even more odiously, this was not a case where the enforcement of a local ordinance ended up silencing a speaker, abridging his or her right to free expression. The speaker would then assert his or her First Amendment rights as a defense against the enforcement of that ordinance. Such is the usual way in which free speech cases come before the law.

In *Snyder*, however, the case originated with a civil tort action in state court. The government was not involved at all—aside from supplying the courthouse and the machinery of justice and granting a permit that made the placement of their signs, and their positions at the funeral, lawful. The state had not abridged speech; in fact, it had facilitated it. The case was brought by a private citizen, suing for damages on account of his emotional distress, against a defendant who a jury found to have acted outrageously. What business even was this of the Supreme Court? No statutory law was being invoked to silence a speaker. The town of Westminster, Maryland, took no position opposing the protest and a permit was granted. The government had not acted against the Westboro Baptist Church to censor its speech by either granting injunctive relief to ban its protest or imposing a severe fine that would have shut it down. A man was burying his son. A decidedly un-Christian church group wished to disrupt the funeral by making a number of very public, and outrageous, anti-gay statements. The First Amendment had nothing to do with this legal matter between private citizens.

In a shameless act of twisted legal and moral reasoning, the Fourth Circuit and the Supreme Court, in overturning that jury verdict, added insult to injury by imposing court costs and legal fees against Snyder in the amount of $16,500. The compensatory and punitive damage awards disappeared, and now Snyder, the bereaved father, was himself being punished.

With such a lopsided majority decision—eight to one in favor of Phelps and his band of pious gay bashers—the Supreme Court delivered a strong message of how far the First Amendment can be extended to protect the most repugnant of speakers. Free speech absolutists, of course, cheered the outcome. But something more was being vindicated. There seemed to be a consensus, shared by free speech zealots, that *Snyder v. Phelps* reaffirmed a principle of American exceptionalism and demonstrated the health of our constitutional democracy and respect for the rule of law. The right of free speech was so precious, it governed disputes even among private citizens. And a grieving father of a dead serviceman was required to bow before it.

Yet, it does not make America exceptional. It makes us look ridiculous—like a nation of unfeeling lunatics possessed by a robotic adherence to an interpretation of a liberty that no other democracy on the planet follows. There were other sensible pathways to relief in *Snyder*. For instance, the Supreme Court could have:

1. Carved out a "zone of grief" that would apply to funerals that no First Amendment speech right could penetrate;
2. Imposed "time, place, and manner restrictions" on the protest, essentially ruling that the local government, had it chosen to, could have withheld the permit without violating the Constitution;

3. Ruled that a civil tort action where a jury awarded damages does not present First Amendment concerns at all;
4. Crafted yet another proscribed category under *Chaplinsky*,
this one dealing with protests at funerals.

None of these options were considered. The Supreme Court
could have taken a firm stand in advancing the civilizing aspects of
the First Amendment. While speech may be free, it is not without
reciprocal obligation. The Court could have set a new direction in
the evolution of the Free Speech Clause by ruling that behavior so
coarse and morally destructive may not benefit from First Amendment protection. Instead, the Snyders' emotional distress claim,
bizarrely, became the violator of the church's constitutional
rights.[298]

Zechariah Chafee said it best, although in the context of the
disrespect to the American flag, which eventually became
lawful, when he wrote that "[t]his [flag desecration] is a state
but not a federal crime, for the United States has no criminal
jurisdiction over offenses against order and good manner."[299]
Yes, that is exactly right: It was the task of a state court jury to
distinguish between merely a breach of "good manners" and a
vile display of uncivil "outrageousness." The citizens of
Maryland had a right, under tort law, to compensate Snyder for
the emotional distress he experienced from the Westboro
Baptist Church's protest at his son's funeral. This was an
appropriate matter for a state court and jury. The Roberts
Court took that right away from them.

All except for Justice Samuel Alito, the one justice on the
Supreme Court who dissented in *Snyder v. Phelps*. He, alone, saw
the case for what it was. Justice Alito forcefully wrote: "Our
profound national commitment to free and open debate is not
a license for the vicious verbal assault that occurred in this
case."[300] And he focused on an appeal to reason and common
sense—the obvious argument that never seems to carry the day

with free speech zealots: the difference between a sensible restriction on how speech can be delivered and a complete ban on the making of an argument altogether. Just because a local government might decide to outlaw cross-burnings does not mean that a member of the KKK is prevented from writing an op-ed in the local paper explaining why he or she is opposed to racial preferences in public education, hiring, and housing. Banning neo-Nazis from marching in brown shirts in front of Holocaust survivors is very different from prohibiting them from running for local elected office wearing conventional clothes, should they wish to present themselves as something other than as hate-filled characters from an execrable 1940s newsreel, and make policy proposals rather than poison the democratic process. A church group can demonstrate their opposition to gays serving in the military without behaving in such a hateful, uncivilized manner.

Justice Alito made this very point when he wrote that there are "almost limitless opportunities to express their views. They may write and distribute books, articles and other texts; they may create and disseminate video and audio recordings; they may circulate petitions; they may speak . . . in public forums and in any private venue that wishes to accommodate them; they may picket peacefully in countless locations, . . . appear on television and speak on the radio; they may post messages on the Internet and send out e-mails."[301] Justice Alito quoted from *Cantwell v. Connecticut,* decided in 1940, in reminding his fellow justices that "personal abuse is not in any proper sense communication of information or opinion safeguarded by the Constitution."[302]

The Westboro Baptist Church was not without options in exercising its First Amendment freedoms. Stopping a church group from torpedoing a military funeral is not an outright ban on making their opinions known. It merely required them to choose another venue and another manner of speaking—and in an acceptably civilized tone.

Arkes explained that "*Chaplinsky* . . . suggested that these statements conveyed nothing of substance that could not be conveyed in some other way. Since it was possible to express the same substance in another manner, it did not seem to threaten the free flow of ideas to require avoidance of the grosser forms of profanity and defamation, out of some respect for the sensibilities of others in a public place."[303]

Let us return to that simple test I suggested earlier: What would George Washington do? Or, more likely, what would he say? Do we really believe that the man who had led the Colonial Army to its improbable military victory over the British Empire imagined that the Bill of Rights would one day enable a group of protesters to disrespect the funeral of a young man killed while serving his country in battle? In what way are we honoring the Founders' moral clarity and generosity of spirit in protecting people who hold up signs that read: "God Hates Fags"?

The question may never have been put to Justice Alito in this fashion, but he probably would have responded with what he wrote in *Snyder*—that the First Amendment does not mean that a speaker "may intentionally inflict severe emotional injury on private persons at a time of intense emotional sensitivity by launching vicious verbal attacks that make no contribution to public debate."[304] Alito recognized the gravity of the harm inflicted on the Snyders and the absurdity of the Court's ruling in favor of the Westboro Baptist Church. "Respondents' outrageous conduct," he wrote, "caused petitioner great injury, and the Court now compounds that injury by depriving petitioner of a judgment that acknowledges the wrong he suffered."[305]

One wonders what made Alito see this case so differently from his brethren. Why was free speech for him subject to commonsense limits and not exempt from standards of human decency?

The authors of the book *Words That Wound* were correct back in 1993 when they wrote, "It is a fight for a constitutional community where 'freedom' does not implicate a right to degrade and humiliate another human being any more than it implicates a right to do physical violence to another or a right to enslave another or a right to economically exploit another in a sweatshop, in a coal mine, or in the fields."[306]

# 32

# OTHER CASES WHERE THE SUPREME COURT PRIVILEGED SPEECH OVER PAIN

Free speech is both a cherished and an idealized liberty, but it cannot remain oblivious to the direct and harmful effects that such involuntary exposure to certain words and images can cause.

*S*NYDER V. PHELPS remains, for the time being, the quintessential example of how little regard the legal system has for the emotional pain of victims brutalized by liberties taken under the constitutional cover of free speech. I fear there may be more such examples in our future. In considering the *Snyder* decision, Professor Schauer observed starkly that, "[h]owever much pain the protests had caused the Snyders, . . . the First Amendment would not permit a restriction on the speakers who caused it, especially where the pain was caused in the process of engaging in 'public discourse' on matters of 'public import.' . . . [T]he First Amendment protects even personally harmful speech . . . [and] require[s] victims to endure such harm."[307]

The *Snyder* opinion, to some extent, recalls an earlier decision before the Supreme Court—one that provided endless amusement to the broader culture. In 1983, during the rise of the Moral Majority led by the Reverend Jerry Falwell, *Hustler* magazine published a parody of an advertisement that implied that Reverend

Falwell had lost his virginity by having had sexual relations with his mother in an outhouse. Falwell brought suit, alleging that the parody was libelous, invaded his privacy, and also constituted an intentional infliction of emotional distress. At the federal district court level, Falwell prevailed on the libel and emotional distress claims and was awarded damages in the amount of $150,000. A federal appeals court for the Fourth Circuit affirmed. The Supreme Court rejected both the emotional distress and libel claims. As for libel, given that Falwell was a public figure, the legal standard under *New York Times v. Sullivan* made such a claim more difficult to prove. But more crucially, the Court ruled that parody is protected speech under the First Amendment.[308]

The fact that Falwell never committed an act of incest with his mother, making the ad patently false and therefore libelous, meant little to the unanimous Court. Similarly, the Court had very little interest in the emotional distress claim, especially since it had already ruled that *Hustler*'s First Amendment protections were paramount. The Constitution required Falwell to manage his emotional distress, which was subordinated to the free speech rights of a pornographic magazine. One can surely imagine how such a depraved portrayal in a national magazine could emotionally injure a religious man. No matter. *Hustler* magazine had the superior right. The lower court's jury verdict awarding Falwell damages for the intentional infliction of emotional distress was overturned, as it was in *Snyder v. Phelps*.

I am not comparing the emotional injuries of the two plaintiffs. A parody advertisement in a magazine such as *Hustler* is distinguishable from the disruption of a military funeral. Falwell was a public figure, after all, and even if he had suffered emotional distress from *Hustler*'s parody, the magazine had a First Amendment right to publish the ad—absurd and insulting though it was. The Snyders were not public figures; they were just a grieving family. What these two cases demonstrate, however, is that the Supreme Court will seemingly always protect speech, regardless of how provocative or painful it might be, over the tortious injury suffered by the plaintiff.

Similarly, in *Cohen v. California*, a Vietnam protestor wearing a jacket emblazoned with the message "Fuck the Draft" as he walked through the corridors of a state courthouse was convicted of disturbing the peace. The Supreme Court overturned the conviction and ruled that the jacket was protected political speech and not conduct, however much the words may have offended the sensibilities of those present at the courthouse.[309] But the mere fact that the message was political in nature does not mean that no other considerations should apply. After all, *Brandenburg v. Ohio*, decided after *Chaplinsky* in 1969, stands for the proposition that a speaker cannot engage in the "incitement of imminent lawless action" and expect to rely on First Amendment safeguards even though a political message of some sort is contained in his or her act of incitement.[310] *Brandenburg* outlaws the speech regardless.[311] *Cohen* is a tougher case from a harm-based perspective. "Fuck the Draft" is clearly political, albeit profane. But Cohen did not wear the jacket with any particular, singular target in mind. The courthouse on that day could have been filled with dissidents opposed to the Vietnam War. They would have cheered him on. Even if some disapproved of America's policies in Vietnam, they could have simply walked away rather than allowed the message to evolve into an emotional disturbance. Not true, of course, in the matters of Falwell and Snyder, who were clearly the targets of the messages directed at them, and they were not free to leave or avoid the assault.

The intentional infliction of emotional distress is not only a lowly, disfavored tort, it also generates little sympathy in First Amendment jurisprudence—even though emotional harm caused by speech has become fundamentally easier to prove. There are many harm-based, consequentialist approaches to free speech. After all, speech can cause tangible emotional or physical harm to the intended target. It can threaten and intimidate a vulnerable audience. It can cause the kind of devastating humiliation that degrades if not obliterates citizenship, reducing the targets to social outcasts too broken to rejoin the community and engage in the democratic experience. Each of these should warrant further scrutiny into the limits of the First Amendment. Free speech that is responsible for leaving behind such human misery has perhaps outworn its welcome and gone too far in abusing its constitutional privilege. If the harm is tangible, the fact that it arises from another's speech does not make it beyond the scope of government regulation. Burning a flag is symbolic speech with strong political overtones, although a Supreme Court Chief Justice, dissenting in the flag-burning case, believed that such a violent gesture "is the equivalent of an inarticulate grunt or roar that, it seems fair to say, is most likely to be indulged in not to express any particular idea, but to antagonize others."[312]

Regardless of how one feels about the symbolic act of such political dissent, it is hard to argue that burning the same flag in front of a family that lost a loved one who died defending that flag is the same. Such expressive conduct is an act of violence that a decent society would not countenance out of some misguidedly romantic attachment to First Amendment convictions. Free speech is both a cherished and an idealized liberty, but we cannot remain oblivious to the direct and harmful effects that such involuntary exposure to certain words and images can cause. The same analysis should be true for marching Nazis, cross-burning Klansmen, Muslim-bashing white supremacists, and homophobes who enjoy disrupting the sanctity of family funerals.

Yet, courts are still unpersuaded that speech which inflicts emotional harm is incompatible with civil society. All of these seminal post-1960s free-speech cases, however, preceded the development of neuroscience that now unequivocally establishes an empirical link between assaultive speech and bodily and psychological damage. Emotional harm continues to be minimized and trivialized, and the Supreme Court continues to resist applying the plain language of

Justice Murphy in *Chaplinsky* more liberally—that there, indeed, are some words "which by their very utterance inflict injury."

It remains true, nonetheless, that listeners assume the risk for a speaker's provocative language. As Professor Arkes noted, "It is now apparently more reasonable to ask the auditors to turn away or to make some effort to avoid the offensive speech—something that is not always easy to do in public streets or buildings—rather than to ask the speaker to accept some restraints on his behavior in public."[313] *Chaplinsky* placed the speaker on notice not to speak ill-advisedly because he or she may hit upon a word or word combination that inflicts injury. *Cohen* shifted the burden onto the listener to always be on alert and to avert one's gaze or walk away if they should find themselves staring at a jean jacket sporting a profane patch.[314] Speech deemed presumptively political, as it was in *Cohen*, will seemingly always override a state law claim in civil tort for emotional distress.

It does not have to be this way. In *Chaplinsky*, words, by their very utterance, can inflict injury and, in such circumstances, stand nakedly without First Amendment safeguards—even without having to show that a breach of the peace had also occurred. In *Cohen*, it is the listener who is being told to "effectively avoid further bombardment of their sensibilities simply by averting their eyes."[315] Schauer reminds the *Cohen* Court, however, that "one cannot avert one's eyes until one's eyes have seen what one would want to avert them from."[316]

The famous phrase Justice John Marshall Harlan II wrote for the majority in *Cohen*, that "one man's vulgarity is another's lyric,"[317] is certainly convincing. It is invoked to assert the impossibility of knowing what configuration of words will cause certain offense in an individual. Searching for the idiosyncrasy of emotional hurt is a fool's errand, we are told. Insults are subjective; feelings are ephemeral. But it is simply not true, as Harlan also wrote, that "governmental officials cannot make principled distinctions" in all areas involving harmful speech.[318]

Justice Harlan denied that there was any way to standardize speech because it depended entirely on the subjective feelings of the people who hear it. Yet, there is a marked difference between the generalized offense one may experience after reading "Fuck the Draft," and being invaded, personally, by Nazis on the village green or having homophobes protesting at your son's funeral. The first is merely a vulgarity addressed to no one in particular, a split-second sighting of something that will likely be ignored or soon forgotten.

"Fuck the Draft" does not single anyone out personally. It does not threaten or intimidate an individual. The other examples are verbal assaults that are personal in nature. They might lead to an immediate, retaliatory, and violent response. And they are likely to result in harm to the intended target. Verbal assaults are delivered to lay claim to the mental state of their victims. If there is a political message to be teased out of the malice, it is merely incidental to its intended purpose. Schauer astutely wrote that, "[t]he word 'offense' is rarely used by the target. The word is typically used by others to downplay the magnitude of what the targets are more likely to describe as 'harm.'"[319]

At least the *Snyder* case generated the kind of public reaction that might have led, for the time being, to a political solution. Since *Snyder v. Phelps* was decided, Congress enacted a measure in 2006 that would make it a crime to willfully disturb "the peace and good order" of a funeral held at a national cemetery for a period of one hour both before and after the burial.[320] Acting on Congress' lead, state legislatures have taken matters into their own hands by passing laws that create protest-free zones at funerals, whereby protesters must maintain a distance of 1,000 feet for one hour both before and after funerals. (The federal law requires only 150 feet.) The supreme courts of at least three states—Nebraska, Missouri, and Minnesota—have upheld these laws. The Iowa legislature voted one hundred to zero to adopt such a measure. "You do not have a constitutional right to infringe on the constitutional rights of the families who are laying fallen loved ones to rest," State Representative Bobby Kaufmann said. One suspects the "constitutional rights" of grieving families, to which Representative Kaufmann is referring, is a penumbral right to privacy, because the right to grieve is not among the Bill of Rights.[321]

# 33

# WHEN NAZIS IN THE UNITED STATES WERE SHOWN THE RESPECT THEY SURELY DID NOT DESERVE

Wearing hoods, marching in goosestep, and carrying tiki torches like the protestors in Charlottesville in August 2017 are not the actions of sincere debaters in possession of ideas. They are, instead, the fully realized tactics of would-be criminals seeking to evoke fear in otherwise vulnerable citizens.

JUST THIRTY-TWO YEARS after the liberation of Auschwitz, in 1977, neo-Nazis obtained permits to march on the Village of Skokie, Illinois, with its disproportionate number of Holocaust survivors as residents. People who had barely escaped the crematoria discovered a new brand of Nazis wishing to torment them—across an ocean—in Illinois. The neo-Nazis had no intention of engaging in a civilized debate in the public square. Instead, they handed out advance leaflets with the words: "WE ARE COMING!" They were targeting the Holocaust survivors, reminding them that they should not get too comfortable in the Midwest. The master race was apparently portable. A thug can, seemingly, shout "Heil Hitler!" anywhere. They had a knack for instilling fear. Other leaflets read: "Where one finds the most Jews, there one will find the most Jew haters." The neo-Nazis produced drawings of swastikas with hands outstretched, choking a stereotypical Jew.

So much for the marketplace of ideas.

The expected outcome did not disappoint. The buildup to a march that, in the end, would never even take place because it had already achieved its purpose, reinvigorating in the minds of Skokie's Holocaust survivors the psychological trauma of past persecution. One survivor, Erna Gans, said in 1978, "Yes, it did terrorize us. It brought back many hours of anguish. Something we thought we left behind. . . . This realization brought back a terror. . . . [H]ere we are again, in the same position. . . . [F]or some it was very realistic—it is here today and I am going to kill them."[322] The Corporation Counsel for Skokie, Harvey Schwartz, interviewed a year after the case, recalled the state of mind of the survivors on the day when the neo-Nazis came closest to actually entering the Village: "[T]hey were changed people: fanatical, irrational, frightened, angry. No one could possibly appeal to them with any reasonable argument. . . . They were possessed, some of them. It was as if they had repressed something for twenty years that was now loose. It was very disturbing. *At this point I realized that the First Amendment theory grossly underestimated the impact on these people.* This was not the 'exchange of ideas'; it was literally an *assault.* . . . People there on that Saturday were injured, damaged—I dare say even physically."[323]

The Village filed a claim for the intentional infliction of emotional distress. None of the various opinions that led up to *Collin v. Smith*, the captioned case, paid much attention, however. The Seventh Circuit noted this "'new tort' of intentional infliction of severe emotional distress," but went on to say that, even if specific individuals were to bring such an action, the court speculated, as if foreshadowing *Snyder v. Phelps*, that it might be barred under the First Amendment.[324] Not unlike *Cohen v. California*, the Holocaust survivors were dismissively informed that they always had the option to avert their eyes by "simply avoid[ing] the Village Hall for thirty minutes on a Sunday afternoon."[325] The court recognized with "certainty" that the "historical associations [the neo-Nazis] would bring with them to Skokie, many people would find their demonstration extremely mentally and emotionally disturbing."[326] But it went on to note that "[t]he problem with engrafting an exception on the First Amendment for such situations is that they are indistinguishable in principle from speech that 'invite[s] dispute . . . induces a condition of unrest, creates dissatisfaction with conditions as they are, or even stirs people to anger.' Yet these are among the 'high purposes of the First Amendment.'"[327]

That conclusion is simply and demonstrably wrong. It is not the same at all. Skokie was a case involving "targeted intimidation posing as free speech."[328] Acts of intimidation like the conduct of the neo-Nazis in Skokie, the Westboro Baptist Church in *Snyder v. Phelps*, the burning of crosses in front of African-Americans, such as in *Virginia v. Black*, and the burning of flags before families who have lost relatives during wartime serving their country have nothing at all to do with symbolic speech and have everything to do with unadulterated, unmerciful violence. Wearing hoods, marching in goosestep, and carrying tiki torches like the protestors in Charlottesville in August 2017 are not the actions of sincere debaters in possession of ideas. They are, instead, the fully realized tactics of would-be criminals seeking to evoke fear in otherwise vulnerable citizens.

Is there any wonder that the general public has lost faith in its public institutions—and especially the legal system—when courts cannot seem to make a sensible distinction between someone who wishes to raise ideas and argue points for the public good and another who wants nothing more than to terrorize Holocaust survivors, African-Americans, homosexuals, and even an innocent family who merely wants an uninterrupted moment to bury their son? Stanley Fish was correct when he wrote, "It is hard when reading these opinions not to feel that the entire enterprise has gone off the rails and that you are in the hands either of charlatans or idiots."[329]

Some courts, however, are capable of getting it right. In the early 1980s in Galveston Bay, Texas, the KKK decided that recently resettled Vietnamese fishermen were unwelcome and would make for a nice target to intimidate. Wearing military regalia and brandishing weapons, the Klan exercised their First Amendment rights by burning in effigy a Vietnamese, offering a message that the Vietnamese were not then, nor would ever be, Texans. Try to tease out the content, much less ideas, in that manner of expression.

The Vietnamese brought suit in federal district court, seeking injunctive relief and asserted violations of several civil rights statutes, along with claims of intimidation and the infliction of emotional distress and tortious interference with contract. They prevailed on the two claims other than the one for emotional distress, largely because the plaintiffs were unable to show an accompanying intentional tort with a physical dimension, such as trespass or assault. In 1981, that is how emotional distress claims were routinely decided. Without a more tangible harm, the emotional distress claim could not stand alone. But the court did rule that, through their actions, the KKK targeted the Vietnamese community of Galveston and therefore had engaged in conduct, and not speech. The burning of a Vietnamese in effigy was ruled to be non-speech.[330] The court did not, however, examine whether the provocative actions of the KKK were, under *Chaplinsky*, tantamount to "fighting words," where no First Amendment protection would apply.

# 34.

# EMOTIONAL DISTRESS CLAIMS
# CAUSED BY SPEECH THAT
# PREVAILED

The outrageousness of these remarks surely should satisfy
the elements of an intentional infliction of emotional distress.
These are not unfortunate misunderstandings or momentary
slips of the tongue taken out of context.

*T*HE VIETNAMESE CASE from Galveston involved injunctive
relief on behalf of an entire community of victimized citizens. While the court did not grant the claim for emotional
distress, such civil tort actions have found success in other courtrooms. In *Alcorn v. Anbro Engineering, Inc.*, an action in California in
1970, an African-American employee instructed a colleague not to
drive a truck to a job site because that employee was not a union
member. Once the supervisor learned of the encounter, he
shouted, "You goddam 'niggers' are not going to tell me about the
rules. I don't want any 'niggers' working for me. I am getting rid
of all the 'niggers'; go pick up and deliver that 8-ton roller to the
other job site and get your paycheck; you're fired."[331]

The court awarded the plaintiff damages for the intentional infliction of emotional distress, finding that the emotional encounter,
and the subsequent sustained shock, left him unable to work. Specifically, the court ruled that the "defendant's conduct was *extreme
and outrageous*, having a *severe and traumatic* effect upon plaintiff's

*emotional tranquility*. Intentionally *humiliated* the plaintiff, insulted his race . . . all without just cause or provocation. Although it may be that mere insulting language, without more, ordinarily would not constitute extreme outrage, the aggravated circumstances alleged by the plaintiff seem sufficient to uphold his complaint."[332]

*Gomez v. Hug* is another case where a court in 1982 awarded the plaintiff employee damages for the intentional infliction of emotional distress. The cause of his injury was a dressing-down from his employer, which included the following exchange: "You are a fucking spic. . . . A fucking Mexican greaser like you, that is all you are. You are nothing but a fucking Mexican greaser, nothing but a pile of shit. Are you going to do something, you coward, you greaser, you fucking spic? What are you going to do? Don't stand there like a damn fool because that is all you are is a pile of shit."[333] Similarly, in *Baily v. Binyon* in 1984, the plaintiff's employer called him a "nigger" several times and then said, "All you niggers are alike." The plaintiff apparently responded to his employer by asserting that he wanted to be treated like a human being and did not appreciate how he was being spoken to. His employer responded with, "You're not a human being, you're a nigger."[334]

Maybe the French have it right. Such encounters with vicious employers must be rejected as crossing the line on human dignity.

The "outrageousness" of these remarks surely should satisfy the elements of a claim for the intentional infliction of emotional distress. These are not unfortunate misunderstandings or momentary slips of the tongue taken out of context. Anyone and everyone should be able to see not only that free speech liberties cannot possibly safeguard such extreme deviations from ordinary civility, but also that anyone on the receiving end of such verbal violence would understandably be left emotionally impaired. If we should not accept it at work, then it should be impermissible in the public square, as well. An act of violence, disguised as a political message, cannot run for cover under the First Amendment.

Sticks and stones is a rhyme without reason. Such severe name-calling should be recognized as beyond the pale, as a matter of law. What these men endured on the job was far worse than a schoolyard taunt. And it does not require a brain scan to authenticate. These were full-blown character assassinations, a kind of withering annihilation. These two state courts should be commended for compensating these plaintiffs for the emotional distress they endured.

In a wrongful termination action in Washington, a worker was subjected to humiliation, embarrassment, racial jokes, and slurs that were delivered on the job site and during working hours. The Supreme Court of Washington found in 1977 that the plaintiff had sustained injury in the form of the intentional infliction of emotional distress.[335] The court went on to explain the evolution of these emotional distress claims, with a special recognition of the harm done to vulnerable minorities. "As we are a nation of immigrants, . . . racial epithets which were once part of the common usage may not now be looked upon as 'mere insulting language.' Changing sensitivity in society alters the acceptability of former terms."[336]

Law professor Cass Sunstein argued that racist speech is antithetical to the promises of the Thirteenth, Fourteenth, and Fifteenth Amendments. In abolishing slavery, and in guaranteeing equality before the law, the Constitution has essentially eliminated second-class citizenship. What would be the point of introducing these amendments into the constitutional mix if racist speech was protected under the First Amendment? To allow for racist speech is tantamount to accepting that not all Americans are to be treated equally as citizens. The First Amendment cannot be asserted in ways that devalue the citizenship and rights also owed to others under the Constitution.[337]

In light of the special sensitivity that must be afforded under the law given this nation's dreadful, racist past, and with the ultimate sin of once permitting the ownership of slaves, Sunstein accounts for the unique harm that arises from racist speech. He wrote, "No one should deny that distinctive harms are produced by racist speech, especially when it is directed against members of minority groups. It is only obtuseness—a failure of perception or emphatic identification—that would enable someone to say that the word 'fascist' or 'pig' or even 'honky' produces the same feelings as the word 'nigger.'"[338]

When it comes to the First Amendment, the question should always be the same: Is the purpose of the speech intended to foster an idea, appeal to reason, and inform the public, or is it to threaten others, incite violence, and cause emotional trauma? The *Chaplinsky* Court introduced not just categories of proscribed speech that the First Amendment would not shield, but also the concept that some words, uttered in a particular way to a particular audience, inflict injury simply by saying them. It was a *per se* rule with a noble purpose. We need to start reclaiming the wisdom of Justice Murphy's vision of a gentler, bigger-hearted, less-rambunctious First Amendment. And we also have to empower victims of indignity and psychological harm, through private civil tort actions, to defend themselves—to become their own public prosecutors and private attorneys general—especially in situations where local governments are too timid to enter into the morass of the First Amendment and courts are jurisprudentially captive to an absolutist free speech agenda. And we need courts to take the intentional infliction of emotional distress seriously, free from the impediments of free speech and the accompanying proof of physical harm.

Today there is hypersensitivity about the Second Amendment. No one (we hope even card-carrying members of the NRA) seriously doubts the consequences of gun violence—surely not after the death toll continues to mount from mass shootings in Parkland, Las Vegas, Orlando, Newtown, Dayton, Pittsburgh, Columbine, El Paso, and elsewhere—even if there is disagreement about what should be done about it, and even if some righteously believe that the Framers wanted all Americans to become gun owners. Those who argue for change in the political culture of gun rights, expressed avidly in yet another national outcry for sensible gun regulatory reform, are treated with the same sneering contempt by the gun lobby as those who, by their insistence on hate speech legislation, embitter and ignite the self-righteous fury of First Amendment absolutists. Absolutists everywhere are out in full force on behalf of their respective cherished constitutional beliefs. Their inflexibility has created ideological gridlock with no solution in sight.

Just think about that.

# 35

# WHEN CARTOONS ARE NOT FUNNY BUT SHOULD STILL CONSTITUTE PERMISSIBLE SPEECH

Poking fun at a religion, even calling it ridiculous, is an altogether different message from defaming its followers or threatening them with harm.

*I* VERY MUCH HESITATED to write a book that would be perceived as critical of the First Amendment. World events, in fact, caused me to set the book aside. Free speech has been very much on everyone's mind, what with political correctness, identity politics, intersectionality, trigger warnings, microaggressions, hate speech codes, and the global controversy associated with the Danish cartoons. Everyone seems to be fearful of what they are—and are not—permitted to say. How can free speech actually exist amid such a battery of cultural, religious, social, morally self-imposed, and often legally enforced restrictions?

The hope of clearing up some of the confusion and clarifying my own position on free speech seemed like a risky undertaking. This book has been arguing for a kinder, gentler, more respectful First Amendment—a vision of free speech that, in some respects, would more resemble the European model. I am not in favor of placing restrictions on robust political debate. Ideas should never be burdened by sensitivity protocols. Ideas are expected to agitate and cause uneasy feelings. This is generally true with political speech and is what the American Founding Fathers had in mind when they established a liberty centered around speech. To qualify for the full complement of free speech safeguards, however, it should involve a sincere attempt to say something meaningful about the politics of the day. Appealing solely to emotion with words and actions intended to threaten violence and cause harm are not First Amendment priorities.

Here is what the First Amendment should never be called upon to protect: groups of nativists shouting, "Muslims Go Home"; neo-Nazis marching through a hamlet where Holocaust survivors have sought to settle in peace; burning crosses on the lawns of African-Americans; showing up to a military funeral with placards intended to make one's hatred of homosexuals plainly known while destroying a moment of mourning. None of these exercises in expression involve a debate about ideas. They are, in fact, neither ideas nor debates. They are orgies of hate that amount to non-speech. And for these patently obvious reasons, they should not be the concern of the First Amendment.

Let's stop pretending that we cannot tell the difference.

And yet, confusion abounds. Perhaps the best example of it, the one that leaves people wondering whether free speech has either gone too far or not far enough, are the events that surrounded the various instances in which the Prophet Muhammad was caricatured in Western newspapers. Muslims complain that any visual representation of the Prophet is blasphemy. Conservatives tend to regard the cartoons as free expression. Some liberals believe the cartoons to be racist.

If drawn in the United States, would they fall within the protections of the First Amendment, despite the fact that some people consider them to be sinister representations that induce incitement and hate?

In Europe, laws that were designed to protect vulnerable minorities were being used to defend fundamentalist religious practices. A political dilemma presented itself: The European Union could not capitulate to this religious edict from a minority population while, at the same time, maintaining and upholding Western principles of free speech.

The Danish cartoons forced the European continent to confront whether it actually respected free speech after all. These liberal democracies had no tolerance for racism. Neo-Nazis were not welcome either. Were cartoonists in the same category? Perhaps freedom of expression was ultimately irreconcilable with the competing demands of pluralism and multiculturalism. And what if Muslims, sharing their newfound Western freedom with people from other nations and cultures, were rejecting some of the freedoms that their adopted homelands were offering? How to accommodate them without applying double standards and separate rules? By 2008, the European Union had apparently decided to side with the sensitivities and mandates of its minority Muslim population. Suddenly, the EU implemented religious hate speech laws that prohibited "religious insult[s]," sought to "preserve social peace and public order," and spoke of "increasing sensitivities" toward "certain individuals" who "reacted violently to criticism of their religion."[339]

Europe's once proud open societies were looking a bit shuttered from all that shuddering. The operating manual for freedom of speech soon changed all throughout the Netherlands, Denmark, Italy, Austria, and Germany. Criminal investigations were opened against novelists, editors, legislators, philosophers, filmmakers, and, of course, cartoonists, followed by convictions for engaging in anti-Islamic speech. Islam simply would not tolerate any criticism of its religious tenets on women's rights, child marriages, punishments for homosexuality, and animal cruelty. And those who spoke out in favor of immigration limits against Muslims were prosecuted, too.

In the United Kingdom, a public-television segment on radical Muslim clerics became the subject of a police investigation that accused the network of engaging in hate speech. A Christian church located in a newly populated Muslim neighborhood found itself convicted on a charge of public disorder for singing hymns on Sunday morning. In 2009, a husband and wife who owned a hotel were hauled into court after one of their guests, a Muslim woman, overheard their breakfast conversation, which apparently included a pejorative remark, and walked away insulted. In Finland, a city council member in Helsinki was convicted for blog entries that disparaged Mohammad's marital history. In Austria, a woman was convicted of defaming the Prophet after discussing some of her own work experiences in Iran and Libya. Similarly, in Austria, a woman was found guilty of "disparaging religious doctrine" when she suggested that Muhammad might have been a pedophile given the fact that he consummated his marriage to a nine-year-old girl.

Under French law, insulting people based on their religion is a crime punishable with six-months' jail time and a $22,500 fine. Famed French movie actress and animal rights activist Brigitte Bardot has been convicted on numerous occasions for defaming and provoking hatred against Muslims—often with the pretext of criticizing their food-slaughtering practices, but the charges always implicated the incitement in her rhetoric: "They will slit the throats of . . . our sheep, they will slit our throats one day and we will have earned it."[340]

Countries that criminalize hate speech, such as Germany, the Netherlands, the United Kingdom, Sweden, and Canada, have unwittingly let it be known that resorting to violence is a proper and expected way to respond to words and images that offend.

In the United States, censorship masquerading as free speech sensitivity was on full display at the PEN Literary Gala—the very year after the murders at *Charlie Hebdo*. The PEN Center decided to honor the slain cartoonists with its Freedom of Expression Courage Award. Most unexpectedly, six literary hosts of the evening declined to attend—as an act of protest against the recipients. PEN is an international organization devoted to the freedom of writers to report upon and represent the world in which they live—either through journalism or art. The purpose behind the award was to honor the very thing that cost the lives of the nine cartoonists who had been gunned down for expressing an idea and criticizing a religion's truth.

The writers who decided to skip the annual PEN Literary Gala in protest saw something else: a French newspaper that had gone too far. The cartoons that appeared in *Charlie Hebdo* were, in their opinion, insulting and threatening to Muslims. The images offended and targeted Muslims—a community already marginalized, underrepresented in power, and overrepresented in prison. Moreover, Muslims are stigmatized by laws that prohibit their religious displays, such as banning headscarves and face-covering veils in both schools and public places. Salman Rushdie—who after all knows a little something about being threatened by those offended by his writing—appalled by the fact that these writers would seemingly side with those who, ultimately, do not believe in freedom of expression at all, mused that they were "six authors in search of character."[341]

Many reading this book might think that I, too, would support this campaign against freedom of speech, with the PEN Literary Gala serving as the perfect occasion to change the conversation about free speech. The United States nearly always protects the speaker over the feelings of the listener. How appropriate for some esteemed members of PEN to take the lead in defense of marginalized Muslims. Here we have gutsy writers taking a righteous stand against their own interests. The Supreme Court would be dumbfounded by the gesture.

And so am I. The controversy over the cartoons illustrates precisely what I am *not* proposing. Any action taken against the cartoonists, whether under the law or through violent means, is censorship—pure and simple. Hurt feelings do not entitle the murder of those who presumably caused the offense. *Charlie Hebdo* was making a statement through satire about some of the tenets of

Islam. The way to respond, in hopes of either rebutting or reaching a common understanding, is not by resorting to murder. One who asks for greater sensitivity cannot expect to rely on violence to win over hearts and minds. In the United States, the cartoons would be protected First Amendment expression, regardless of the insult some Muslims might feel. The cartoons address ideas that invite debate or discussion, not death.

A basic tenet of one's religion cannot be that it will not tolerate any insult or offense from either its disciples or nonbelievers. No religion, political ideology, or set of beliefs or ideas can hold the world hostage with commandments everyone must follow. But that is seemingly what devout Muslims are demanding of the world: Accept our beliefs as the word of our God, or we will bring violence or unreasonable special pleadings that overturn the liberal premises of your open societies.

Taking offense—whether it be from its inside reformers or outside critics—is something a religion must tolerate under principles of free speech. This is particularly true in the case of Islam, which, unlike Hinduism, Christianity, Judaism, and the other world religions, serves as a political movement with some of its most devout followers of Muhammad seeking to impose a caliphate around the world. With such political aspirations, Islam cannot be exempt from political criticism.

Free speech is free not just for the speaker; it creates a wider freedom from which we all benefit. Its purpose is to allow for the free flow of ideas. Mocking the Prophet of Islam or making him look foolish, however, does not attack Muslims personally or threaten them as a people. Nor does it malign Muslims, make them targets, or subject them to opprobrium. And while it might insult some, it does not cause harm to anyone.

What that fateful issue of *Charlie Hebdo* achieved—and what the Danish cartoons represented before them—was to question the beliefs of Islam in a satirical manner. Poking fun at a religion, even calling it ridiculous, is an altogether different message from defaming its followers or threatening them with harm. The cartoons did not incite violence—either imminent or sometime in the future. The only violence that occurred was the reaction from incensed Muslims.

People can mock Ash Wednesday or the eating of matzah on Passover as much as they wish. In the Bible Belt there are reports of billboards with the image of Jesus recommending a local dealership for those in the market for a new truck. Jesus also makes cameo appearances in country music songs.

Jews are comfortable with jokes about Moses, one of their prophets, dropping the Ten Commandments as if he slipped on a banana peel. Buddha's desperate failure to stick with a diet has made the rounds of comedy circuits for as long as stand-ups have delivered jokes on the pieties of the divine.

The *Book of Mormon*, which is still running on Broadway and which captured nine Tony Awards in 2011, including one for Best Musical, could not possibly have an equal anywhere in its hilarious takedown of a world religion. The creation myth of Mormonism and the Church of Jesus Christ of Latter-day Saints is skewered to scandalous effect. The history of its founding and the tenets of its belief are savaged mercilessly. And yet, nowhere—not on Broadway, not on any of the national tours, or the productions mounted in London's West End, or in Oslo, Stockholm, Melbourne, or Copenhagen—are angry Mormons standing outside theaters, pumping their fists and shouting, "Death to Broadway!" or "Death to *South Park*!" No one in Utah has issued the Mormon equivalent of a *fatwa* against Trey Parker and Matt Stone, the musical's creators (who also write and produce *South Park*). Indeed, when the play first opened, the Church of Jesus Christ of Latter-day Saints took out a full-page ad in the *Playbill* program, which read: "You've seen the play. Now come to one of our churches and see the difference."[342]

All this commotion over cartoons is confusing liberals in Western democracies about the true meaning of free speech. Absolutists are appalled that free speech is being compromised out of fear of offending a religion. Progressives believe that if Muslims are insulted, then that is reason enough to condemn cartoonists as racists. Curiously, the issue is rarely framed in terms of protecting Muslims from violence—the usual way in which restrictions on speech are justified.

Jeremy Waldron has noted the "basic distinction between an attack on a body of beliefs and an attack on the basic social standing and the reputation of a group. . . . In every democratic society, we distinguish between the respect accorded to a citizen and the disagreement we might have concerning his or her social and political convictions."[343]

A critique of an ideology, even in the form of an insult, is not the same as a threat made against its adherents. Ideas, whether they be religious beliefs, political ideologies, economic theories, social welfare policies, or art and culture, must always be subject to critical review. Shouting, "Muslims are degenerates! They rape and steal! We want them out of our communities!" is unabashed hate speech and should never be tolerated, just as "Mexicans coming over the border are rapists" is also hate speech that should be unlawful. The Nation of Islam's firebrand leader, Louis Farrakhan, gave a controversial sermon in March 2018 during which he preached, "Farrakhan, by God's grace, has pulled the cover off of that Satanic Jew and I'm here to say your time is up, your world is through."[344] This is classic hate speech. Incitement that calls for violence against groups ("your time is up"), references to the "N-word," threats made against homosexuals, or refrains among Palestinians that Jews are descendants of monkeys and pigs are all examples of hate speech. Implicit in civilization is the protection of individuals and groups from assaults. Competing objectives often clash. Sometimes ideas offend. Civilization means that we know the difference between an actual assault and an idea that merely offends.

And when there is an assault that is expressive in nature, it should be treated no differently than a physical battery. Hate speech laws, drafted narrowly so as to present no constitutional impediment, should be relied upon to criminalize weaponized speech. And civil tort actions for emotional distress should be more readily filed and treated with the respect they deserve. It is the job of the juries to decide, both in criminal and civil courts, whether the expressive activity is more than an insult or an offense, and therefore falls outside the protection of the First Amendment.

# 36

# HATE SPEECH IS A HATE CRIME

A hate crime, which might leave less of a hateful signature, is punished without ambivalence—it is treated, undoubtedly, as a crime. . . . Inexplicably, however, hate speech, more violent and impressionable, receives a pass.

*H*ATE SPEECH IS a crime throughout Europe. Canada has its own hate speech law. In Canada, it is a criminal offense to communicate a "statement in any public place [which] incites hatred against any identifiable group where such incitement is likely to lead to a breach of the peace."[345] That language does not sound all that much different from *Chaplinsky*, but for the fact that Canada has an explicit hate speech law, which recognizes that hate in the form of speech is a human rights violation. Canada does not mince words. The United States, by contrast, minces like a sous chef. It will not compromise much on its free speech protections. In a sign of misplaced priorities, to deny someone the right to utter hateful speech in the United States might itself be deemed a human rights violation. Hate speech laws are perceived as un-American.

Yet, the United States does have hate crime statutes. These laws have no necessary relationship to speech and, in fact, are not necessarily triggered by speech. The difference between hate crimes and hate speech codes are significant. The former provides statutorily enforced enhancement penalties for certain crimes animated by hate. An ordinary crime that evidences hate as a motive is punished more severely. A physical assault against an African-American where the "N-word" was uttered during the commission of the act is a perfect example of the interconnectedness between an ordinary crime and a hate crime. The hate crime element justifies an enhanced penalty.

Hate speech, by contrast, is perfectly lawful under the First Amendment. Hate speech is often directed to the public at large in keeping with the public nature of these offenses—the scarring of the public landscape with messages targeting a specific group of people defined by race, religion, ethnicity, and sexual orientation. Hate crimes are more often directed to their intended targets as individuals, and have no ostensible political agenda or message. This may explain why courts are more forgiving of hate speech—because it is easier to attribute a political dimension that often, undeservingly, draws First Amendment protection.

The contradiction is baffling. The presence of hate in the commission of the crime can be used to enhance a criminal penalty, but hate speech is a privileged anomaly of the First Amendment. Hate does not convert free speech into restricted speech. What makes hate speech unassailable, while hate displayed in conjunction with a crime deserves a more severe penalty? The Supreme Court in *Wisconsin v. Mitchell*, in 1993, put a fine point on that distinction by declaring that penalty enhancements for racially motivated crimes do not violate the First Amendment.[346] Under this ruling, a crime motivated by racial animus against, say, an African-American, is punished more harshly than the same crime committed against a white person. It is not the act that is subject to an increased punishment, but rather the wrongdoer's decision to choose a victim who is protected under the hate crime statute—provided he or she makes known the reason why this particular victim was chosen.

Does that not violate the wrongdoer's First Amendment rights? If hate speech is protected without an accompanying crime, why then should the same words lose their First Amendment guarantees all on account of a hate crime—and, at the same time, enhance the underlying penalty? It is one thing to be punished for committing a crime; it is something else entirely for the punishment to be increased simply because words of hatred were spoken during its commission—words that, by themselves, would be regarded as free speech. The Supreme Court justified penalty enhancements for hate crimes by ruling that "although the government can't punish abstract beliefs, it can punish a vast array of depraved motives. . . . [Hate crime statutes do not] prohibit people from expressing their views, nor punish them for doing so."[347]

But they do. A wrongdoer who articulates hatred right before committing a crime is doubly punished for it. Where is the free speech in that? In the case of cross-burnings, the crime of trespass or arson on the victim's property does not result in an enhanced penalty even though the act is hateful and establishes a motive for the crime. It is treated instead as political speech protected under the First Amendment, despite the existence of actionable and simultaneous crimes such as arson and trespass. The *Mitchell* Court inadvertently highlights this inconsistency by noting that hate crimes are more severe than non-bias-motivated crimes because they are "more likely to provoke retaliatory crimes, inflict distinct emotional harm on their victims, and incite community unrest."[348]

But that is exactly what the Supreme Court said about hateful speech in *Chaplinsky, Brandenburg, Virginia v. Black*, and *Beauharnais v. Illinois*, the group libel case.[349] The reason why the First Amendment does not shield the speakers in those cases is because the words are deemed provoking, inciting, intimidating, threatening, and harmful—precisely the reactions that hateful speech tends to elicit and incite. It is what hate itself can do and what hateful speech often does. There is no reason for the First Amendment to protect *hate speech* if *hate crimes* are singled out for special punishment. Hate speech should be treated no differently from a hate crime. The Supreme Court has ruled that hate is acknowledged to be a problem that requires penalty enhancements. When hate mixes with speech, however, then it loses its moral urgency, and not only does it require no penalty enhancement—it requires no penalty at all. In either case, however, the offender was speaking the language of hate. Hate animated the crime and imposed a higher cost on the victim—in damaged dignity, traumatic memory, and broken citizenship. For this it merited an increased punishment for the wrongdoer. Yet, for some reason, hate speech without an underlying crime imposes no cost at all.

Solitary speech becomes the magic prophylactic.

This disparate treatment seems wholly unjustified. We have long acknowledged the pathologies of hate—in any form. There is no principled reason why one manifestation of hate gets elevated to its own enhanced crime while, in another form, hateful speech is treated as the cost of doing business in a liberal democracy—and constitutes no criminal act at all. As columnist Charles Blow has written, "When the debate devolves into invectives born of hate— racist, misogynistic, homophobic or otherwise—it ceases to be healthy or productive and instead dredges up the worst of who we are and, in some cases, remain."[350]

Hate speech is simply not speech. It adds no value or meaning to the public sphere. The prefix of hate tips its hand and tells you everything you need to know about the purported speech. Professor Heyman stated the obvious when he wrote, "Public hate speech is not entitled to constitutional protection because it violates the principles that should govern democratic debate."[351] And without constitutional protection, it is avowedly no better than the hate that justifies the special sanction of a hate crime.

The only logical conclusions one can draw from the Supreme Court's rulings on the First Amendment are that, in the opinion of the many justices who have sat on the bench since the 1960s, hate itself is worth debating, the founders of our freedoms believed that the hatred of other citizens is a debatable subject, and that the hated should be placed in the intolerable position of arguing for their own existence. In one of the seminal cross-burning cases, *R.A.V. v. St. Paul*, decided in 1992, the Court overturned an ordinance that outlawed the kind of "fighting words" that amounted to hate speech. The Court regarded the St. Paul ordinance as essentially viewpoint discrimination—as if the hate of another is a political point of view that must be protected under the First Amendment.[352] Justice Byron White's concurrence was particularly disturbing, leaving the impression that the racial and ethnic animus of the speaker is entitled to more governmental protection than the peace and tranquility of the targeted group. By essentially treating hateful "fighting words" as an appropriate subject for debate, it placed hate speech itself on the same level of importance as political and cultural discourse.[353]

There is obviously great trepidation about legislating hate speech laws itself without an underlying hate crime. Libertarians, of course, mistrust government involvement in any enterprise. Regulating speech leaves them particularly fearful of a censorial Big Brother. Liberals have little faith in government, too, what with memories of anti-immigration and segregation laws, which President Trump has only helped revive and magnify. The government cannot be given an opportunity to stifle debate. Otherwise the actions it takes will be without recourse. That is what hate speech code detractors, who are contemptuous of majority rule, always say.

Jeremy Waldron observed that what these cases have in common are majorities acting against vulnerable minorities. "But hate speech laws," he wrote, "represent almost exactly the opposite: a legislative majority bending over backward to ensure that vulnerable minorities are protected against hatred and discrimination that might otherwise be endemic in society."[354]

A hate crime is, by itself, only a misnomer. Hatred of the actual victim is not necessarily present or essential for the crime to take place and for the enhancement to be warranted. Hate crime statutes serve the purpose of penalizing hateful beliefs, attitudes, and feelings that are prevalent in society and manifested in the choice of the intended target of the crime—and the words uttered, or actions taken, during the commission of the crime. In desecrating a synagogue, the offender does not also have to scream, "Die Jews," for the crime to take place and the enhancement to apply. We do not actually measure or even care how hateful the perpetrators of these crimes actually are.

But hate speech in and of itself is different. Hate speech is always revealing of the hater; the message is always unmistakable and undeniable. A prejudiced person can openly declare his or her bigoted beliefs in the public square without violating any law. Notwithstanding reasonable time, place and manner restrictions, the First Amendment can always be called upon to protect hateful words or conduct—whether in the form of marching neo-Nazis and white supremacists, the burning of crosses, the building of extremist websites, or the writing of books that advance racial hatred. Yet a hate crime, which might leave less of a hateful signature, is punished without ambivalence—it is treated, undoubtedly, as a crime. With this form of hate, government regulation is seemingly unobjectionable. It deserves criminal punishment. Inexplicably, however, hate speech, more violent and impressionable, receives a pass.

The reasons to punish hate crimes are manifold. They differ from other, non-bias-related crimes in the degree of violence that results, the severe harm brought to the victim, and the social blight on the community. Hate crimes are statistically more likely to be committed against persons rather than property and are more likely to be violent in nature—90 percent amount to assaults as compared with 20 percent for ordinary crimes, according to the Uniform Crime Report; 45 percent are aggravated assaults versus 30 percent for ordinary crimes, which means that a weapon was involved in the crime and the degree and extent of injury was substantially greater. The psychological impact of hate crimes is more severe; after five years, there are significantly greater levels of depression, traumatic stress, anxiety, and anger. Socially, the victims of hate crimes try to become less visible and often experience greater physical trauma—indeed, they are three times more likely to require hospitalization.[355]

Law professor Mari Matsuda has argued for many years that victims of hate propaganda experience severe forms of scarring: "physiological symptoms and emotional distress ranging from fear in the gut, rapid pulse rate and difficulty in breathing, nightmares, post-traumatic stress disorder, hypertension, psychosis and suicide."[356] The research and medical data makes no distinction between hate speech and hate crimes. They are equally harmful. Bigotry manifested as speech acts or as criminal acts has lasting physical and psychological consequences. The ethos of European democracy is overly mindful of hate and its scarring of society and the harm it brings to vulnerable individuals and groups. In the United States, our laws address hate crimes through enhanced penalties while hate speech itself is treated as a quaint artifact of the First Amendment—unpunished, its harmful consequences are minimized or outright denied.

The criminality of hate speech already exists in Supreme Court precedents. In *Beauharnais v. Illinois*, ten years after its decision in *Chaplinsky*, the Court upheld the constitutionality of a group libel criminal statute that prohibited the dissemination of written materials that "portrays depravity, criminality, . . . or lack of virtue of a class of citizens, of any race, color, creed, or religion," and that exposes such a group of citizens to "contempt, derision, or obloquy or which is productive of breach of the peace or riots."[357] A white supremacist, Beauharnais, as president of the White Circle League of America, Inc., distributed leaflets that referred to African-Americans as rapists and robbers, among other defamatory statements. The Supreme Court actually, and correctly, referred to the language in the leaflet as "violent." Beauharnais was convicted under the statute, a decision that was affirmed by the Illinois Supreme Court.

The United States Supreme Court noted the long history of racial tension and violence in the Midwest related to the great northern migration of African-Americans in the early part of the twentieth century. One could not find fault with the state legislature's effort to "curb false or malicious defamation of racial and religious groups, made in public places and by means calculated to have a powerful emotional impact on those to whom it was presented." The purpose of Beauharnais' leaflet was to incite violence "in order to deprive others of their equal rights to the exercise of their liberties."[358] Justice Felix Frankfurter, writing for the majority of the Court, recognized how one set of liberties can casually cancel the rights of other citizens in the exercise of their own. Such is not a just outcome in a nation that has equal protection as a foundational principle of its existence.

The Supreme Court adopted the *Chaplinsky* Fighting Words Doctrine, quoting from it extensively—the "utterances" that "are no essential part of any exposition of ideas," with its "slight social value as a step to the truth," and that are clearly "outweighed by the social interest in order and morality"—and combined it with criminal libel law, ruling that utterances that would be subject to criminal sanctions if directed at an individual do not suddenly become lawful once delivered to a group.[359]

*Chaplinsky* and *Beauharnais*, neither of which has ever been overruled, can be read together to furnish the constitutional framework to conclude that verbally provocative assaults—against individuals and groups—are not protected under the First Amendment.

# 37

# THE ALTERNATIVE UNIVERSE OF
# THE COLLEGE CAMPUS

People who watch in horror at what has happened on campus are understandably skeptical about expanding these already crippling sensitivities beyond the academy.

WHAT PASSES FOR hate on a college campus does not resemble what most people believe hate speech to be. This perhaps explains why the public has such trouble appreciating the harm it causes. What they see on campus is an image not of real harm, but rather the trivialization of harm—a species of hate that plays well on the campus green but looks ridiculous to people who peer into the college bubble in astonishment. The only true injury is the self-inflicted one to the reputation of the ivory tower.

All across the country there are variations on hate speech codes and other curtailments on speech that are celebrated on college campuses as essential to the educational mission. Most of these deal with protections against offenses and insults or ideas and images that cause discomfort and upset, all of which seems so out of place given the amount of tuition everyone is paying. What is being censored on campus is largely unfamiliar to people in the trenches of public life who have experienced actual harm. A college campus is a world unto its own—with its own set of rules, representative culture, and vocabulary comprised of words and ideas that, apparently, raise all sorts of destabilizing havoc in a student's life.

The public is growing more accustomed to hearing anecdotes from academia, with its "microaggressions," "trigger warnings," "safe spaces," and fragile student bodies attached to, apparently, even more brittle brains. These are all new terms of art that describe a sinister form of victimization on campus—a shared misery of verbal afflictions from within the academy that require a much more delicate handling of speech. *Caveat emptor* has left the Latin lab and now pervades the entire collegiate experience. Institutions of higher learning have become places where the free exchange of ideas is no longer welcome because students are not emotionally rugged enough to hear them. And students, often encouraged by faculty, are not silent about their weakened immune systems. Speakers invited to campus with views out of lockstep with a more progressive agenda are summarily disinvited. Speakers who slip by campus censors are shouted down. Books are removed from syllabi or are given un-kosher warning certifications, all on account of passages, words, or opinions that the "intersectional" thought police have deemed too traumatizing, or personally insulting, for students to read. Intellectual thought and the imperatives of art are being sacrificed to some paternalistic notion that students are better off living in sanitized echo chambers than in more grating but challenging environments.

College was once regarded as the gateway to adulthood. Now, it seems, colleges have become the enablers of arrested development and the infantilizing of an entire generation of prickly Peter Pans.

Greg Lukianoff, the president and CEO of FIRE, and Jonathan Haidt, a social psychologist, have written eloquently and critically about this phenomenon. Their main thesis is that, like many righteous causes that lose their way, here, too, the good intentions of seeking to protect students from ideas that might arouse but also upset them is disastrous for both the state of education and the overall mental health of the student. The former president of the ACLU and now law professor Nadine Strossen argues that "current campus censorship threatens even more speech than the invalidated 'hate speech' codes of the past. . . . [T]oday's capacious understanding of 'hate speech' is often understood as encompassing the expression of any idea that some students consider objectionable."[360]

This is how bad things have gotten and why there is such hand-wringing and head-scratching about restrictions on speech. America's sense of humor on its college campuses has been hijacked by "intersectional" censors wagging fingers at every conceivable faux pas. Affection verboten. Stereotypes unmentionable. Analogies are anathema. Proportion is gone. Harmless ribbing is treated like grand theft ego. No one can seemingly tell the difference between a marching Nazi with murder on his mind and a comedian telling a joke about Asians possessing superior math skills.

Feelings are that raw.

Tenured professors live in fear of unwittingly saying the wrong thing during a lecture, which in this era could devolve into a Title IX action. In 2015, at the ten campuses of the University of California, the deans and department chairs were presented with examples of "microaggressions," defined as indirect, subtle, and unintentional discriminatory statements directed at marginalized groups, which were to be strictly avoided in classroom discussions. Two of the worst offenders: "America is the land of opportunity" and "I believe the most qualified person should get the job." Where is the aggression in that? It is not micro; it is downright invisible! Librarians from Simmons College have graciously done the legwork and created an Anti-Oppression Guide, which outlines a list of verbally hostile, derogatorily negative slights routinely committed against Muslims, which now include such benign phrases as: "God Bless You" and "Merry Christmas." According to the Guide, these phrases would impart to a Muslim a perceived dominance of Christianity over Islam.[361]

The *macro*aggression, like genocides, is all but forgotten in this new subculture of finding fault with every magnified slight. The micro is the new macro, and the possibility of overreaction is given no quarter. So fragile are these students that their entire collegiate experience is suddenly being confined to one single "safe space"—a rarefied prophylactic that does not exist in the real world and is as intellectually dishonest as it is suffocating.

At Tufts, a conservative newspaper was singled out for committing "harassment" simply for *quoting accurately* from the Koran and for publishing facts about the lives of women in Saudi Arabia. Lukianoff humorously observed that Tufts may have set a precedent for "find[ing] someone guilty of harassment for stating verifiable facts directed at no one in particular."[362]

Lukianoff and Haidt write that colleges have created an atmosphere where students believe they have a right not to be offended. Worse still, "[a] claim that someone's words are 'offensive' is not just an expression of one's own subjective feelings of being offended. It is, rather, a public charge that the speaker has done something objectively wrong. It is a demand that the speaker apologize or be punished."[363]

In a December 2014 report produced by FIRE, more than 55 percent of the 437 colleges and universities in the United States maintain speech codes that infringe upon the free speech rights of students.[364] When challenged in court, however, each one was ruled to be unconstitutional.[365]

Anyone observing from beyond the ivy-covered walls would assume that the First Amendment no longer applies in university life. Universities are now becoming the marketplaces of the least offensive ideas. People who watch in dismay at what has happened on campus are understandably skeptical about expanding these already crippling sensitivities beyond the academy. The contours of the First Amendment have different, often contradictory, meanings depending on whether one is on or off campus. At universities, offenses and insults that force students out of their comfort zones must be quarantined; outside of the campus, separated from the womb of the "safe space" college existence, all bets and gloves are off. Sensitivities are rare sightings in a world of human indignity and assaultive speech. The new look of free speech on campus serves neither the imperatives of a liberal education nor the goals of deliberative democracy.

We are simply not preparing college students for life outside of the academy, and we are confusing everyone else about the true meaning of free speech. Upon graduation, students make their way into new social settings and places of employment where the rules of civility and fair play are different and where they can expect to find no sheltering safe spaces. Universities are under no obligation to protect students from, as columnist Judith Shulevitz craftily wrote, "feeling bombarded by a lot of viewpoints that really go against their dearly and closely held beliefs or generally had their feelings hurt."[366] It used to be that the mandate of institutions of higher learning was to assist evolving minds to confront new ideas and to test settled beliefs.

In April of 2018, at the City College of New York, over twenty students from the local chapter of Students for Justice in Palestine ("SJP") chose to commemorate the "Nakba," which translates from the Arabic into "catastrophe" and relates to the creation of the State of Israel, with a public demonstration. During the lunch hour, when everyone was either crossing the campus or milling about the open lawn, the SJP members, after offering some preliminary remarks, decided to chant, "Intifada! Intifada! Intifada!"

Intifada is not a call for peace or social justice. It poses neither a political idea nor an inspirational message nor even the hope for national aspirations. The word translates, literally, to "tremor" or "shivering." By now, most people know that it actually means a violent campaign to kill Jews—most of whom are Israeli civilians. If you are chanting the word "intifada," you are calling for the murder of Jews. The word has nothing to do with Palestinian rights and everything to do with Jewish annihilation. It is chanted as a means of incitement. Its recitation is purposeful and provocative.

When Jewish students complained to CCNY's president, Vincent Boudreau, wondering perhaps whether "safe spaces" also applied to them or whether a genocidal macroaggression should be a concern of the university, they were informed that chanting "intifada" on campus, with the specific purpose of influencing the minds of gathering students, is protected speech under the First Amendment.

To openly call for the killing of Jews is a permissible form of political speech? Is that not the very model of incitement to violence that *Brandenburg v. Ohio* sought to restrict from First Amendment consideration?[367]

Hurt feelings are treated like crimes against humanity; true threats and intimidation that rise to the level of actual aggression are casually dismissed as the give-and-take of political discourse. Ironically, during the same month in April 2018, a Nazi living in the United Kingdom was sentenced to three years in prison for stirring up racial hatred in two speeches he delivered at alt-right rallies in 2015 and 2016. Among other obscenities, he described Jews as "parasites," called for them to be "eradicated," and said that they are the "real enemy" of the British people. The court wrote about the defendant that "[h]e seeks to raise street armies, perpetrate violence against Jewish people and ultimately bring about genocide."[368]

In a widely debated essay, Ulrich Baer, a vice provost for faculty arts, humanities, and diversity at New York University, wrote, "Some things are unmentionable and undebatable, but not because they offend sensibilities of the sheltered young. Some topics, such as claims that some human beings are by definition inferior to others, or illegal, or unworthy of legal standing, are not open to debate because such people cannot debate them on the same terms."[369]

If speech is to be regulated, a good place to start would be in protecting the dignity of human beings who have been exposed to injurious speech. There is the protection of copyrights, laws against false advertising, libel and defamation, and the deliberate use of fraudulent information in a business transaction. Of course, these particular exceptions to the general rule of free speech disproportionally benefit the privileged and the powerful. False advertising and fraudulent information in business transactions are "high-class problems"—they do not protect vulnerable minorities but rather financial interests.[370] Law professors Richard Delgado and Jean Stefancic wondered why a "black undergraduate subjected to vicious abuse while walking late at night on campus" is not entitled to at least the same consideration as a business transaction.[371]

And as much as students and faculty cannot be allowed to censor ideas that the First Amendment would otherwise protect, professors cannot hide under the mantle of academic freedom when what they are producing is shoddy scholarship that has no relationship to ideas, aesthetics, or the pursuit of truth. This raises yet another misapplication of free speech on college campuses. Ideas deemed as microaggressions are censored; meanwhile, some faculty believe that academic freedom protects almost anything they say—even if it has nothing to do with academia or the search for the truth.

The same liberty that does not protect the shock comic Dieudonné onstage should not be protecting an academic like Steven Salaita on campus.

In 2014, Salaita accepted a tenure track position at the university of Illinois at Urbana-Champaign. That offer was eventually rescinded as soon as the chancellor of the university received a preview of some of Salaita's Twitter postings, replete with vile comments wholly unworthy of an academic. He wrote, for instance, after three Israeli teenagers were kidnapped and murdered by Hamas in 2014, that "I wish all fucking West Bank settlers would go missing." There is more. He tweeted that anyone supporting Israel during the last Gaza War was "an awful human being." And this: "Zionists: transforming 'anti-Semitism' from something horrible into something honorable since 1948." Salaita was unrepentant and fully assumed that the university would stand beside him. Liel Leibovitz, a columnist, wondered how Salaita would have fared at a university if his tweet referred to African-Americans as "transforming 'racism' from something horrible into something honorable since 1964."[372]

Many did, in fact, rush to Salaita's defense, on both First Amendment and academic freedom grounds. The University of Illinois is a public institution, after all. His freedom to speak should be constitutionally protected. Yet, why should his tweets merit constitutional protection? They are of a piece with incitement and hatred. While speech may be free, that does not mean that it cannot be critically judged—especially when its quality is as poor as Salaita's Twitter offerings and has the potential to generate actual physical harm by third parties reading them.

The exercise of free speech is always undertaken at one's own peril. There is a reason people are advised to keep their mouths shut. What gets said may fall outside the law; it could also elicit a black eye. Caution is warranted. How speech will land, what effect it might have, and what harm it might bring is often unknown. Salaita chose to share his language and quality of mind with the Twitter universe. His employer had every reason to question both his intellectual rigor and his awful judgment. This was not a proper occasion in which to invoke academic freedom, mostly because those tweets showed no affinity for the academy whatsoever.

Writing about the cherished platform that universities provide, Jason Blum wrote: "Worthy speech is both intellectually and morally responsible . . . demonstrating a basic level of respect for one's interlocutors. We are not required to provide a soapbox for every blowhard with a following on Twitter."[373]

One may have a First Amendment right to speak or write in any form desired, but not without critical review—particularly in an academic setting that places a premium on peer review. The marketplace of ideas must impose an insistence on quality. Barriers to entry must exist. The seriousness of mind is what makes one worthy of inclusion. Having a right to free speech does not guarantee a university platform in which to deliver that speech— for teachers or for invited guests. Colleges and universities render all kinds of judgments regarding what students should read and what gets left off the syllabus. The selection process is not an exercise in censorship. It comes down to the curatorial prerogatives of the academy and the ability to judge excellence. Under the best of circumstances, what gets left off the syllabus and who is refused a platform to speak is a matter of making the grade and earning the right to be read and to speak. There are no other free speech entitlements.[374]

38.

---

# THE RIGHT TO MAKE A BOMB

---

In the United States, Homeland Security receives a busy signal every time they try to request from Facebook and Twitter information on detected terrorist chatter.

IRST AMENDMENT ABUSE on the Internet is rampant and potentially murderous. Some information accessible on the Internet has redeeming value only if one wishes to hasten the end of days. The inviolability of the online universe can have deadly consequences. Passion runs hot in places where participants are virtually anonymous. The Internet is yet another facilitator of speech that could surely benefit from regulatory oversight. But here, too, the First Amendment is flashed like a golden ticket that staves off governmental intrusion.

James Madison might as well have been the inventor of Facebook.

On October 31, 2017, a terrorist who had rented a pickup truck from Home Depot mowed down eight people and injured eleven more along a bicycle path in Lower Manhattan. Halloween in Manhattan took a more ghoulish turn. The terrorist was not wearing a mask or costume for the occasion. Everything about him was in plain view—including how he came to plan his murderous outing on the streets of New York. Apparently, the recipe was readily available for anyone with jihadist fantasies and an Internet connection. He simply followed the directions on how to leave the longest "trail of carnage" possible after having read an online magazine devoted to jihad. The article can be found on Rumiyah's website—ISIS' very own magazine and how-to guide—this one with the title: "Just Terror Tactics." Beneath a photo of a Hertz rental truck, the text reads gruesomely: "Very few actually comprehend the deadly and destructive capability of the motor vehicle and its capacity of reaping large numbers of casualties if used in a premeditated manner."[375]

Recruit and indoctrinate willing followers, add water, and presto: mass murder.

The Internet has become a terrorist's best friend.[376] It is online where recruitment, propaganda, advocacy, indoctrination, and incitement takes place and where instructional videos on anything from beheadings to bomb-making to setting a murderous rampage in motion can be found. There is no shortage of websites devoted to assisting a would-be terrorist. At least there are TSA personnel at airports to provide security. The Internet is policed by no one— no metal detectors, body scanners, pat-downs, or profiling. Anyone with a cell phone and a hot spot can plot a terrorist attack. Terrorist platforms can be accessed through social media, chat rooms, message boards, Twitter accounts, and, of course, text messaging. Cyberspace is where the Islamic cleric Anwar al-Awlaki, through his widely viewed sermons on YouTube, influenced the Fort Hood shooter and Boston Marathon bombers.

All thanks to free speech.

All throughout Europe—as they do with hate speech—other liberal democracies take a much tougher stance in prosecuting terrorist activities over the Internet. In the United States, Homeland Security receives a busy signal every time they try to request from Facebook and Twitter information on detected terrorist chatter. Apple fears cooperating with the NSA lest they alienate the online community, where Edward Snowden and Julian Assange are digital deities, the lethal consequences of their actions to American national security notwithstanding. America is not likely to follow Germany's lead in passing a law that imposes large fines against social media platforms that fail to remove hate speech within twenty-four hours of notification. The German Network Enforcement Law has codified twenty-one types of content that are deemed "manifestly illegal." This new online hate speech law has forced social media platforms, such as Facebook, to create deletion centers where as many as 1,200 employees serve as content moderators—deleting everything from terrorist propaganda, Nazi symbols, and child abuse. Facebook has been particularly aggressive in its compliance, removing illegal hate speech from its website at an improved rate of 100 percent, yet even it still has a way to go to be scrubbed clean, as will be noted below.

Perhaps there should be no surprise that these actions are taking place in Germany. After all, for much of its postwar, democratic history, with the Holocaust always haunting its moral conscience, Germany made sure that its commitment to free speech would never provide a license for the dissemination of hate speech. Hitler's *Mein Kampf*, for instance, was mostly outlawed and is available today only in an annotated version. Swastikas are unlawful; so, too, is Holocaust denial. German government leaders understood, immediately, that if hate speech is unlawful in the public square, the same should hold true on social networks. The public square and the online community must play by the same rules. For this reason, a tweet sent from a far-right politician on December 31, 2017, accusing the Cologne police of appeasing "barbaric, Muslim, gang-raping groups of men," was removed from Twitter.[377]

Following Germany's lead, France's Parliament is debating a similar legislative measure. Laetitia Avia, a member of the lower house of Parliament and the sponsor of the bill, said, "There is no reason that comments that would not be tolerated on a bus, in a café or in school—basically in 'real life'—should be tolerated on a website or network."[378]

Neither terrorist incitement nor garden-variety hate speech should be welcome on the Internet. In June 2018, a British judge sentenced a blogger to twenty weeks' imprisonment for posting anti-Semitic songs and threatening messages on her YouTube channel. In addition to rantings in which she repeatedly denied the Holocaust, she sang songs defaming and threatening Holocaust survivors. The UK's Crown Prosecution Service charged her with two counts of sending offensive, indecent, or menacing messages over a public communications network. A third charge was related to one of her songs posted on YouTube.[379]

Even Afghanistan, surely no free speech mecca, acting on a tip about the Taliban, swiftly shut down WhatsApp and Telegram in order to disrupt a budding terrorist threat.[380] In France, the Union of Jewish French Students brought an action against Twitter seeking $50 million in damages for allowing anti-Semitic tweets to circulate in cyberspace. Twitter eventually deleted the tweets, although it refused to divulge the identities of the users who created the messages.[381]

The European Union, in partnership with Facebook, Twitter, YouTube, and Microsoft, and in the direct aftermath of the terrorist attacks in Paris and Brussels, created a Code of Conduct to deal with illegal hate speech and jihadist propaganda online—specifically in Europe.[382] The European Convention on the Prevention of Terrorism, which includes forty-seven countries, was created, in part, to prosecute the growing threats posed by terrorism without compromising freedom of expression. Article 5 requires each signatory state to criminalize the "public provocation to commit a terrorist offence."[383]

Several European countries went even further in drafting laws, specifically to address digital terrorist propaganda, terrorist videos, and articles found in al-Qaeda's magazine, *Inspire*. The UK Data Retention and Investigatory Powers Act of 2014, the Netherlands General Civil Penal Code Article 147c, and Canada's statute C-51 all contain elements that make it easier for their respective governments to regulate terrorist speech and propaganda over the Internet. After an investigation into the attempted assassination of a member of the British Parliament, England discovered that the would-be assassin had been radicalized by al-Awlaki's sermons. The United Kingdom demanded that YouTube remove and block some of al-Awlaki's sermons that are available on its site.

The United States has made no such request of YouTube despite the direct link between these sermons and the murders at Fort Hood and at the Boston Marathon.[384]

In a very influential law review article regarding terrorist speech on social media, Alexander Tsesis reported that Facebook refused requests to disable a Community page called "Stab Israelis," which depicted various images of Palestinian men holding large knives pointed at Hasidic Jews along with the message: "There is nothing greater than a knife penetrating the heads of the Jews." Given Facebook's lack of cooperation while insisting on its First Amendment obligation to ensure freedom of speech, and with nowhere else to turn, twenty thousand Israelis filed a class action lawsuit against Facebook for "allowing Palestinian terrorists to incite violent attacks against Israelis on its internet platforms."[385]

That lawsuit was doomed from the start. A similar civil suit against Facebook, also brought by Israelis who sought to hold the social network responsible for Hamas Facebook pages that led to violent attacks, was rejected at both the trial and appellate court levels. In the United States, Internet providers are largely shielded from civil liability under Section 230 of the Communications Decency Act of 1996, which grants immunity to websites for the content created by their users. Not only do social media companies stand defiantly on First Amendment grounds in not policing lethal content should the government seek their cooperation, they are also protected from civil liability pursuant to a federal law that has been "construed broadly in favor of immunity."[386]

Another proscribed category could be added to the *Chaplinsky* catalog, this one excluding terrorist incitement over the Internet from First Amendment protection (the Patriot Act itself could be of some use here, too, or separate legislation dealing, specifically, with the Internet). Of course, such judicial activism would mobilize free speech absolutists on the same constitutional crusade that occurs whenever hate speech is discussed as ripe for regulatory reform. Frederick Schauer has observed that, when it comes to terrorism, the First Amendment apparently requires all Americans to assume the risk of a catastrophe rather than curtail the rights of a speaker—even a genocidal one. The principle is that it is "better to be safe than sorry." But safe from what—a censoring regulator or a murderous terrorist? With terrorism, it is more likely that we will end up being "more sorry than safe."[387]

Even cyberbullying, which has also become a fan favorite on the Internet, and which accounts for needless tragic suicides every year, probably has its slippery-slope adherents who would fume at the mention that it, too, should be restricted. For them, the Internet was designed as a modern public square, imbued with the virtues of real-time debate and political advocacy. Yes, but it also enabled Russia's cyber-misinformation campaign against the United States in its 2016 presidential election. The Internet is no innocent. All throughout the Cold War, the Soviets never managed such a calculated and coordinated strike against the United States. Its irreversible influence over our electoral process was an act of war launched much more easily than any prior Russian military campaign.

Ironically, for all the assertions of First Amendment liberties, the Preamble to the Constitution provides for the "common defence," "secur[es] the Blessings of Liberty," and places national security at the forefront of the government's obligations to its citizens.[388] Given this nonnegotiable national security mandate, it is not clear why the First Amendment rights of some should impede the government's duty to protect all. Adhering strictly to the Constitution does not mean that the government must bypass its obligation embodied in the Preamble of the Constitution where national defense actually precedes the right to free speech. Most assuredly, "terrorist incitement is not what the First Amendment was ever meant to safeguard; moreover, terrorist incitement is most decidedly *not* free speech. . . . [It] does not involve the debating of ideas in some imaginary marketplace. . . . Would-be terrorists are not looking for chatrooms as confessionals where they can express their ambivalence, if not profound regret, as to how Islam became both a religion of peace and also a prodigious killer of Muslims."[389]

There is already a lower standard of First Amendment guarantees for low-value speech. Is that not what defines so much of the traffic on the digital highway? What is more "low value" than the keystrokes of a low-rent Internet troll, especially one who is a wannabe terrorist? In the best case, it is spam; in the worst, it is a bomb. As Professor Leiter has pointedly written, "The self-congratulatory rhetoric of bloggers and tweeters notwithstanding, the unmediated blather that is so much of cyberspace has added little net value to the world. . . . [T]he internet has lowered the cost of communication, but it is far from clear what has been good, since it has lowered the cost (and increased the visibility) for ignoramuses, fools and propagandists of all stripes. . . . [T]he crowds are as likely to be wrong as right, foolish as wise, ignorant as well-informed."[390]

Undeniably, the Internet is responsible for making information available and communication possible in unsurpassable ways. But the unintended consequences of its misuse must also be acknowledged.

In the 2019 El Paso massacre in a Walmart that claimed twenty-two lives, the gunman posted a hateful manifesto on the website 8chan shortly before going on his shooting spree. This was not the first time that a mass murderer took to social media to announce his murderous intentions with unabashed hate speech. This time, however, the use of the Internet for this murderous purpose caused some to wonder why we don't hold Internet providers accountable to their role in providing a digital soapbox, one that could be used to prevent such killings rather than declaim them.[391]

Hate speech—whenever it is uttered, wherever it is found, in whatever form it takes, and on which platform it makes itself known—must be treated like obscenity: subject to Justice Potter Stewart's aphorism, "I know it when I see it."[392] The stakes are too great otherwise, and the injuries from speech have been neglected for far too long. Professor Waldron summed it up well when he wrote, "A motivation oriented purely to protect people's feelings against offense is one thing. But a restriction on hate speech oriented to protecting the basic social standing—the elementary dignity as I have put it—of members of vulnerable groups, and to maintaining the assurance they need in order to go about their lives in a secure and dignified manner, may seem like a much more compelling objective."[393]

We are living in strangely political and cultural times where people are afraid to make a misstep in their speech. There is a great deal of self-censorship going around for a nation that prides itself on freedom of expression. Behind every free speech absolutist lurks a cyberspace bully and college campus censor. And we have seen how moral condemnation is meted out swiftly to those who violate the new ethos of political correctness, with its social niceties, unforgiving pieties, and irredeemable white privileges.

Will we survive this era in which moral whiplash and the gridlock of already made-up minds continues to mangle the fundamental liberty of free expression?

# 39

# TOLERATING SKID MARKS ON
# THE SLIPPERY SLOPE

Absolutists might actually feel that we would all be better off
if we lived in a society without hate speech or one that
banned high-magazine-capacity assault rifles. But they cannot allow that desirable outcome to take hold of their senses
because they are fixated on the horror that awaits us all at
the bottom of that improbably lubricated slope.

NOT UNLIKE DEBATES about the Second Amendment, the First Amendment is riddled with slippery-slope delusions. Indeed, both the NRA and the ACLU would not exist without slippery-slope thinking—the doomsday scenario that can only be avoided by doing nothing at all. NRA supporters hold fast to arguments such as, "If guns are outlawed, only outlaws will have guns," or "If they come for my semi-automatic assault weapon, the next thing you know they'll show up and confiscate my deer hunting rifle or small handgun." Those on the other side of the argument see nothing but hysterics playing politics with their singular obsessions—all to the detriment of the rest of us. Opposing the slippery slope requires making those who live according to such zero-sum thinking look positively unhinged. Only a crazy person would point to a slippery slope in order to put their overreaction under solid ground. Stanley Fish wrote that, "to most people, the slippery-slope argument sounds paranoid. So, the anti-gun side achieves a strategic objective: making the NRA and its allies look first unreasonable and then disreputable."[394]

Invoking the slippery slope is an effective, metaphorical way to excuse not taking a moral position all due to an exaggerated fear that one step in the wrong direction might unleash a cascade of causality. It anticipates a parade of horribles, an unstoppable force of unforeseen calamity, instigated by pulling on a single thread from the status quo. It is a rhetorical technique that infuses rational argument with an emotional consequence, "an ominous or threatening warning about the alleged government policies or intentions that most of the audience of the speech would be likely to view with alarm."[395] Fish said it best in explaining the slippery slope as "what begins as a small and limited restriction may in time flower into full-fledged tyranny. This is known in the trade as the 'slippery slope' argument, and it says that, given the danger of going down the regulatory road, it is safer to never begin." It is a species of "worst case scenario[s] . . . [which] assumes that there is nothing in place, no underbrush, to stop the slide. . . . Slippery slope trajectories are inevitable only in the *head*, where you can slide from A to B to Z with nothing to retard the acceleration of the logic. In the real world, . . . the chances of ever getting to Z are next to nothing."[396]

With the First Amendment, the concern is that censorship, in any form and no matter how slight, once permitted, will lose all fail-safe protocols to prevent the future regulation of almost anything that might come out of a speaker's mouth. "Sure, take away a Klansman's right to burn a cross, but then the next thing you know, any criticism of the government will be outlawed as sedition. We won't be allowed to say anything!"

Calm down. Not likely. We have already created a few limited exceptions to the First Amendment. And Americans are still, apparently, speaking freely. We have already taken a few measured steps down the slope without tumbling. We continue to live in a thriving, free-speech society. *Absolutism on free speech, no matter what*

*First Amendment diehards wish to believe, has already been rejected.* We all know there are some things that cannot be said. And liberty functions just fine.

The slippery slope paralyzes us with line-drawing trepidations—where, exactly, to draw the line without stifling political speech and making a disastrous mistake. But drawing the lines on speech should not be so terrifying to imagine. After all, arbitrary yet workable lines are drawn and accepted in every other area of the law without the world coming to an unavoidable end—had only we exercised the good sense to draw that fateful line elsewhere. Indeed, all of *stare decisis* is a line-drawing exercise. Defining the standard of care in negligence. Determining the *mens rea* in premeditated murder. Establishing the meeting of the minds in the formation of a contract. All those areas of the law have been structured to accept definitional lines. And there are firm lines already drawn under First Amendment law that separate protected speech from the proscribed categories of libel and defamation, obscenity, "true threats," "fighting words," and "the incitement of imminent lawlessness." Not being permitted to shout "Fire!" in a crowded theater is separated by a line that demarcates other words that *can* be yelled in a packed house, such as "Bravo!" at the closing curtain. These admonitions were created somewhere along the slope. A line was drawn and a stake pitched. And the ground held. Ankles remained unbroken despite the perceived overblown adventure downward. Schauer has written that, "[i]t is not when we are *at* the bottom, but only when we are at the top of the slope and afraid of sliding *to* the bottom, that we need a slippery slope argument."[397]

Why do we not fear the slippery slope that exists in the opposite direction—as in not venturing any step at all, of doing nothing? There are costs to living in perpetual fear of the slippery slope— morally, if not legally. After all, the whole argument that gives the slippery slope its trajectory is based on the unexpected improbable extreme. It is the legal equivalent of the boogeyman. Yet, no one can live a meaningful life always on guard for the worst-case scenario. Such skittish behavior does not make for good law, either. With respect to the First and Second Amendments, by allowing stasis to prevail, and with no deviation from the general rule that allows free speech and permissive gun ownership, we have surrendered to a permanent state of both verbal and gun violence without reprieve—all because we live in mortal terror of cascading down the slippery slope. After all, any time a slippery-slope argument is made, there is an implicit concession that the envisioned change in the law is eminently reasonable, if not favorable, in and of itself. We know we *should* do it—but for the slippery slope. Absolutists might *actually* feel that we would all be better off if we lived in a society without hate speech or one that banned high-magazine-capacity assault rifles. But they cannot allow that desirable outcome to take hold of their senses because they are fixated on the horror that awaits us all at the bottom of that improbably lubricated slope.

The phantom abyss prevents policy proposals that would benefit us all. Law professor Susan Bandes correctly diagnosed the central flaw in the logic of the slippery slope by observing that "for fear of the wrong result later, the Court chooses the wrong result now, based on the mistaken belief that by preserving the status quo it has not acted; that by choosing a rough form of justice it has avoided the question of justice entirely."[398]

Schauer raised the very real possibility that, with a prohibition of all pornography, for instance, the Western world might never have seen the publications of *Ulysses* or *Lady Chatterley's Lover*. The raunchiest porn movie may never have flickered on a screen, but would that be worth the absence of *Tropic of Cancer*? Absolutism against obscenity would have made the world poorer culturally. Absolutism on free speech can devastate the assurances of citizenship and do lasting damage to victims of violence done with words. Absolutism on unregulated gun ownership is an invitation for mass shootings. Distinctions and allowances must be made; otherwise the dark side of the slippery slope will cast its shadow on precautions not taken.

Justice John Marshall Harlan, in *Cohen v. California*, famously wrote that "one man's vulgarity is another's lyric."[399] Justice Lewis F. Powell, in *Gertz v. Welch*, was equally lionized for having penned, "There is no such thing as a false idea."[400]

Both statements, however, are wrong. A vulgarity is properly named because it cannot be set to music. It is atonal and jarring, incompatible with the synchronicity of an actual melody. No lyric will be inspired by it. No words can be put to it. And many ideas are false—easily disproved, poorly reasoned, maliciously formed, nonsensical, and idiotic at their inception.

Yet, we continue to cling to these judicial pronouncements because they help justify the extreme liberties taken by the First Amendment. What they have in common is the dead-end, defeatist propositions: "When it comes to words, how can we know what it all means?" "Who can really say?" "Everything is subjective." "The eye of the beholder is blind." In such a climate of zero-sum uncertainty, courts have cozily taken the position that free speech simply should not be curtailed. Flooding society with speech is the safer bet. Regulating speech carries too much risk and will turn a fool's errand into a full-time job.

And so, judges and juries are deemed incapable of deciding on such matters as drawing a red line between speech and non-speech. This cavalier attitude behind the relativism of vulgar lyrics and false ideas is an outright surrender to a "no-go zone" of constitutional interpretation. Leave the First Amendment alone. The government should not be interfering with speech, we are told. As Professor Fish has written, it all suggests "a self-imposed incapacity to make distinctions that would seem perfectly obvious to any well-informed teenager."[401]

Instead, we resign ourselves to the view that this is the price we all must pay for living in a liberal democracy. A great deal of indignity must be endured in order to earn the freedoms we have been granted. Law professor Eugene Volokh has written that even murder itself is worth the price. "The First Amendment requires us to run certain risks to get the benefits that free speech provides. . . . These risks may include even a mildly elevated risk of homicide— for instance, when speech advocates homicide, praises it, weakens social norms against it. . . . Each such crime is of course a tragedy, but a slightly increased risk even of death . . . is part of the price we pay for the First Amendment."[402]

Murder is an acceptable compromise for having free speech? The Framers would be shocked by how we have twisted ourselves into embarrassing knots of misguided thinking. I prefer what Professor Leiter wrote in response to this slippery-slope stranglehold. He wonders why we should all accept the "irresponsible libertarian position that we should tolerate the damage to truth and to the well-being of victims of bad speech as necessary costs to be born on behalf of insuring the *possibly* true, non-harmful and otherwise valuable speech might be heard, even though unpopular."[403] Fish correctly noted that the price we have to pay for living in a democracy is that injury or harm to others is something we should all learn to live with. Those who say this are almost never themselves paying the price.[404]

# CONCLUSION

King George III's prior restraints, laws of sedition, and tariffs on tea and stamps left us all a little brain damaged—we have become tarred and feathered in mind. We do not trust the government to regulate our lives, and we never really have.

$S$ UCH A SAD state of affairs is the condition of the First Amendment. Exploited by immoderate, hostile speakers. Undefended by those who lack the moral courage and independence of mind to rein it in. Defenseless against slippery-slope projections. We see this in many aspects of First Amendment law—an unwillingness to defend with moral conviction a line that *can* actually be drawn, one that would separate speech from non-speech. Doing so would give the First Amendment a far nobler purpose than as an unapologetic defender of neo-Nazis, Klansmen, white separatists, and other groups of haters with violence in their heads.

For too long now we have treated the Free Speech Clause of the First Amendment as both an article of faith and a leap of faith. We say it requires no further improvements. We disable our reason rather than insist on reform. But we must remember that it is itself only an amendment. Moses did not carry it down from Mt. Sinai. It was absolutely written by men and can surely be changed by women and men. Indeed, it came to life because of the need for a change in doing away with authoritarian governments. But that enlightened project did not come to an end. It was designed with further tinkering in mind. Literature professor Ulrich Baer wrote that "[f]reedom of expression is not an unchanging absolute. When its proponents forget that it requires the vigilant and continuing examination of its parameters, and instead invoke a pure model of free speech that has never existed, the dangers to our democracy are clear and present."[405]

The grand, evolving American experiment that the Framers wished for our new republic did not begin and end with self-government and representative democracy. It also included foundational laws. We have been trained, from our revolutionary beginnings, to cast aside the tyranny of monarchs and their unjust laws that violate our natural rights. This is the legacy we adopted from having separated, forcefully, from King George III. His prior restraints, laws of sedition, and tariffs on tea and stamps left us all a little brain damaged—we have become tarred and feathered in mind. We do not trust the government to regulate our lives, and we never really have.

But somebody has to be in charge, minding the store and enforcing discipline and responsible citizenship. That is the essence of our democracy, too. Fair play and equality are no lesser freedoms than speech. Our Founding Fathers did not give birth to a new nation so as to permit the purveyors of hate and raiders of dignity to turn the Constitution into the sort of detested document that starts a revolution.

We could have all simply remained subjects of King George III if that is what they wanted.

So what to do now then?

We could add a new amendment to our Constitution—one that reflects the values of human dignity that are found in nearly all other liberal democracies—a constitutional right to dignity that would offset the free speech priorities of the First Amendment.

After all, we added the Thirteenth, Fourteenth, and Fifteenth Amendments immediately following the Civil War precisely to redress the gross injustices of slavery and to invoke a new set of rights that would acknowledge that dark American past.

It could be done here with dignity.

But we do not have to go that far and take such action. The right to privacy that has been read into the penumbras of several amendments to the Constitution did not result in an amendment that granted women reproductive freedom over their bodies, or men and women the right to choose same-sex partners. The Supreme Court made those interpretations straight from the existing amendments and, for the time being, these rights are now settled law. Privacy was read into the Constitution; it was not put there by amendment.

The Supreme Court could similarly find a right to dignity in the penumbras of the existing amendments. It could also elevate dignity—and the right not to be assaulted by the free expression of another—as yet another element of the right to privacy, alongside abortion, homosexuality, and marriage.

But the Court does not have to go that far either. Supreme Court case law already exists that could place restrictions on assaultive, weaponized, and threatening speech, simply by expanding some of the proscribed categories already listed in *Chaplinsky, Beauharnais,* and *Brandenburg,* and the low-value speech identified in *Virginia v. Black.*

Hate speech, narrowly defined by the Supreme Court as that which is not really speech at all because it is absent of ideas and therefore contentless—and delivered in such a manner and with such nefarious intention that its purpose is only meant to harm another, to render citizenship meaningless, and to make venturing out in public a hazardous enterprise—could be disqualified from First Amendment safeguards altogether. Local communities that pass such ordinances would then no longer have them invalidated by a Supreme Court that only has eyes for speech and is blind to human dignity.

And, finally, now that neuroscience has allowed us entry into the once mysterious workings of the human brain, and we know the physical and emotional consequences of weaponized words, damages for the intentional infliction of emotional distress should not find themselves overturned by a free speech defense that should have no place in a civil action, as it did in *Snyder v. Phelps*.

But what we most certainly should *not* do is nothing.

# ACKNOWLEDGMENTS

*I*T TAKES A *shtetl* to write a book. Well, not a whole *shtetl*, but certainly a good number of fine people. To my mind, an Acknowledgments page has but one purpose: to recognize those who helped make it possible, or easier, for this book to be written. If you are not on this list, please do not despair. It doesn't mean we are not friends, or even family. It simply means that your friendship didn't involve carrying some of the burdens that went into this most recent Thane Rosenbaum project. (There are no enemies on this list.)

So with that in mind, I would like to thank:

Sam Ashner, Hugo Barecca, Judy Berkman, Warren Bloom, Marty Bodzin, Benjamin Brafman, Steve "Bubba" Cohen, Jeffrey Epstein, Joe Feshbach, Samuel G. Freedman, Carolyn Gilbert, Ben Goldhagen, Gil Goldschein, Mark Golub, Sol Haber, Tom Hameline, Angela Himsel, Robert Hollweg, Tracey Hughes, Annette Insdorf, Thomas Kaplan, Alan Kadish, Barbara Feshbach Katz, Bill and Andrea Kirsh, George Klein, Andy Kovler, Carolyn Jackson, Jim Leitner, Jeffrey Lenobel, Alex Mauskop, Kate Moore, Geoffrey Pantone, Brett Paul, Tom Portzline, Paula Rackoff, Patricia Salkin, Sanjay Sethie, Joel Simon, David Stern, Esther Tendy, John Thomas, and Susan Wessen.

A special gratitude to: Michael and Susan Ashner, Danny and Sarah Goldhagen, Danny Retter, Eric Wasserman and Robert Wertheimer.

My longstanding agent, Ellen Levine.

The always agile and forever loyal FOLCS team: Sara Gajic, Olivia Simon and Shervin Abachi.

I had a group of fine research assistants over the years: from Fordham Law School, Anastasia Sushko; and from NYU Law School, Tochukwu Chikwendu, Benigna Ejimba and the stupendous and invaluable Valeria Vegh Weis.

NYU Law Library was quite helpful and I would like to single out: Gretchen Feltes and Jessica Freeman.

My publisher and editor on this book, the multi-talented, level-headed, clear-eyed, novelistic and courageous Fredric Price, the best book steward an author could ever hope to have. And a winning part of the Fig Tree Books experience included the wonderful design work of Christine Van Bree and the skillful eyes and hand of D. J. Schuette.

And my children, Basia Tess, Zofii Anna, Elska Bette and Solènne Rose.

# ENDNOTES

1. Andrew Marantz, "How Social-Media Trolls Turned U.C. Berkeley into a Free-Speech Circus," *New Yorker*, July 2, 2018, *available at* https://www.newyorker.com/magazine/2018/07/02/how-social-media-trolls-turned-uc-berkeley-into-a-free-speech-circus?reload=true.

2. Raymond Ibrahim, "How the US Army War College Surrendered to CAIR," *Algemeiner*, June 17, 2019, *available at* https://www.algemeiner.com/2019/06/17/how-the-us-army-war-college-surrendered-to-cair/.

3. 117 *Harvard Law Review* (2004), 1765, 1790.

4 "Judge rules Charlottesville alt-right rally can go on," CBS News/AP, August 11, 2017, *available at* https://www.cbsnews.com/news/judge-rules-charlottesville-alt-right-rally-can-go-on/.

5. Joseph Goldstein, "After Backing Alt-Right in Charlottesville, A.C.L.U Wrestles With Its Role," *New York Times*, Aug. 17, 2017, *available at* https://www.nytimes.com/2017/08/17/nyregion/aclu-free-speech-rights-charlottesville-skokie-rally.html.

6. Wendy Kaminer, "The ACLU Retreats from Free Expression," *Wall Street Journal*, June 20, 2018, *available at* https://www.wsj.com/articles/the-aclu-retreats-from-free-expression-1529533065.

7. Alex Blasdal, "How the resurgence of white supremacy in the US sparked a war over free speech," *Guardian*, May 31, 2018, *available at* https://www.theguardian.com/news/2018/may/31/how-the-resurgence-of-white-supremacy-in-the-us-sparked-a-war-over-free-speech-aclu-charlottesville.

8. Blasdal, "How the resurgence of white supremacy in the US sparked a war over free speech."

9. Zechariah Chafee, *Free Speech in the United States* (Boston: Harvard University Press, 1941).

10. *Palko v. Connecticut*, 301 U.S. (1937), 319, 327.

11. *Texas v. Johnson*, 491 U.S. (1989), 397.

12. *Collin v. Smith*, 432 U.S. (1977), 43.

13. *R.A.V. v. St. Paul*, 505 U.S. (1992), 377.

14. *Snyder v. Phelps*, 562 U.S. (2011), 443.

15. Marantz, "How Social-Media Trolls Turned U.C. Berkeley into a Free-Speech Circus."

16. Chafee, *Free Speech in the United States,* 5 (emphasis added).

17. Chafee, *Free Speech in the United States,* 5 n.2.

18. Henry Samuel, "French comedian Dieudonné sentenced to two months in prison," *Telegraph*, Nov. 25, 2015, *available at* https://www.telegraph.co.uk/news/worldnews/europe/belgium/12015954/French-comedian-Dieudonne-sentenced-to-two-months-in-prison.html.

19. Dan Bilefsky, "Court Rules Against French Comedian Dieudonné in Free-Speech Case," *New York Times*, Nov. 10, 2015, *available at* https://www.nytimes.com/2015/11/11/world/europe/dieudonne-mbala-mbala-france-european-rights-court.html?searchResultPosition=1.

20. Melissa Eddy and Aurelien Breeden, "The El Paso Shooting Revived the Free Speech Debate. Europe Has Limits," *New York Times*, Aug. 6, 2019, *available at* https://www.nytimes.com/2019/08/06/world/europe/el-paso-shooting-freedom-of-speech.html.

21. Alexander Tsesis, "Dignity and Speech: The Regulation of Hate Speech in a Democracy," 44 *Wake Forest Law Review* (2009), 497, 527 fn. 216–17.

22. Jeremy Waldron, "Dignity and Defamation: The Visibility of Hate," 123 *Harvard Law Review* (2010), 1597, 1643.

23. Eric Posner, "The World Doesn't Love the First Amendment," *Slate*, Sept. 25, 2012, *available at* http://www.slate.com/articles/news_and_politics/jurisprudence/2012/09/the_vile_anti_muslim_video_and_the_first_amendment_does_the_u_s_overvalue_free_speech_.html.

24. Adam Liptak, "Hate speech or free speech? What much of the West bans is protected in the U.S.," *New York Times*, June 11, 2008, *available at* http://www.nytimes.com/2008/06/11/world/americas/11iht-hate.4.13645369.html.

25. Thane Rosenbaum, "Should Neo-Nazis Be Allowed Free Speech?" *Daily Beast*, January 30, 2014, *available at* https://www.thedailybeast.com/should-neo-nazis-be-allowed-free-speech.

26. John Villasenor, "Views among college students regarding the First Amendment: Results from a new survey," Brookings Institute, Sept. 18, 2017.

27. Jeffrey M. Jones, "More U.S. College Students Say Campus Climate Deters Speech," Gallup, March 12, 2018, *available at* http://news. gallup.com/poll/229085/college-students-say-campus-climate-deters-speech.aspx?version=print; *also*: Richard Perez-Pena, Mitch Smith, and Stephanie Saul, "University of Chicago Strikes Back Against Campus Political Correctness," *New York Times*, Aug. 26, 2016, *available at* https:// www.nytimes.com/2016/08/27/us/university-of-chicago-strikes-back-against-campus-political-correctness.html; *also*: Cecilia Capuzzi Simon, "Fighting for Free Speech on America's Campuses," *New York Times*, Aug. 1, 2016, *available at* https://www.nytimes.com/2016/08/07/education /edlife/fire-first-amendment-on-campus-free-speech.html.

28. *FIRE*, "Spotlight on Speech Codes 2015: The State of Free Speech on Our Nation's Campuses," *available at* https://www.thefire.org /resources/spotlight/reports/spotlight-speech-codes-2015/; *also*: Haley Hudler, "New Survey Exposes Threat to Free Speech on Campus," *FIRE*, October 28, 2015, *available at* https://www.thefire.org/new -survey-exposes-threats-to-free-speech-on-campus/.

29. Thomas Fuller, "Berkeley Cancels Ann Coulter Speech Over Safety Concerns," *New York Times*, April 19, 2017, *available at* https://www .nytimes.com/2017/04/19/us/berkeley-ann-coulter-speech-canceled. html; *also*: Susan Svriuga, William Wan, Elizabeth Dwoskin, "Ann Coulter Speech at Berkeley cancelled, again, amid fears for safety," *Washington Post*, April 26, 2017, *available at* https://www.washingtonpost.com/news /grade-point/wp/2017/04/26/ann-coulter-speech-canceled-at-uc -berkeley-amid-fears-for-safety/?utm_term=.a30ce0e2f3e2.

30. Marantz, "How Social-Media Trolls Turned U.C. Berkeley into a Free-Speech Circus."

31. Emma Kerr, "As Protests Mount, U. of Chicago Plans for a Visit From Steve Bannon," *Chronicle of Higher Education*, Feb. 6, 2018, *available at* https://www.chronicle.com/article/As-Protests-Mount-U-of/242463.

32. Allison Stanger, "Understanding the Angry Mob at Middlebury That Gave Me a Concussion," *New York Times*, March 13, 2017, *available at* https://www.nytimes.com/2017/03/13/opinion/understanding-the -angry-mob-that-gave-me-a-concussion.html.

33. Liam Stack, "Yale's Halloween Advice Stokes a Racially Charged Debate," *New York Times*, Nov. 8, 2015, *available at* https://www.nytimes.com/2015/11/09/nyregion/yale-culturally-insensitive-halloween-costumes-free-speech.html.

34. Manny Fernandez and Richard Perez-Pena, "As Two Oklahoma Students Are Expelled for Racist Chant, Sigma Alpha Epsilon Vows Wider Inquiry," *New York Times*, March 10, 2015, *available at* https://www.nytimes.com/2015/03/11/us/university-of-oklahoma-sigma-alpha-epsilon-racist-fraternity-video.html.

35. Joel Brinkley and Ian Fisher, "U.S. Says It Also Finds Cartoons of Muhammad Offensive," *New York Times*, Feb. 4, 2006, *available at* https://www.nytimes.com/2006/02/04/politics/us-says-it-also-finds-cartoons-of-muhammad-offensive.html.

36. Patricia Cohen, "Yale Press Band Images of Muhammad in New Book," *New York Times*, Aug. 12, 2009, *available at* https://www.nytimes.com/2009/08/13/books/13book.html?mtrref=www.bing.com.

37. Richard Perez-Pena, "After Protests I.M.F. Chief Withdraws as Smith College's Commencement Speaker," *New York Times*, May 12, 2014, *available at* https://www.nytimes.com/2014/05/13/us/after-protests-imf-chief-withdraws-as-smith-colleges-commencement-speaker.html; *also*: Jacque Wilson, "UC Berkley students petition to drop Bill Maher from commencement," CNN, Oct. 28, 2014, *available at* http://www.cnn.com/2014/10/28/living/bill-maher-commencement-speaker/index.html; *also*: "List of Campus Disinvitation Attempts: 2000–2014," *FIRE*, Jun. 3, 2014, *available at* https://www.thefire.org/list-of-campus-disinvitations-2000-2014/.

38. Anna Silman, "Ten famous comedians on how political correctness is killing comedy: 'We are addicted to the rush of being offended,'" *Salon*, June 10, 2015, *available at* https://www.salon.com/2015/06/10/10_famous_comedians_on_how_political_correctness_is_killing_comedy_we_are_addicted_to_the_rush_of_being_offended/.

39. Valier Strauss, "Is professor's #NRA tweet a firing offense or protected speech?" *Washington Post*, Sept. 29, 2013, *available at* https://www.washingtonpost.com/news/answer-sheet/wp/2013/09/29/is-professors-nra-tweet-a-firing-offense-or-protected-speech/?utm_term=.e8964d194a85.

40. Nicholas Kristof, "Stop the Knee-Jerk Liberalism That Hurts Its Own Cause," *New York Times*, June 29, 2019, *available at* https://www.nytimes.com/2019/06/29/opinion/sunday/liberalism-united-states.html.

41. John Koblin, "Roseanne Barr Incites Fury with Racist Tweet, and Her Show Is Cancelled by ABC," *New York Times*, May 29, 2018, *available at* https://www.nytimes.com/2018/05/29/business/media /roseanne-barr-offensive-tweets.html?rref=collection%2Fissuec ollection%2Ftodays-new-york-times&action=click&contentColle ction=todayspaper&region=rank&module=package&version=hi ghlights&contentPlacement=2&pgtype=collection.

42. Daisuke Wakabayashi, "Google Legally Fired Diversity-Memo Author, Labor Agency Says," *New York Times*, Feb. 16, 2018, *available at* https:// www.nytimes.com/2018/02/16/business/google-memo-firing.html.

43. Rob Bluey, "This CEO Made a Political Donation, Then Lost His Job Because Liberals Didn't Like It," *Daily Signal*, April 4, 2014, *available at* https://www.dailysignal.com/2014/04/04/ceo-made -political-donation-lost-job-liberals-didnt-like/; *also*: Associated Press, "Mozilla CEO resignation raised free speech issues," *USA Today*, April 4, 2014, *available at* https://www.usatoday.com/story/news /nation/2014/04/04/mozilla-ceo-resignation-free-speech/7328759/.

44. Leanna Garfield, "Pro-LBGT-rights Consumers vow to boycott Chick-fil-A after it announces its opening in Toronto—here's why the fast-food chain is so controversial," *Business Insider*, July 27, 2018, *available at* https://www.businessinsider.com/chick-fil-a-lgbt-twitter-jack-dorsey -apology-marriage-equality-2018-6/.

45. Natalie Wolfe, "Celeb costumes that were rude, racist or downright offensive," News.com.au, Oct. 31, 2016, *available at* https://www .news.com.au/entertainment/celebrity-style/wardrobe-malfunction /celeb-costumes-that-were-rude-racist-or-downright-offensive/news -story/c63ac15dc9b972bcc9a53a0ec5d3b7dc.

46. Peter Sblendoria, "Justin Timberlake accused of black appropriation after tweeting about Jesse Williams' BET Awards speech," *New York Daily News*, June 27, 2016, *available at* https://www.nydailynews.com /entertainment/music/justin-timberlake-accused-black-appropriation -tweet-article-1.2689560.

47. Bethany Mandel, "The Angry Left Is Turning Me Into A Trump Supporter," *Forward*, June 12, 2018, *available at* https://forward.com/opinion/402998 /the-angry-left-is-turning-me-into-a-trump-supporter/?utm_content =opinion_Newsletter_MainList_Title_Position-1&utm_source =Sailthru&utm_medium=email&utm_campaign=Opinion%20-%20 automated%20-%20wednesday%202018-06-13&utm_term=Opinion.

48. Rob Goldberg, "Jerry Jones Says that Any Cowboys Player Who 'Disrespects' The Flag Won't Play," *Bleacher Report*, Oct. 8, 2017, *available at* https://bleacherreport.com/articles/2737631-jerry-jones -says-a-cowboys-player-who-disrespects-the-flag-wont-play.

49. *Schenck v. United States*, 249 U.S. (1919), 47.

50. Stanley Fish, *There's No Such Thing as Free Speech: And It's a Good Thing, Too* (Oxfordshire: Oxford University Press, 1994); *also*: Kalefa Sanneh, "The Hell You Say: The new battles over free speech are fierce, but who is censoring whom?" *New Yorker*, Aug. 10 & 17, 2015, *available at* https://www.newyorker.com/magazine/2015/08/10/the-hell -you-say.

51. Lincoln Caplan, "The Embattled 1st Amendment," *American Scholar*, Spring 2015 (citing Professor Ronald K.L. Collins' list of forty-three additional categories).

52. Alexander Tsesis, "The Empirical Shortcomings of First Amendment Jurisprudence: A Historical Perspective on the Power of hate Speech," *Santa Clara Law Review* (2000), 729, 776.

53. *Abrams v. United States*, 250 U.S. (1919), 616, 630 (Holmes, J., dissenting) (emphasis added).

54. Alexander Meiklejohn, *Political Freedom: The Constitutional Powers of the People* (Oxfordshire: Oxford University Press, 1960), 73.

55. *New York State Board of Elections v. Lopez Torres*, 552 U.S. (2008), 196, 208.

56. *Whitney v. California*, 274 U.S. (1927), 357, 376–77 (emphasis added).

57. *Gertz v. Robert Welch, Inc.*, 418 U.S. (1974), 323, 339–40 (emphasis added).

58. Sindre Bangstad, *Anders Breivik and the Rise of Islamophobia* (London: ZED Books, 2014).

59. Frank Bruni, "The Lecture that Donald Trump Needs," *New York Times*, Sept. 26, 2017, *available at* https://www.nytimes.com/2017/09/26 /opinion/sessions-free-speech-trump.html?rref=collection%2Fsection collection%2Fopinion-columnists (emphasis added).

60. Fish, *There's No Such Thing as Free Speech*, 125.

61. *United States v. Dennis*, 183 F.2d 201 (2nd Circuit 1950), 213.

62. *Id.* (emphasis added).

63. Thane Rosenbaum, "The Internet As Marketplace of Madness—and a Terrorist's Best Friend," 86 *Fordham Law Review* (2017), 591, 594.

64. Alvin I. Goldman and James C. Cox, "Speech, Truth and the Free Market for Ideas," *Legal Theory* (1996), 2, 29–32.

65. Alexander Meiklejohn, *Free Speech: and Its Relation to Self-Government* (New York: Harper & Brothers, 1948), 87.

66. *Terminiello v. Chicago*, 337 U.S. (1949), 1, 23–24 (Jackson, J., dissenting).

67. Lyrissa Barnett Lidsky, "Nobody's Fool: The Rational Audience as First Amendment Ideal," *University of Florida Law Review* (2010), 799, 815.

68. Derek E. Bambauer, "Shopping Badly: Cognitive Biases, Communications, and the Fallacy of the Marketplace of Ideas," 77 *University of Colorado Law Review* (2006), 649, 696, 709.

69. Sharon Begley, "People Believe a 'Fact' That Fits Their Views Even if It's Clearly False," *Wall Street Journal*, Feb. 4, 2005, *available at* https://www.wsj.com/articles/SB110746526775045356.

70. Chip Heath and Jonathan Bender, *When Truth Doesn't Win in the Marketplace of Ideas: Entrapping Schemas, Gore, and the Internet* (Stanford: Stanford University Press, 2003), 209.

71. Lyrissa Barnett Lidsky, "Nobody's Fool: The Rational Audience as First Amendment Ideal," *University of Florida Law Review* (2010), 799, 832.

72. Lidsky, "Nobody's Fool: The Rational Audience as First Amendment Ideal," 828.

73. Andrew Romano, "How Ignorant are Americans?" *Newsweek,* March 20, 2011, *available at* http://www.newsweek.com/how-ignorant-are -americans-66053.

74. Tom Nichols, *The Death of Expertise: The Campaign Against Established Knowledge and Why It Matters* (Oxfordshire: Oxford University Press, 2017); *also:* Tom Nichols, "America's Cult of Ignorance," *Daily Beast*, May 5, 2017, *available at* https://www.thedailybeast.com/americas -cult-of-ignorance.

75. Yuval Harari, "People Have Limited Knowledge. What's the Remedy? Nobody Knows," *New York Times*, Apr. 18, 2017, writing about Steven Sloman & Philip Fernbach, *The Knowledge Illusion: Why We Never Think Alone* (2017). *See generally* Christopher H. Achen & Larry M. Bartels, *Democracy for Realists: Why Elections Do Not Produce Responsive Government* (Princeton: Princeton University Press, 2016); *also:* Bryan Caplan, *The Myth of the Rational Voter* (Princeton: Princeton University Press, 2008).

76. Nicholas D. Kristof, "With a Few More Brains . . . ," *New York Times*, March 30, 2008, *available at* https://www.nytimes.com/2008/03/30/opinion/30kristof.html.

77. Larry E. Tise, *Proslavery: A History of the Defense of Slavery in America, 1701–1840* (Athens: University of Georgia Press, 1987), 8.

78. Charles R. Lawrence III, "If He Hollers Let Him Go: Regulating Racist Speech on Campus," in *Words That Wound: Critical Race Theory, Assaultive Speech, and the First Amendment* (Boulder: Westview Press, 1993), 75, 77.

79. Sheen Iyengar et al., "How Much Choice Is Too Much: Contributions to 401(k) Retirement Plans" (Pension Research Council, Working Paper No. 2003-10), 9.

80. Jordan Malter, "Alt-Tech Platforms: A haven for fringe views online," CNN, Nov. 10, 2017, https://money.cnn.com/2017/11/10/technology/culture/divided-we-code-alt-tech/index.html.

81. U.K. News, "Critics argue that safe space policies at British universities have become a direct threat to freedom of speech," *The Week*, May 3, 2015.

82. Jerome A. Barron, "Access to the Press—A New First Amendment Right," *Harvard Law Review* (1967), 1641, 1678.

83. R. H. Coase, "The Market for Goods and the Market for Ideas," 64 *American Economic Review* (1964), 384, 385.

84. R. H. Coase, "Advertising and Free Speech," 6 *Journal of Legal Studies* (1977), 1, 4.

85. David Folkenflik, "Sinclair Broadcast Group Forces Nearly 200 Station Anchors to Read Same Script," NPR, April 2, 2018, *available at* https://www.npr.org/2018/04/02/598916366/sinclair-broadcast-group-forces-nearly-200-station-anchors-to-read-same-script.

86. *Bethel School District No. 403 v. Fraser*, 478 U.S. (1986), 675.

87. *Hazelwood School District v. Kuhlmeier*, 484 U.S. (1988), 260.

88. Adeel Hassan, "Photo of More Than 60 Students Giving Apparent Nazi Salute Is Being Investigated," *New York Times*, Nov. 12, 2018, *available at* https://www.nytimes.com/2018/11/12/us/nazi-salute-wisconsin-students.html.

89. Kathryn Schumaker, "Why school administrators were wrong not to punish students who gave the Nazi salute," *Washington Post*, Nov. 29, 2018, *available at* https://www.washingtonpost.com/outlook/2018/11/29

/why-school-administrators-were-wrong-not-punish-students-who-gave
-nazi-salute/?noredirect=on&utm_term=.03360f55e7a9.

90. Genevieve Lakier, "The Invention of Low-Value Speech," 128 *Harvard Law Review* (2015), 2166, 2172 (emphasis added).

91. *United States v. Stevens*, 559 U.S. (2010), 560, 567.

92. *Roth v. United States*, 354 U.S. (1957), 476, 484 (emphasis added).

93. *Miller v. California*, 413 U.S. (1973), 15, 24.

94. *Chaplinsky v. New Hampshire*, 315 U.S. (1942), 568, 571–72 (emphasis added).

95. *Id.* (emphasis added).

96. *Cantwell v. Connecticut*, 310 U.S. (1940), 296, 309–10 (emphasis added).

97. *Jones v. Opelika*, 316 U.S. (1942), 584, 593, *reversed* 319 U.S. (1943), 103 (emphasis added).

98. *Texas v. Johnson*, 491 U.S. (1989), 397, 418.

99. Genevieve Lakier, "The Invention of Low-Value Speech," 128 *Harvard Law Review* (2015), 2166, 2203 (emphasis added).

100. *Chaplinsky v. New Hampshire*, 315 U.S. (1942), 568, 571–72.

101. Brian Leiter, "The Case Against Free Speech," 38 *Sydney Law Review* (Dec. 18, 2016), 407, *available at* SSRN: https://ssrn.com/abstract=2450866.

102. *Feiner v. New York*, 340 U.S. (1951), 315, 320 (emphasis added).

103. *FCC v. Pacifica Foundation*, 438 U.S. (1978), 726, 743 n.18.

104. Frederick Schauer, "The Hostile Audience Revisited," Knight First Amendment Institute, Emerging Threats Series (2017).

105. Sanneh, "The Hell You Say."

106. Tim Wu, "How Twitter Killed the First Amendment," *New York Times*, Oct. 27, 2017, *available at* https://www.nytimes.com/2017/10/27/opinion/twitter-first-amendment.html.

107. Shiri Moshe, "Rutgers President Defends 'Academic Freedom' of Three Professors Blasted for Comments on Israel, Jews," *Algemeiner*, Nov. 20, 2017, *available at* https://www.algemeiner.com/2017/11/20/rutgers-president-defends-academic-freedom-of-three-professors-blasted-for-comments-on-israel-jews/.

108. Peter Salovey, "Free Speech, Personified," *New York Times*, Nov. 26, 2017, *available at* https://www.nytimes.com/2017/11/26/opinion/free-speech-yale-civil-rights.html.

109. Daniel Retter, "Humiliating, *Gehinnom Bava Matzia*, 58b," *HaMafteach® Talmud Bavli Indexed Referenced Guide* (English Edition, September 2014), 287.

110. Primo Levi, *Survival in Auschwitz* (Italy: DeSilva, 1947), 25.

111. Patricia J. Williams, "Spirit-Murdering the Messenger: The Discourse of Fingerpointing as the Law's Response to Racism," 42 *University of Miami Law Review* (1987), 127, 129.

112. Thane Rosenbaum, *The Myth of Moral Justice: Why Our Legal System Fails to Do What's Right* (New York: Harper Collins, 2004).

113. Lisa Feldman Barrett, *How Emotions Are Made* (Boston: Mariner Books, 2017), 241.

114. Immanuel Kant, *Foundations of the Metaphysics of Morals* (Lewis W. Beck, trans., ed., New York: Macmillan, 1990), 434–35 (1785).

115. Kant, *Metaphysics of Morals*, 462.

116. Kant, *Metaphysics of Morals*, 329–30.

117. Kant, *Metaphysics of Morals* (Mary Gregor trans., Cambridge: Cambridge Univ. Press, 1991), 236–37, 332–33, 462–64 (1797).

118. Richard Hurowitz, "Remembering the White Rose," *New York Times*, Feb. 21, 2018, *available at* https://www.nytimes.com/2018/02/21/opinion/white-rose-hitler-protest.html.

119. Steven J. Heyman, *Free Speech and Human Dignity* (2008), 145, *available at* SSRN: https://ssrn.com/abstract=1107254.

120. Richard Delgado, "Words That Wound: A Tort Action for Racial Insults, Epithets, and Name Calling," in *Words That Wound* (Boulder: Westview Press, 1993), 91.

121. Jeremy Waldron, *The Harm in Hate Speech* (Cambridge: Harvard University Press, 2012).

122. Delgado, *Words That Wound*, 94.

123. Waldron, *The Harm in Hate Speech*, 84.

124. Editorial, "Europe's Expanding 'Right to be Forgotten,'" *New York Times,* Feb. 4, 2015, *available at* http://www.nytimes.com/2015/02/04/opinion/europes-expanding-right-to-be-forgotten.html.

125. James Q. Whitman, "The Two Western Cultures of Privacy: Dignity versus Liberty," 113 *Yale Law Journal* (2004) 1151, 1162, 1165.

126. Gabrielle S. Friedman and James Q. Whitman, "The European Transformation of Harassment Law: Discrimination Versus Dignity," 9 *Columbia Journal of European Law* (2003), 241, 260.

127. *Wachenheim v. France, CE Ass.*, Oct. 27, 1995, Rec. Lebon 372, *aff'd* Communication No. 854/1999, Human Rights Commission, July 8-26m (2002), CCPR/C/75/D/854/1999.

128. Tom Heneghan, "Sarkozy asks Muslims not to feel hurt by veil ban," Reuters, May 19, 2010, *available at* https://uk.reuters.com/article/uk-france-veil/sarkozy-asks-muslims-not-to-feel-hurt-by-veil-ban-idUKTRE64I3RZ20100519.

129. Universal Declaration of Human Rights, General Assembly Resolution 217 (III) A, United Nations Document A/RES/217(III), at article 1 (Dec. 10, 1948) (emphasis added).

130. The International Covenant on Civil and Political Rights, General Assembly Resolution 2200A (XXI), Preamble United Nations Document 52-58, U.N. GAOR 21sr Sess., Supp. No. 16, U.N. Doc. A/6316 (Dec. 16, 1966).

131. Australian Human Rights Commission, "At a Glance: Racial Vilification under sections 18C and 18D of the Racial Discrimination Act 1975 (Cth)," Dec. 12, 2013, *available at* https://www.humanrights.gov.au/our-work/race-discrimination/projects/glance-racial-vilification-under-sections-18c-and-18d-racial.

132. Aharon Barak, *Human Dignity: The Constitutional Value and the Constitutional Right* (Cambridge: Cambridge University Press, 2015), 51, 59.

133. Martha C. Nussbaum, "Constitutions and Capabilities: 'Perception' Against Lofty Formalism," 121 *Harvard Law Review* (2007), 4, 7.

134. Declaration of the Rights of Man and of the Citizen, article 11 (France, 1789) *available at* https://constitution.org/fr/fr_drm.htm.

135. Doreen Carvajal and Alan Cowell, "French Rein In Speech Backing Acts of Terror," *New York Times*, Jan. 15, 2015, *available at* https://www.nytimes.com/2015/01/16/world/europe/french-rein-in-speech-backing-acts-of-terror.html?searchResultPosition=1.

136. Eddy and Breeden, "The El Paso Shooting Revived the Free Speech Debate."

137. *Id.*

138. Press Law of 1881, section 24 (France, 1881) *available at* https://www .legal-project.org/issues/european-hate-speech-laws.

139. Valerie Strauss, "Florida principal reassigned after refusing to call the Holocaust a 'factual, historical event,'" *Washington Post*, July 8, 2019, *available at* https://www.washingtonpost.com/education/2019/07/08 /florida-principal-reassigned-after-refusing-call-holocaust-factual-historic -event/?noredirect=on&utm_term=.1fc993369dec.

140. *Switzman v. Elbling*, Supreme Court Reports (Canada, 1957), 285, 326 (emphasis added).

141. *Regina v. Keegstra*, 3 Supreme Court Reports (Canada, 1990), 697, 698.

142. *Regina,* 697, 746–47.

143. *Taylor v. Canadian Human Rights Commission*, 3 Supreme Court Reports (Canada, 1990) 892, 919.

144. South Africa Constitution 1996, chapter 2, section 10.

145. Israel, Basic Law, Human Dignity and Liberty, 1994, S.H. 90 articles 2, 4.

146. HCJ 7015/02 *Ajuri v. IDF Commander in the West Bank* (2002) *Israeli Law Review* (2002), 1.

147. Mephisto, BVerfGE 30, 173 (1971) (F.R.G.), *translated in* 2 Decision of the Bundesverfassungsericht—Federal Constitutional Court—Federal Republic (1958) of Germany (pt. 1), at 156 (1998).

148. Basic Law for the Federal Republic of Germany (Christian Tomuschat & David P. Currie, trans., 2008), *available at* https://www.btg- bestellservice.de/pdf/80201000.pdf.

149. Grundgesetz article II, paragraph 1.

150. Guy E. Carmi, "Dignity—The Enemy from Within: A Theoretical and Comparative Analysis of Human Dignity as a Free Speech Justification," 9 *University of Pennsylvania Journal of Constitutional Law* (2007), 957, 998.

151. Sara Lipton, "The Words That Killed Medieval Jews," *New York Times,* Opinion, Dec. 11, 2015, *available at* https://nyti.ms/1Z375xs.

152. *Virginia v. Black*, 538 U.S. (2003), 343, 357.

153. Ben Cohen, "Houston Imam's Apology for Sermon Urging Muslims to 'Fight the Jews in Palestine' Falls Short for Local Jewish Leaders," *Algemeiner*, Dec. 27, 2017, *available at* https://www.algemeiner.com /2017/12/27/houston-imams-apology-for-sermon-urging-muslims -to-fight-the-jews-in-palestine-falls-short-for-local-jewish-leaders/.

154. *See generally* Alexander Tsesis, "Dignity and Speech: The Regulation of Hate Speech in a Democracy, 44 *Wake Forest Law Review* (2009), 497, 502.

155. Gordon W. Allport, *The Nature of Prejudice* (New York: Basic Books, 1979), 57, 60.

156. *Lauro v. Charles*, 219 F.3d (Second Circuit, 2000), 202.

157. *Schmerber v. California*, 384 U.S. (1966), 757, 767.

158. *Miranda v. Arizona*, 384 U.S. (1966), 436, 460.

159. *Atkins v. Virginia*, 536 U.S. (2002), 304, 311–12.

160. *Lawrence v. Texas*, 539 U.S. (2003), 558, 567, 575 ("retain their dignity as free persons"); *also*: *Hollingsworth v. Perry*, 570 U.S. 693 (2013) ("adversely affecting the status and dignity of the members of a disfavored class").

161. *Cohen v. California*, 403 U.S. (1971), 14, 24.

162. *Screws v. United States*, 325 U.S. (1945), 91, 135.

163. *Duncan v. Kahanamoku*, 327 U.S. (1946), 304, 334.

164. Stephen J. Wermiel, "Law and Human Dignity: The Judicial Soul of Justice Brennan," 7 *William and Mary Bill of Rights Journal* (1998), 223, 226–28, *available at* http://scholarship.law.wm.edu/wmborj/vol7/iss1/5.

165. Montana Constitution, "Declaration of Rights," Article II, section 4 (1972).

166. Barak, *Human Dignity,* 192–93; *also*: Wermiel, "Law and Human Dignity," 223, 224.

167. *Paul v. Davis*, 424 U.S. (1978), 693, 734 (emphasis added).

168. *Furman v. Georgia*, 408 U.S. (1972), 238, 270 (emphasis added).

169. *Lawrence v. Texas*, 539 U.S. (2003), 558 (emphasis added).

170. *United States v. Windsor*, 570 U.S. (2013), 744, 764.

171. *Obergefell v. Hodges*, 576 U.S. ___ (2015), 135; Supreme Court, 2584, 2693–95.

172. *Roper v. Simmons*, 543 U.S. (2005), 560, 551.

173. *Glover v. United States*, 531 U.S. (2000), 98, 104.

174. William J. Brennan, Jr., "The Constitution of the United States: Contemporary Ratification," delivered at Georgetown University Law Center (Oct. 12, 1985); *also*: William J. Brennan, Jr., "The Constitution of the United States: Contemporary Ratification," 27 *South Texas Law Review* (1986), 433, 438 (emphasis added).

175. Nomination of William Joseph Brennan, Jr.: Hearing Before the Senate Commission On the Judiciary, 85th Congress (1957), 8.

176. *See generally* Charles Lane, "Justice Kennedy's unifying theme was dignity," *Washington Post,* Opinion, June 28, 2018, *available at* https://www.washingtonpost.com/opinions/there-was-one-unifying -theme-of-anthony-kennedys-jurisprudence/2018/06/28/650aa740 -7adf-11e8-80be-6d32e182a3bc_story.html?noredirect=on&utm _term=.d471a4bcfda0; *also*: Liz Halloran, "Explaining Justice Kennedy: The Dignity Factor," NPR.org, June 28, 2018, *available at* https://www .npr.org/sections/thetwo-way/2013/06/27/196280855/explaining -justice-kennedy-the-dignity-factor=.

177. Barak, *Human Dignity*, 206.

178. Jeremy Waldron, "Free Speech & the Menace of Hysteria," 55 *New York Review Books*, May 29, 2008, *available at* http://www.nybooks.com /articles/21452; *also*: Jeremy Waldron, "Dignity and Defamation: The Visibility of Hate," 123 *Harvard Law Review* (2009), 1597, 1601; *also*: Waldron, *The Harm in Hate Speech*, 39.

179. Thomas Hobbes, *Leviathan* (Richard Tuck ed., Cambridge: Cambridge University Press, 1991), 63–64; 88; 107; 206–7 (1651).

180. Waldron, "Dignity and Defamation," 1627.

181. Tsesis, "Dignity and Speech," 497, 513 n.111.

182. Robert C. Post, "Racist Speech, Democracy, and the First Amendment," 32 *William & Mary Law Review* (1991), 267, 284.

183. Steven J. Heyman, "Righting the Balance: An Inquiry into the Foundations and Limits of Freedom of Expression," 78 *Boston University Law Review* (1998), 1275, 1380.

184. Heyman, "Righting the Balance," 1313 (citing John Locke's, *Two Treatises of Government*, II secs. 6, 57 [Peter Laslett ed., Cambridge: Cambridge University Press 1988] (1698), and Kant, *Metaphysics of Morals* [Cambridge: Cambridge University Press, 1996], 230–33.

185. Thomas G. West, "Free Speech in the American Founding and in Modern Liberalism," 21 *Social Philosophy and Policy* (2004), 310, 323, *available at* https://www.hillsdale.edu/wp-content /uploads/2017/07/2004-free-speech-in-the-founding-and-in- modern-liberalism.pdf.

186. Pennsylvania Constitution, 1790, article 9, section 7.

187. "Philodemos," *Pennsylvania Gazette*, May 7, 1788, reprinted in Merrill Jensen, ed., *The Documentary History of the Ratification of the Constitution: Ratification of the Constitution by the States*, volume 2 supplemental (Madison: State Historical Society of Wisconsin, 1976).

188. *Respublica v. Oswald*, 1 U.S. (Pennsylvania, 1788), 319, 324.

189. *Updegraph v. Commonwealth*, 11 Serg. & Rawle (Pennsylvania, 1824), 393, 408–9.

190. *People v. Ruggles*, 8 Johns. (New York Supreme Court, 1811), 290, 292.

191. Cass Sunstein, *Democracy and the Problem of Free Speech* xviii (New York: The Free Press, 1993).

192. St. George Tucker, "Of the Right of Conscience; and of the Freedom of Speech, and of the Press," 1 William Blackstone, note G, at 11 (emphasis added), in 4 William Blackstone, *Commentaries on the Law of England* (St. George Tucker ed., Philadelphia: Young & Small, 1803), 151–52.

193. 8 *Annals of Congress* (1798), 75.

194. Thomas C. West, "Free Speech in the American Founding and in Modern Liberalism," *Social Philosophy and Policy*, 21, no.2 (Summer 2004), 313, 316.

195. Letter from Thomas Jefferson to Francis W. Gilmer (June 7, 1816), in 15 *Writings of Thomas Jefferson* (Andrew A. Lipscomb & Albert Ellery Bergh eds., 1905), 23, 24.

196. John Locke, *Two Treatises of Government,* book II, sections 4, 6, 57, 63 (Peter Laslett ed., Cambridge: Cambridge University Press, 1988) (1690).

197. Locke, book II, sections 95–96, 128.

198. Steven J. Heyman, *Free Speech and Human Dignity* (New Haven: Yale University Press, 2008), 20.

199. Heyman, *Free Speech and Human Dignity,* 176.

200. Heyman, *Free Speech and Human Dignity,* 39.

201. *Alcorn v. Mitchell,* 63 Illinois (1872), 553, 554 (emphasis added).

202. *Fisher v. Carrousel Motor Hotel*, 424 S.W. 2d (Texas 1967), 627, 628–29 (emphasis added).

203. Louis D. Brandeis and Samuel Warren, "The Right to Privacy," 4 *Harvard Law Review* (1890), 193, 195, 266.

204. Andrew Ross Sorkin, "Peter Thiel Is Said to Bankroll Hulk Hogan Suit Against *Gawker,*" *New York Times*, May 25, 2015, *available at* https://www.nytimes.com/2016/05/25/business/dealbook/peter-thiel-is-said-to-bankroll-hulk-hogans-suit-against-gawker.html.

205. Brandeis and Warren, "The Right to Privacy," 193, 196.

206. *Restatement (Second) of Torts*, sections 642B, 652C, 652D, 652E.

207. *Chaplinsky v. New Hampshire*, 315 U.S. (1942), 568, 572.

208. Heyman, *Free Speech and Human Dignity,* 144.

209. Cass R. Sunstein, "What If the Founders Had Free Speech Wrong?" *Bloomberg*, December 14, 2017, *available at* https://www.bloomberg.com /view/articles/2017-12-14/what-if-the-u-s-has-free-speech-all-wrong.

210. Jud Campbell, "Natural Rights and the First Amendment," 127 *Yale Law Journal* (2017), 246, 283, *available at* https://www.yalelawjournal.org /article/natural-rights-and-the-first-amendment.

211. Campbell, "Natural Rights and the First Amendment," 276.

212. *Id.*

213. Campbell, "Natural Rights and the First Amendment," 273.

214. *Id.*

215. Campbell, "Natural Rights and the First Amendment," 260.

216. *Respublica,* 319, 325 (emphasis added).

217. Campbell, "Natural Rights and the First Amendment," 310.

218. Robert H. Bork, "Neutral Principles and Some First Amendment Problems," 47 *Indiana Law Journal* 1 (1971), 20.

219. Heyman, *Free Speech and Human Dignity,* 177.

220. Proposal by Sherman to House Committee of Eleven, July 21–28, 1789, in *The Complete Bill of Rights: The Drafts, Debates, Sources, and Origins* (Neil H. Cogan, ed., 1997), 83 (emphasis added).

221. Adam Liptak, "How Conservatives Weaponized the First Amendment," *New York Times*, June 30, 2018, *available at* https://www.nytimes.com /2018/06/30/us/politics/first-amendment-conservatives-supreme -court.html.

222. David Goldberger, "Sources of Judicial Reluctance to Use Psychic Harm as a Basis for Suppressing Racist, Sexist and Ethnically Offensive Speech," 66 *Brooklyn Law Review* (1991), 1165, 1166.

223. Alexander M. Bickel, *The Morality of Consent* (New Haven, Yale University Press, 1975), 72.

224. Robin Abcarian, "Just as we thought: Richie Incognito bullied Jonathan Martin," *Los Angeles Times*, Feb. 14, 2014, *available at* http://www .latimes.com/local/abcarian/la-me-ra-report-miami-dolphins

-jonathan-martin-bullied-by-richie-incognito--20140214-story
.html#axzz2v0vKKjyb; *also*: Barry Petchesky, "The Worst Stuff From
The Miami Dolphins Investigation," *Deadspin*, Feb. 14, 2014, *available at*
http://deadspin.com/the-worst-stuff-from-the-dolphins-investigation
-epdai-1522846626.

225. Ken Belson, "Ex-Dolphin Jonathan Martin Is Detained After Social
Media Posts Shuts School," *New York Times*, Feb. 23, 2018, *available at*
https://www.nytimes.com/2018/02/23/sports/football/jonathan
-martin.html.

226. *Commonwealth v. Carter*, No. 15YO0001NE (Massachusetts Juvenile
Court, June 16, 2017).

227. Lawrence Tribe, *American Constitutional Law* section 12-8 (1978), 605–6.

228. *Brandenburg v. Ohio*, 395 U.S. (1969), 444, 447.

229. Hadley Arkes, "Civility and the Restriction on Speech: Rediscovering the
Defamation of Groups," 1974 *Supreme Court Review* (1974), 281, 306.

230. *Chaplinsky*, 315 U.S., 572.

231. *Chaplinsky*, 315 U.S., 571–72.

232. Rodney A. Smolla, "Words 'Which by Their Very Utterance Inflict
Injury': The Evolving Treatment of Inherently Dangerous Speech in Free
Speech and Theory," 36 *Pepperdine Law Review* (2009), 317, 319, *available
at* https://digitalcommons.pepperdine.edu/plr/vol36/iss2/4/.

233. *Restatement (Second) of Torts* (1965), section 46, comment d.

234. *Knierim v. Izzo*, 22 Illinois 2d (1961), 73, 85, 174 N.E.2d 157, 164.

235. Hadley Arkes, "Civility and the Restriction on Speech: Rediscovering the
Defamation of Groups," 1974 *Supreme Court Review* (1974), 281, 324.

236. Arkes, "Civility and the Restriction on Speech," 333.

237. Feldman Barrett, *How Emotions Are Made*, 241.

238. Feldman Barrett, *How Emotions Are Made*, 201.

239. Feldman Barrett, *How Emotions Are Made*, 206.

240. R. Douglas Fields, "Sticks and Stones—Hurtful Words Damage the
Brain," Oct. 30, 2010, *Psychology Today*, The New Brain, *available at*
https://www.psychologytoday.com/blog/the-new-brain/201010
/sticks-and-stones-hurtful-words-damage-the-brain.

241. Vivian Parry, "How emotional pain can really hurt," BBC News, July 21,
2008.

242. Feldman Barrett, *How Emotions Are Made*, 200, 202.

243. Lisa Feldman Barrett, "When Is Speech Violence?" *New York Times*, Opinion, July 14, 2017, *available at* https://nyti.ms/2ukaVf4.

244. Arkes, "Civility and the Restriction on Speech," 281, 300.

245. Feldman Barrett, *How Emotions Are Made*, 204.

246. Robert T. Carter, "Racism and Psychological and Emotional Injury: Recognizing and Assessing Race-Based Traumatic Stress," *The Counseling Psychologist*, Jan. 26, 2007, *available at* https://journals.sagepub.com /doi/pdf/10.1177/0011000006292033.

247. Feldman Barrett, *How Emotions Are Made*, 242.

248. Feldman Barrett, "When Is Speech Violence?"

249. Greg Lukianoff, "A Dozen Things 'The New Yorker' Gets Wrong about Free Speech (And Why It Matters)," *Huffington Post*, Aug. 21, 2015, *available at* https://www.huffpost.com/entry/a-dozen-things-the-new -yo_b_8021046.

250. *Page v. Smith*, AC 155, House of Lords (1996), 2.

251. *Restatement (Third) of Torts: Liability for Physical and Emotional Harm* (2012), section 47 n.1 comment f.

252. *Restatement (Third) of Torts: Liability for Physical and Emotional Harm* (2012), section 45 comment a.

253. Erica Goldberg, "Emotional Duties," 47 *Connecticut Law Review* (2015), 809, 827.

254. Betsy J. Grey, "Neuroscience and Emotional Harm in Tort Law: Rethinking the American Approach to Free-Standing Emotional Distress Claims," 1; *also in*: *Law and Neuroscience* (Oxfordshire: Oxford University Press, 2011), *available at* https://asu.pure.elsevier.com/en/publications /neuroscience-and-emotional-harm-in-tort-law-rethinking-the-americ.

255. *Allen v. Bloomfield Hills School District*, 281 Michigan Appellate (2008), 49, 57.

256. Grey, "Neuroscience and Emotional Harm in Tort Law," 18.

257. Robert Pear, "House Approves Bill on Mental Health Parity," *New York Times*, March 6, 2008, *available at* http://www.nytimes. com/2008/03/06/washington/06health.html.

258. Grey, "Neuroscience and Emotional Harm in Tort Law," 13.

259. Grey, "Neuroscience and Emotional Harm in Tort Law," 11.

260. Grey, "Neuroscience and Emotional Harm in Tort Law," 12; *also*: Benno Roozendaal, Bruce S. McEwen, and Sumantra Chattarji, "Stress, Memory and the Amygdala," 10 *Nature Reviews Neuroscience* (2009), 423, 465.

261. Grey, "Neuroscience and Emotional Harm in Tort Law," 13.

262. Grey, "Neuroscience and Emotional Harm in Tort Law," 17.

263. Joseph E. LeDoux, "Emotional Circuits in the Brain," 23 *Annual Review of Neuroscience* (2000), 155, 156–57.

264. *Restatement (Second) of Torts* (1965), section 46 (emphasis added).

265. *Restatement (Third) of Torts* (1987), section 45.

266. *Restatement (Third) of Torts*, section 46.

267. Deana Pollard Sacks, "Constitutionalized Negligence," 89 *Washington University Law Review* (2012), 1065, 1118.

268. "Study Finds Hate Speech on Commercial Talk Radio Could Negatively Impact Listeners' Health," *Hispanically Speaking News*, August 25, 2012.

269. Hermes Garban, Francisco Iribarren, Chon Noriega, Nicholson Barr, and Widong Zhu, "Using Biological Markers to Measure Stress in Listeners of Commercial Talk Radio," UCLA Chicano Studies Research Center, Working Paper, August 2012, *available at* http://www.chicano.ucla.edu/files/WP03_Using-Biological-Markers.pdf.

270. Katrin Bennhold, "Germany Acts to Tame Facebook, Learning From Its Own History of Hate," *New York Times*, May 19, 2018, *available at* https://www.nytimes.com/2018/05/19/technology/facebook-deletion-center-germany.html.

271. Gregory Herek, "The Impact of hate crime victimization," Department of Psychology, University of California, Davis, *available at* http://www.lgbpsychology.org/html/summary.pdf.

272. J.C. Weiss, H.J. Ehrlich, and B.E.K. Larcom, "Ethnoviolence at Work," *Journal of Intergroup Relations*, Vol. 18, No. 4 (1991–1992), 28–29.

273. David van Mill, "Getting Rid of Hate Speech," in *Free Speech and the State* (London: Palgrave Macmillan, Cham, 2017), *available at* https://link.springer.com/chapter/10.1007/978-3-319-51635-6_4.

274. Robert Emery and Jim Coan, "What causes chest pain when feelings are hurt?" *Scientific American* MIND, March 1, 2010, *available at* https://www.scientificamerican.com/article/what-causes-chest-pains/.

275. Maia Szalavitz, "New Test Distinguishes Physical From Emotional Pain in Brain for First Time," *Time*, May 6, 2013, *available at* http://healthland .time.com/2013/05/06/a-pain-detector-for-the-brain/.

276. Association for Psychological Science, "Could acetaminophen ease psychological pain?," *Science Daily*, Dec. 25, 2009, *available at* www .sciencedaily.com/releases/2009/12/091222154742.htm.

277. Delgado, "Words That Wound," 92; *also*: Rodney Clark, Norman B. Anderson, Vernessa Clark, David R. Williams, "Racism as a Stressor for African-Americans: A Biopsychosocial Model," *American Psychologist*, 54 (1999), 805–16, *available at* https://scholar.harvard.edu /davidrwilliams/dwilliam/publications/racism-stressor-african -americans-biopsychosocial-model.

278. Melissa Healy, "Heartache or headache, pain process is similar, studies find," *Los Angeles Times*, April 4, 2011, *available at* https://www.latimes .com/health/la-xpm-2011-apr-04-la-he-mood-pain-20110404-story .html.

279. Zhansheng Chen, Kipling D. Williams, Julie Fitness, and Nicola C. Newton, "When Hurt Won't Heal: Exploring the Capacity to Relive Social and Physical Pain," *Psychological Science*, August 2008; *also*: Chris Irvine, "Emotional pain hurts more than physical pain, researchers say," *Daily Telegraph*, Aug. 28, 2008, *available at* https://www.telegraph .co.uk/news/newstopics/howaboutthat/2639959/Emotional-pain -hurts-more-than-physical-pain-researchers-say.html.

280. Arkes, "Civility and the Restriction on Speech," 281, 300.

281. Ethan Kross, Marc G. Berman, Walter Mischel, Edward E. Smith, Tor D. Wager, "Social rejection shares somatosensory representations with physical pain," PNAS, April 12, 2011, *available at* http://www.pnas .org/content/108/15/6270.full?sid=758b38cc-b399-4d22-9c37 -3c074cf321be.

282. Matt McMillen, "To the brain, getting burned, getting dumped feel the same," CNN Health, March 29, 2011, *available at* http://www .cnn.com/2011/HEALTH/03/28/burn.heartbreak.same.to.brain /index.html.

283. Jonathan Rottenberg, "Physical Pain and Emotional Pain: More Similar Than You Think," *Psychology Today*, Dec. 23, 2009, *available at* https:// www.psychologytoday.com/us/blog/charting-the-depths/200912 /physical-pain-and-emotional-pain-more-similar-you-think.

284. Jennifer Warner, "Words Really Do Hurt: Study Shows Words Alone May Activate Pain Response in the Brain," WebMD, April 2, 2010, *available at* https://www.webmd.com/pain-management /news/20100402/words-really-do-hurt; *also* https://www.uni-jena .de/en/News/Archiv/Archiv+2010/PM100326_weiss_hurt.html.

285. Fields, "Sticks and Stones."

286. Ann Polcari, Karen Rabi, Elizabeth Bolger, and Martin Teicher, "Parental Verbal Affection and Verbal Aggression in Childhood Differentially Influence Psychiatric Symptoms and Wellbeing in Young Adulthood," 38 *Child Abuse & Neglect* 1 (January 2014), 91–102.

287. Goldberg, "Emotional Duties," 809, 831.

288. Goldberg, "Emotional Duties," 835.

289. Lawrence, "If He Hollers Let Him Go," 74.

290. *Stevens v. United States*, 559 U.S. (2010), 460.

291. Rebecca L. Brown, "The Harm Principle and Free Speech," USC School of Law, Center for Law and Social Science, March 23, 2015, *available at* https://papers.ssrn.com/sol3/papers.cfm?abstract_id=2584080.

292. Chafee, *Free Speech in the United States,* 149 (emphasis added).

293. Chafee, *Free Speech in the United States*, 150, 152 (emphasis added).

294. Fish, *There's No Such Thing as Free Speech,* 125.

295. Arkes, "Civility and the Restriction on Speech," 300.

296. *Snyder v. Phelps*, 562 U.S. (2011), 443.

297. *Snyder v. Phelps*, 131 Supreme Court Reporter (2011), 1207, 1220 (emphasis added).

298. Nathan B. Oman and Jason M. Solomon, "The Supreme Court's Theory of Private Law," 62 *Duke Law Journal* (2013), 1135.

299. Chafee, *Free Speech in the United States*, 150.

300. *Snyder*, 562 U.S., 46.

301. *Snyder*, 562 U.S., 463–64.

302. *Cantwell v. Connecticut*, 310 U.S (1940), 296, 310.

303. Arkes, "Civility and the Restriction on Speech," 317.

304. *Snyder*, 562 U.S., 464.

305. *Snyder*, 562 U.S., 475.

306. Matsuda, *Words That Wound*, 15 (Introduction).

307. Frederick Schauer, "Harm(s) and the First Amendment," *Supreme Court Review* (2011), 81, 90.

308. *Hustler Magazine v. Falwell*, 485 U.S. (1988), 46.

309. *Cohen v. California*, 403 U.S. (1971), 15.

310. *Brandenburg v. Ohio*, 395 U.S. (1969), 444.

311. David Goldberger, "Sources of Judicial Reluctance to Use Psychic Harm as a Basis for Suppressing Racist, Sexist and Ethnically Offensive Speech," 66 *Brooklyn Law Review* (1991), 1165, 1204.

312. *Texas v. Johnson*, 491 U.S. (1989), 397, 432 (Rehnquist, J., dissenting).

313. Arkes, "Civility and the Restriction on Speech," 314.

314. *Cohen*, 403 U.S., 21.

315. *Id.*

316. Schauer, "Harm(s) and the First Amendment," 106.

317. *Cohen*, 403 U.S., 25.

318. *Id.*

319. Schauer, "Harm(s) and the First Amendment," 101 n.83.

320. Respect for America's Fallen Heroes Act, Pub. L. No. 109-228, section 2, 120 Stat. 387 (2006) (codified at 38 U.S.C. section 2413).

321. James. Q. Lynch, "Iowa House unanimously approves limits on funeral protests," *Globe Gazette,* March 27, 2015, *available at* http://globegazette.com/news/local/iowa-house-unanimously -approves-limits-on-funeral-protests/article_588ee652-c576-5bed -ba7b-da626059d465.html.

322. Donald A. Downs, "Skokie Revisited: Hate Group Speech and the First Amendment," 60 *Notre Dame Law Review* (1985), 629, 640 n.50.

323. Downs, "Skokie Revisited," 641 n.50 (emphasis added).

324. *Collin v. Smith*, 578 F.2d (7th Circuit, 1978), 1197, 1206.

325. *Collin*, 578 F.2d, 1207.

326. *Collin*, 578 F.2d, 1200.

327. *Collin*, 578 F.2d, 1206.

328. Downs, "Skokie Revisited," 647.

329. Fish, *There's No Such Thing as Free Speech*, 124.

330. *Vietnamese Fisherman's Association v. Knights of the Ku Klux Klan*, 518 F. Supp. 993 (Southern District of Texas, 1981).

331. *Alcorn v. Anbro Engineering, Inc.*, 2 California 3d (1970), 493, 494, 468 P.2d 216, 217, 86 *California Reporter*, 88, 89.

332. *Alcorn,* 3d 493, 98–99, 468 P.2d 216, 218–19, 86 *California Reporter*, 88, 90–91 (emphasis added).

333. *Gomez v. Hug,* 645 P.2d (Kansas Court of Appeals, 1982), 916, 918.

334. *United States v. Torres*, 583 F. Supp. (Northern District of Illinois, 1984), 923, 925.

335. *Contreras v. Crown Zellerbach*, 88 Washington 2d (1977), 735, 736, 565 P.2d 1173, 1174.

336. *Contreras*, 735, 741–42, 565 P.2d 1173, 1177.

337. Sunstein, *Democracy and the Problem of Free Speech*, 193.

338. Sunstein, *Democracy and the Problem of Free Speech,* 186.

339. Nina Shea, "Hate Speech Laws Aren't the Answer to Islamic Extremism—They're Part of the Problem," *National Review*, Jan. 9, 2015, *available at* https://www.nationalreview.com/2015/01/hate-speech-laws-arent-answer-islamic-extremism-theyre-part-problem-nina-shea/.

340. Erik Bleich, "French hate speech laws are less simplistic than you think," *Washington Post*, Jan. 18, 2015, *available at* https://www.washingtonpost.com/news/monkey-cage/wp/2015/01/18/french-hate-speech-laws-are-less-simplistic-than-you-think/?utm_term=.181ca11b35ba.

341. Adam Gopnick, "PEN Has Every Right to Honor *Charlie Hebdo*," *New Yorker*, April 30, 2015, *available at* https://www.newyorker.com/news/daily-comment/pen-has-every-right-to-honor-charlie-hebdo.

342. Jill Lawless, "Charlie Hebdo Raises the Question: Is Hate Speech Protected in France," CBSNews, Jan. 25, 2015.

343. Waldron, *The Harm in Hate Speech*, 120.

344. Jesse Singal, "Why Won't Women's March Leaders Denounce Louis Farrakhan's Anti-Semitism, *Intelligencer*, March 7, 2018, *available at* https://nymag.com/intelligencer/2018/03/is-it-so-hard-to-denounce-louis-farrakhans-anti-semitism.html.

345. Criminal Code of Canada, Section 319 Canadian Human Rights Act.

346. *Wisconsin v. Mitchell*, 508 U.S. (1993), 476, 479.

347. *Id.*

348. *Mitchell,* 508 U.S., 488.

349. *Beauharnais v. Illinois*, 343 U.S. (1952), 250.

350. Charles Blow, "Accommodating Divisiveness," *New York Times*, Feb. 21, 2014, *available at* https://www.nytimes.com/2014/02/22/opinion/blow-accommodating-divisiveness.html.

351. Heyman, *Free Speech and Human Dignity,* 174.

352. *R.A.V v. St. Paul*, 505 U.S. (1992), 377, 391.

353. *R.A.V.*, 505 U.S., 402.

354. Waldron, "Dignity and Defamation," 1597, 1655.

355. Megan Sullaway, "Psychological Perspectives Hate Crime Laws," 10 *Psychology, Public Policy, and Law* (2004), 250, 261–65.

356. Mari J. Matsuda, "Public Response to Racist Speech: Considering the Victim's Story," 87 *Michigan Law Review*, (1989), 3220, 3235–40.

357. *Beauharnais v. Illinois*, 343 U.S. (1952), 250, 251.

358. *Beauharnais*, 343 U.S., 261.

359. Goldberger, "Sources of Judicial Reluctance," 1165, 1177.

360. Nadine Strossen, *Hate: Why We Should Resist It With Free Speech, Not Censorship* (Oxfordshire: Oxford University Press, 2018), 19.

361. Katherine Timpf, "'God Bless You' Listed among Anti-Muslim 'Microaggressions,'" *National Review*, March 14, 2018, *available at* https://www.nationalreview.com/2018/03/god-bless-you-microaggression-against-muslims/?utm_source=Facebook&utm_medium=Social&utm_campaign=Timpf.

362. George F. Will, "Colleges have free speech on the run," *Washington Post* Opinions, Nov. 30, 2012, *available at* https://www.washingtonpost.com/opinions/george-will-colleges-have-free-speech-on-the-run/2012/11/30/9457072c-3a54-11e2-8a97-363b0f9a0ab3_story.html.

363. Greg Lukianoff and Jonathan Haidt, "The Coddling of the American Mind," *Atlantic*, Sept. 2015, *available at* https://www.theatlantic.com/magazine/archive/2015/09/the-coddling-of-the-american-mind/399356/.

364. Lukianoff, "A Dozen Things '*The New Yorker*' Gets Wrong about Free Speech."

365. Erwin Chemerinsky, "The Free Speech-Hate Speech Trade-Off," *New York Times*, Opinion, Sept. 13, 2017, *available at* https://www.nytimes.com/2017/09/13/opinion/berkeley-dean-erwin-chemerinsky.html.

366. Judith Shulevitz, "In College and Hiding from Scary Ideas," *New York Times*, March 21, 2015 *available at* https://www.nytimes.com /2015/03/22/opinion/sunday/judith-shulevitz-hiding-from-scary -ideas.html.

367. Oshra Bitton, "When Students for 'Justice' Promote Violence," *CAMERA on Campus*, May 17, 2018, *available at* http://cameraoncampus.org /blog/when-students-for-justice-promote-violence/.

368. Daniel Sugarman, "Neo Nazi jailed after calling for genocide on Jews," *Jewish Chronicle*, April 20, 2018, *available at* https://www.thejc.com /news/uk-news/neo-nazi-jailed-for-stirring-up-racial-hatred-after -calling-for-genocide-of-jews-1.462814.

369. Ulrich Baer, "What 'Snowflakes' Get Right About Free Speech," *New York Times*, Opinion, April 24, 2017, *available at* https://www.nytimes .com/2017/04/24/opinion/what-liberal-snowflakes-get-right-about -free-speech.html.

370. Brian Owsley, "Racist Speech and 'Reasonable People': A Proposal for a Tort Remedy," 24 *Columbia Human Rights Law Review* (1993), 323, 326, 350.

371. Richard Delgada and Jean Stefancic, "Ten Arguments Against Hate Speech Regulation: How Valid?" 23 *North Kentucky Law Review* (1996), 475, 484.

372. Liel Leibovitz, "Tweets Cost a Professor His Tenure, and That's a Good Thing," *Tablet*, Aug. 29, 2014, *available at* http://www.tabletmag.com /jewish-news-and-politics/183274/salaita-tweets.

373. Jason N. Blum, "Don't Bow to Blowhards," *Chronicle Review*, Sept. 3, 2017, *available at* https://www.chronicle.com/article/Don-t-Bow-to -Blowhards/241048.

374. Aaron R. Hanlon, "Why Colleges Have a Right to Reject Hateful Speakers Like Ann Coulter," *New Republic*, April 24, 2017, *available at* https://newrepublic.com/article/142218/colleges-right-reject -hateful-speakers-like-ann-coulter.

375. Jim Rutenberg, "Terrorism Is Faster Than Twitter," *New York Times*, Nov. 5, 2017, *available at* https://www.nytimes.com/2017/11/05 /business/media/terrorism-social-networks-freedom.html.

376. Thane Rosenbaum, "The Internet As Marketplace of Madness—and a Terrorist's Best Friend," 86 *Fordham Law Review* (2017), 591.

377. Bennhold, "Germany Acts to Tame Facebook."

378. Eddy and Breeden, "The El Paso Shooting Revived the Free Speech Debate."

379. Ben Cohen, "'Repulsive Anti-Semite' Convicted by UK Judge for Jew-Hating YouTube Videos," *Algemeiner*, June 14, 2018, *available at* https://www.algemeiner.com/2018/06/14/repulsive-antisemite -convicted-by-uk-judge-for-jew-hating-youtube-videos/.

380. Rutenberg, "Terrorism Is Faster Than Twitter."

381. Greg Lukianoff, "Twitter, hate speech, and the costs of keeping quiet," CNET, April 7, 2013, *available at* https://www.cnet.com/news /twitter-hate-speech-and-the-costs-of-keeping-quiet/.

382. Soeren Kern, "European Union Declares War On Internet Free Speech," *Gatestone Institute*, June 3, 2016, *available at* https://www .gatestoneinstitute.org/8189/social-media-censorship.

383. Council of European Convention on the Prevention of Terrorism, Council of Europe Treaty Series, no. 196, May 16, 2005, *available at* https://rm.coe.int/168008371c.

384. Alexander Tsesis, "Terrorist Speech On Social Media," 70 *Vanderbilt Law Review*, (2017), 651, 681.

385. Tsesis, "Terrorist Speech On Social Media," 654.

386. Daisuke Wakabayashi, "Legal Shield for Websites Rattles Under Onslaught of Hate Speech," *New York Times*, Aug. 6, 2019, *available at* https://www.nytimes.com/2019/08/06/technology/section-230- hate-speech.html.

387. Frederick Schauer, "Is It Better to Be Safe Than Sorry?: Free Speech and the Precautionary Principle," 36 *Pepperdine Law Review* (2009), 301, 305.

388. *Holder v. Humanitarian Law Project*, 561 U.S. (2010), 1, 40 (dealing with material support to foreign terrorist organizations pursuant to the USA Patriot Act); *also*: Tsesis, "Terrorist Speech On Social Media," 706–7.

389. Rosenbaum, "The Internet As Marketplace of Madness," 600.

390. Leiter, *The Case Against Free Speech*, 31 n.82.

391. Eddy and Breeden, "The El Paso Shooting Revived the Free Speech Debate."

392. *Jocobellis v. Ohio*, 378 U.S. (1964), 184 (Stewart, J., concurring).

393. Waldron, "Dignity and Defamation," 1597, 1646.

394. Ramesh Ponnuru, "Target Practice: A Media Gun Show," *National Review*, June 14, 1991.

395. Douglas Walton, *Slippery Slope Arguments* (Oxfordshire: Oxford University Press, 1992), 175.

396. Fish, *There's No Such Thing as Free Speech*, 130.

397. Frederick Schauer, "Slippery Slopes," 99 *Harvard Law Review* (1985), 361, 365.

398. Susan Bandes, "The Negative Constitution: A Critique," 88 *University of Michigan Law Review* (1990), 2271, 2335.

399. *Cohen*, 403 U.S., 15, 25.

400. *Gertz v. Welch*, 418 U.S. (1974), 323, 339.

401. Fish, *There's No Such Thing as Free Speech*, 132.

402. Eugene Volokh, "Crime-facilitating Speech," 57 *Stanford Law Review* (2005), 1095, 1174–79.

403. Leiter, *The Case Against Free Speech*, 39.

404. Stanley Fish, "Fraught with Death: Skepticism, Progressivism, and the First Amendment," 64 *University of Colorado Law Review* (1993), 1061, 1086.

405. Baer, "What 'Snowflakes' Get Right About Free Speech."